The Junior
GENERAL
KNOWLEDGE
ENCYCLOPEDIA

The Junior
GENERAL
KNOWLEDGE
ENCYCLOPEDIA

Edited by
Theodore Rowland Entwistle
and Jean Cooke

Foreword by
Magnus Magnusson

TREASURE PRESS

Contents

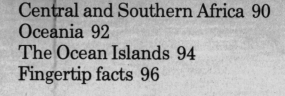

First published in Great Britain by Octopus Books Ltd

This edition published by Treasure Press
59 Grosvenor Street
London W1

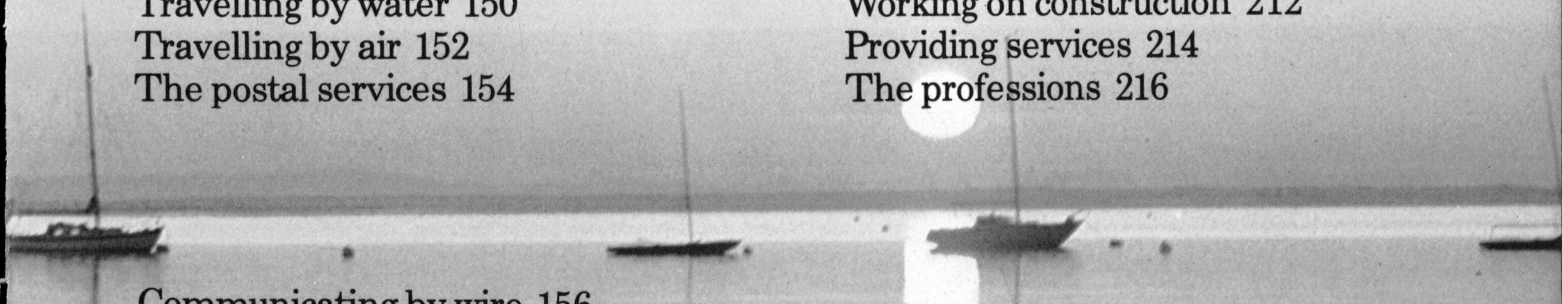

© 1978 Octopus Books Ltd

Revised 1982

Reprinted 1983, 1984

ISBN 0 907407 74 9

Printed in Czechoslovakia

50385/5

Contributors

Jill Bailey MSC
Arthur Butterfield
Jean Cooke
Lionel Grigson BA
Reginald Hammond FRGS
Alan C. Jenkins FZS, FRGS
Mark Lambert
Kenneth E. Lowther MA
Keith L. Lye BA, FRGS
Peter Muccini MA
Jonathan Ormond BA
Theodore Rowland-Entwistle BA, FRGS
Andrew Wilson BA (ECON)

Consultants

Nicholas Badham PhD
University of Southampton
England

Alan Kingdon MBBS MRCS LRCP

Ken Richardson PhD
Educational psychologist
Open University
England

John Swinson PhD
Educational psychologist

Malcolm Arth PhD
Curator of Education
The American Museum of Natural History

Foreword

We can't all be Masterminds; but we can all do a great deal to improve our General Knowledge of the world about us. Whether it's the Universe, or science, or modern technology, or the animal world, or the Arts, or foreign countries (or your own country, come to that), life becomes more vivid and multicoloured if you *know* about things.

The world is infinitely full of marvellous *stories:* stories about how things were and how things are, stories of what happened and why, stories of people and places. Finding out these stories for yourself is not only good for you – it's fun as well.

No matter where you live in the world, this Junior Encyclopedia can give you insights into the rest of the world. All the information is up-to-date and clearly presented, each topic contained within a single spread to give you a clear and concise picture of whatever you want to look up. It gives you, in effect, General Knowledge at your fingertips.

You probably know the old saying, that 'curiosity killed the cat'. Well, it certainly doesn't apply in our household. Our house is packed with reference books of all kinds, so that no matter what subject crops up that our family wants to know more about, we've got the answers somewhere on the book-shelves. We've also got two extremely healthy cats!

An 'encyclopedia' means, literally, 'the circle of human knowledge'. You won't find all human knowledge in an encyclopedia; but in this one you will find all you want to know at first glance – until your curiosity leads you further. The Junior General Knowledge Encyclopedia is both a doorway and a key, an Open Sesame to a new world of awareness.

Use it well, and often, and perhaps I'll have to change that first sentence: yes, we *can* all be Masterminds. Junior Masterminds, anyway.

Magnus Magnusson

The Earth in space

If you look at the sky on a clear night you can see hundreds, perhaps thousands, of stars, pinpoints of light in a dome of bluish black. If you then look through a small telescope or a pair of binoculars even more stars will flash into view – and astronomers using really powerful telescopes can see more still. Even so, some stars are too far away or too faint to see even with the biggest ordinary telescopes, and we have to use radio telescopes to collect radio waves which come from them.

All the stars together, millions upon millions of them, make up the Universe, of which our Earth forms a very tiny part. In this first section of the encyclopedia we shall look at the stars which make up the Universe, at our own star, the Sun, and the planets which circle round it, and in more detail at the Earth itself.

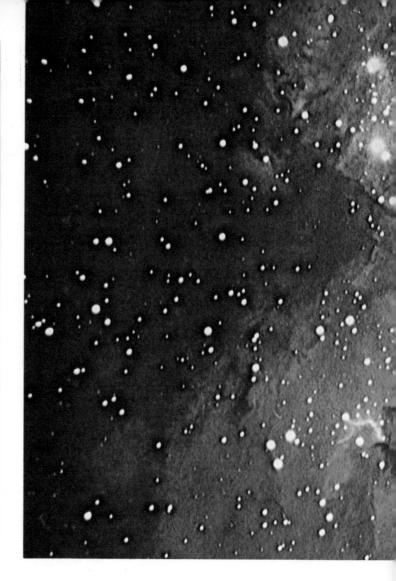

Stars and galaxies

A star is a kind of giant nuclear reactor, producing heat and light. In this way it differs from the Moon or a planet such as Venus, which do not produce light but merely reflect that of the Sun. Another difference is that while the Moon and the planets are solid, a star is so hot that all the chemical elements of which it is made are in the form of gas.

We can tell what elements are present in a star by studying the spectrum of its light. A spectrum is produced by passing the light through a prism which breaks the light up into bands of colours – violet, indigo, blue, green, yellow, orange and red. The width of each band varies according to the element. Astronomers can also tell from a star's spectrum something about its type and size, and even if it is moving away from us.

The stars vary greatly in size. The smallest are about the size of the Earth, while the biggest have a diameter about 25 times the distance from the Sun to Earth. The Sun itself is a star, of medium size. The largest stars are known as giants, but they have a comparatively low mass – that is, the matter of which they are made is more thinly spread out. Dwarf stars, on the other hand, are much denser.

A white dwarf is the smallest kind, and has the dimmest light. Stars go through many changes in the millions of years they exist, and astronomers think that a white dwarf is in a late stage of development. Double stars are pairs of stars that circle around each other.

Astronomers describe conspicuous groups of stars as constellations. There are 88 constellations, and more than 30 of them can be seen by people living in the northern half of the world. The rest can be seen by people living further south. Even bigger groups of stars are called galaxies. Our own Galaxy (with a capital G) is also called the Milky Way, and the Sun and its planets form part of it. The Galaxy rotates around a central point, just as the Earth revolves around the Sun. There are millions of galaxies in space, but without a telescope you can see only one, the Andromeda Nebula.

The stars are an incredibly long way away. To give you some idea, a spacecraft travelling 27 times as fast as the fastest jet-plane takes five months to reach Venus, the planet nearest to Earth. If the spacecraft were to travel at the speed of light, 299,792 km (186,282 miles) a second, the fastest possible speed, it would reach Venus in about 8 minutes. Yet travelling at the same speed as light, the spacecraft would take 3 years and four months to reach the nearest star (called Proxima Centauri by astronomers). The most distant known stars are

hundreds of thousands of times farther away in outer space. The stars appear to move across the sky every night, and to change position during the year, but this movement is due to the Earth's own rotation and its orbit around the Sun. In other words, we are looking at the stars from different positions.

Above: A nebula is a cloud of dust and small particles in space, which shines with the reflected light of the stars around it, or possibly emits light itself. This one is in the constellation Serpens.

Below: Just a few of the constellations seen in the sky. The lines are put in to show how they link up.

Southern Hemisphere

Northern Hemisphere

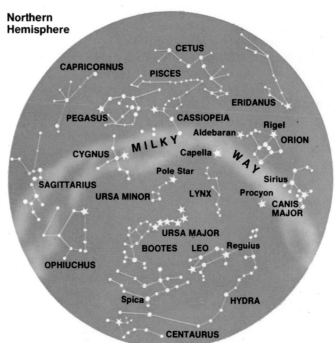

9

The Sun and its planets

Although the Sun is not one of the biggest stars, it is by far the most important to us here on Earth, because it provides us with heat and light. Without the Sun, life on Earth just could not exist. Around the Sun circle nine 'cold' heavenly bodies, which produce neither heat nor light of their own. They are called planets, from a Greek word meaning 'wanderer', because they appear to move about the sky while the stars seem to be always in the same relative positions. Earth is one of the planets. The Sun and planets together make up the solar system, so-called from the Latin word *sol*, Sun.

The Sun is more than one hundred times as large in diameter as the Earth. It spins round on its own axis once every 25 days, but because it is gas and not a solid body the Sun's equator displaces sideways in relation to the polar areas. As part of the Galaxy it hurtles through space at around 70,000 kph (44,000 mph)–though we on Earth are not conscious of this movement because we are moving with the Sun. The heat of the Sun is incredible– about 5500°C at the surface, and almost twice as hot in the centre. Even though the Sun is about 150,000,000 km (93,000,000 miles) away, the heat it radiates would shrivel up every living thing on Earth if it were not filtered by our atmosphere, which acts as an invisible sunshade.

You should never, on any account, look directly at the Sun, even through smoked glass–the glare is so great it could quickly blind you. However, astronomers using specially adapted telescopes can study the Sun, and they have found that there are dark blotches on the surface, called sunspots. These sunspots change in size and position, and when there is a great deal of sunspot activity it can interfere with radio waves on Earth, and may even affect the needles of compasses. The Sun itself emits a constant stream of radio waves.

The nine planets are–in order outward from the Sun–Mercury, Venus, Earth, Mars, Jupiter, Saturn, Uranus, Neptune and Pluto. The first four are comparatively small. There is a large gap between Mars and Jupiter, and in this gap are the Asteroids or minor planets, a large number of very small bodies. Jupiter, Saturn, Neptune and Uranus are called the major planets because of their great size. Pluto, the furthest planet, is about the same size as Mercury, the nearest to the Sun.

Mercury is the smallest planet, and it turns very slowly on its axis–its day lasts about 59 Earth-days.

Its surface is very like that of the Moon, dry, dusty and pitted with craters. The craters were made by meteorites, particles from outer space. Space probes have found no atmosphere, but there may be some active volcanoes.

Venus, which is nearly as big as the Earth, turns on its axis even more slowly than Mercury–once every 243 Earth-days. It rotates in the opposite direction to Earth. It has an atmosphere, but this consists mainly of the gas carbon dioxide, which does not support life. Clouds floating over the planet are believed to consist of sulphuric acid, the corrosive substance found in car batteries. Finally, the surface is so hot it would melt lead.

Mars, which has a diameter roughly half that of the Earth, rotates at about the same speed, once in just over 24 hours. Its year–the time it takes to orbit the Sun–lasts almost two of our years. It has a very thin atmosphere, consisting largely of carbon dioxide, but also containing some water– which Venus does not have. There are ice caps at the poles, as there are on Earth. The surface is a mass of ridges and very deep canyons, like the Badlands of Dakota on a giant scale. The surface of the planet seems to be permanently frozen.

The Asteroids or minor planets total about 2,000

The upper part of the picture shows the relative sizes of the planets and their moons: 1, Mercury; 2, Venus; 3, Earth; 4, Mars; 5, Jupiter; 6, Saturn; 7, Uranus; 8, Neptune; 9, Pluto. The lower part of the picture shows the relative distances of the planets from the Sun. The broad band between Mars and Jupiter represents the asteroids.

—that is, those so far discovered, but there are probably many thousands more. The largest, Ceres, has a diameter of only 687 km (425 miles), and all but a few are less than 100 km (60 miles) across. The Asteroids may be fragments of a planet which broke up millions of years ago, but some astronomers think they are fragments which failed to combine to form a larger body like the other planets.

Jupiter is the largest of the planets, and is eleven times larger than the Earth. It spins very fast, and its day is less than half the length of ours. It appears to have a very thick atmosphere, consisting largely of hydrogen, the lightest of all gases, and there are many storms in this atmosphere. Running around the planet parallel with its equator are a series of coloured bands, ranging from brown to pink. Several light and dark spots occur along these bands. The largest is the Great Red Spot, which moves around the planet. The substance of which Jupiter is made is very light compared with that of the Earth.

Saturn is almost as big as Jupiter. It also revolves quickly, and its day lasts just over 10 hours. It has

Left: A photograph of Jupiter made by the spacecraft Pioneer 11. It shows the Great Red Spot very clearly.

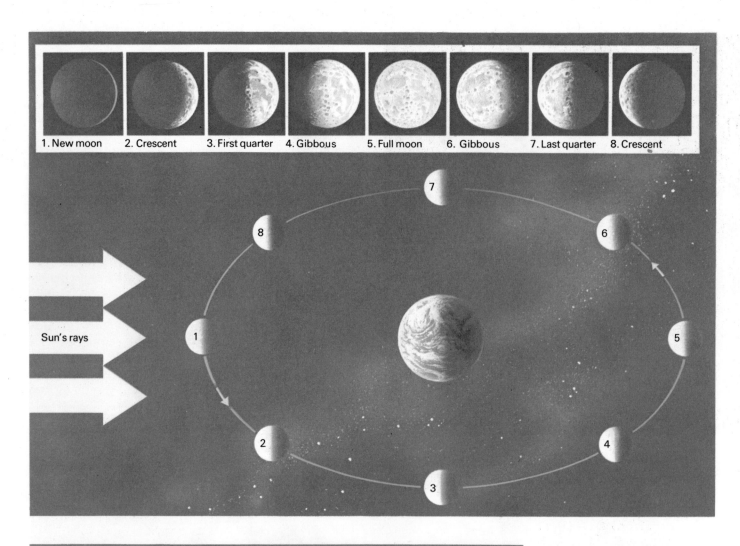

| 1. New moon | 2. Crescent | 3. First quarter | 4. Gibbous | 5. Full moon | 6. Gibbous | 7. Last quarter | 8. Crescent |

Sun's rays

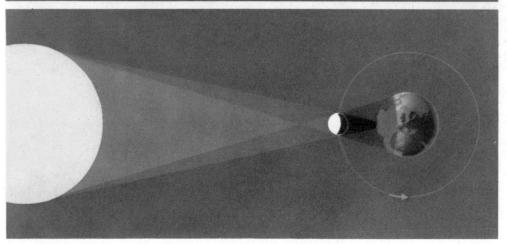

Above: How the Moon appears to change shape in the sky as it goes around the Earth. The lower part of the picture shows how the Sun always lights up half of the Moon's surface. At point 1 the Moon is between Earth and Sun and is almost invisible. At point 5 the Moon is the other side of the Earth and its lit-up face is completely visible. The little panels at the top show what we see at various times.

Left: If the Sun, Earth and Moon are in a straight line the Moon lies in the Earth's shadow, and it is said to be in eclipse. An eclipse can lasts up to 1½ hours. If the shadow only partly covers the Moon it is in a partial eclipse. In the same way, if the Moon is between the Earth and the Sun the Sun can be eclipsed. An eclipse of the Sun does not last more than 7½ minutes, usually less. There are two or three eclipses of the Sun every year, but they are not visible from all parts of the Earth.

a deep atmosphere, consisting mainly of helium, hydrogen and methane. We know very little about its surface, except that it appears to be very cold. Its most striking feature is the series of rings which surround it. There are hundreds of rings, and astronomers think they consist mainly of very small crystals of ice.

Uranus, though huge compared with Earth, is much smaller than Jupiter and Saturn. Its day lasts just under 11 hours. Its atmosphere consists largely of hydrogen and methane, and its surface is very cold.

Neptune is a bit smaller than Uranus, and it can be seen only with a telescope. It was not discovered until 1846. Its day lasts a little less than 16 hours, and it has an atmosphere containing methane.

Pluto, the furthest of the planets, is only a little larger than Mercury. Its day lasts six days and nine hours of our time. Nobody can be sure whether it has an atmosphere, but recent observations suggest that it consists of rock covered with frozen methane gas. It was discovered in 1930.

The Moon

Seven of the planets have satellites circling around them – Jupiter 15, Saturn 15 (besides the rings), Uranus 5, Mars and Neptune two each, Pluto one. Our satellite, the Moon, is the closest heavenly body to us, close enough for men to have landed and explored a little of its surface (see pages 182–183).

The Moon's diameter is just over one quarter that of the Earth. Rocks brought back from the Moon show that it is about the same age as Earth, and was presumably formed at the same time. It may have been a small planet which was 'captured' by the pull of the Earth's gravity, and it now orbits the Earth about every 28 days. It spins on its axis in exactly the same time, so it always presents the same face towards the Earth.

Although the Moon often shines very brightly – so much so that you can even see to read by it – it produces no light of its own. It acts as a large mirror in space, reflecting the light of the Sun. The planets also reflect the Sun's light in the same way. The Moon's apparent changes of shape and the differing amount of light it reflects are due to its journey around the Earth. When the Moon is between Earth and Sun, hardly any light falls on the side we see. That is the phase known as the new Moon. As the Moon's position changes, the Sun illuminates more of its face, and when it is on the opposite side to the Sun, we see the full Moon.

The surface is dry and dusty, a desolate landscape which has remained unchanged for millions of years, because there is no wind or rain to reshape it. There are signs of old volcanoes on the Moon, but no eruptions have taken place for a very long time. There are frequent moonquakes, however, showing that deep inside the Moon is still hot and active. The surface of the Moon is covered by craters left by meteors which have crashed into it over its long life. Few meteors ever reach the Earth's surface, because the friction produced as they hurtle through the atmosphere causes them to burn up, while any traces of meteors before the atmosphere was formed have long since vanished.

The famous meteor crater in north-east Arizona was probably made about 50,000 years ago. It is 1,265 metres (4,150 feet) across, and the meteorite that made it probably weighed about 1,000,000 tonnes.

This photograph of the Earth taken by American Apollo astronauts shows Africa, with Arabia near the top of the picture. Swirling clouds cover much of the globe.

The Earth's structure

As you have seen on pages 10–12, the Earth is one of the nine planets which revolve around the Sun. Because we live on Earth it is the only one of the planets about which we know very much – and even then we do not know a great deal about what happens under the surface. Although we have explored the atmosphere all round us, and even been to the Moon, we have penetrated only a very little way inside the Earth. On land the deepest we have been is about 3·5 km (2 mi.) in a South African mine. In the sea divers have descended almost 11 km (9 mi.) into the Mariana Trench of the Pacific Ocean. When you realise that the diameter of the Earth is over 12,000 km (7,500 mi.), you can see we have barely scratched the surface.

However, scientists have managed to find out quite a lot about the inside of the earth by studying the way in which earthquake shocks travel through it. The shock waves of an earth tremor move at different speeds according to the kind of material through which they are travelling. So by taking a lot of notes and doing some detective work, geologists (the people who study the Earth's structure) and seismologists (who study earthquakes) have built up a picture of the inside of our world, hidden deep beneath our feet.

The Earth is constructed in layers, a little bit like an onion. The outer part, the bit we know, is the crust, which is like the skin of the onion. It is quite thin – about 32 km (20 mi.) under the sea, and as little as 8 km (5 mi.) under some land areas. The crust includes both land and sea. The next layer

If you could see inside the Earth, it would probably look something like this. You can see the onion-like structure. Unlike an onion the Earth's layers are not truly separate but blend one into another.

below the crust is the mantle, a layer of very hot rock – so hot that it can flow about. Under the mantle comes the core, which is in two layers. The outer core is made of hot metals, which are also molten, and the inner core is a solid ball of extremely hot iron and nickel.

The deeper you go into the Earth, the hotter it becomes. The inner core is thought to be 50 times as hot as boiling water!

Gravity also grows stronger the deeper you go. If you put a pile of books on your head, the pile will be heavier the more books you add to it. If you imagine the pile of books extending down into the Earth, you will see that even a few kilometres down the pressure must be very great indeed. Divers know just how much the pressure of water increases under the sea, and for really deep dives they have to be enclosed in very thick steel submarines, or they would be crushed to death. One result of all this pressure deep inside the Earth is that rock and metal behave in different ways. That is why the inner core of the Earth is solid metal, although it is so hot it would otherwise be molten.

Because the Earth has so much iron in it, it is really a giant magnet, which explains why it turns the needle of a compass to point north.

Although the surface of the Earth appears to be unchanging, it is really altering all the time – but so slowly that as a rule you cannot see the changes taking place. The surface is made up of a series of gigantic plates, six or seven of them, which move about. When you look at the map of the world you can see that Africa and South America would fit together if they were close. Once, many millions of years ago, these two continents were actually

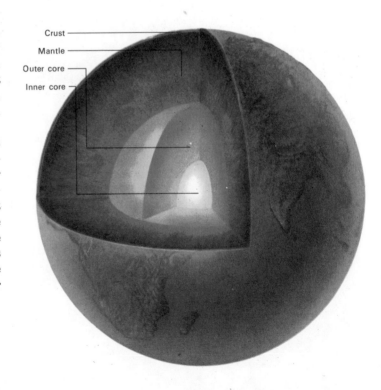

Crust
Mantle
Outer core
Inner core

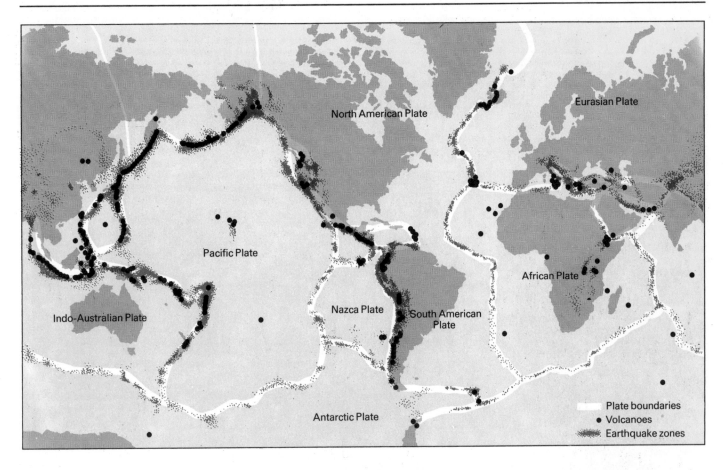

joined, but they split apart and have been moving away from each other ever since. The Atlantic Ocean is growing wider every year, though only by a centimetre or two.

Two of the plates covering the Earth meet under the middle of the Atlantic and come slowly up out of the Earth, with new material added to them all the time. At some other places one plate slides under another and disappears back inside the Earth – generally in deep ocean trenches. In yet other places the edges of the plates just rub together – this causes earthquakes.

Above: The white lines on this map show the boundaries of the plates which cover the surface of the Earth. Volcanoes are represented by black dots, and earthquake zones by red marks. You will notice that most of the volcanoes and earthquakes occur on or very close to plate boundaries.

Left: An earthquake can destroy a building in a matter of seconds. This one was wrecked by a 'quake in the Philippines in August 1976.

The land and its shape

As you saw on the previous page, the Earth's surface is changing all the time because the continents move slowly about. Hundreds of millions of years ago the continents probably formed one great mass of land which gradually split up.

However, the incredibly slow movement of the continents is not the only way in which the surface of our globe is changed. The rocks of which the Earth's crust is made are continually being built up, worn away and reformed. Erosion, which means wearing away, is one of the forces that changes the appearance of the Earth. If you make a heap of sand and pour some water slowly over it you will see tiny rivers forming and washing away some of the sand. That is erosion at work. Water moves sand and soil quickly because they are soft, but it can also wear away even the hardest rock–that can take thousands or millions of years. Newly-formed mountains are often sharp and jagged, but with time they are worn into smoother shapes.

Top: Caps of very hard rock have protected these pillars of soft rock from erosion near Urgup, in Turkey.

Above: The river-carved Grand Canyon in the U.S.A.

16

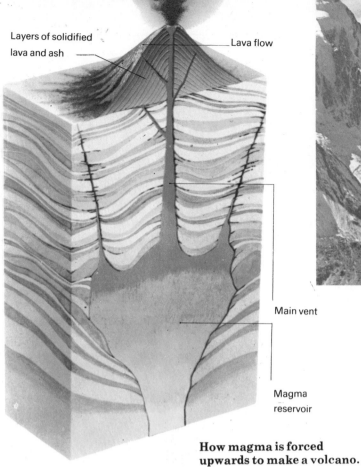

Layers of solidified
lava and ash

Lava flow

Main vent

Magma
reservoir

**How magma is forced
upwards to make a volcano.**

Above: The Alps are a range of folded mountains. They
are slowly being worn down by wind and rain and the
great glaciers—ice rivers—which run down the valleys.

Below: This ribbed volcanic cone is inside the crater
of a much larger volcano, Mount Bromo in eastern Java.

Water—rain, rivers or the sea—is not the only
cause of erosion. In another form, as ice, it also
grinds away rock. Great ice rivers, called glaciers,
have planed off the tops of mountains and left them
smooth, and carried rocks from one place to another.
Wind is another eroding agent, particularly in
deserts where it can lash a rock surface with sand
granules, like rubbing it with coarse glasspaper.

There are many kinds of rocks making up the
Earth, but they fall into three basic groups. Igneous
(firelike) rocks are made from magma, hot molten
rock which has come out of the interior of the Earth
and cooled to become solid. Lava from volcanoes is
an example of one kind of igneous rock.

Sedimentary (settled) rocks are the direct result
of erosion. A river scouring its way through rock
and soil carries a lot of tiny particles—sediment—
suspended in its waters. When it reaches the sea the
particles gradually settle on the bottom, building
up layer after layer. After millions of years these
layers become compressed as rock, such as sand-
stone. Often such rocks contain fossils (the stony
remains) of shellfish and other creatures.

As the Earth's crust moves, some rocks become
absorbed into it and are changed by heat and pressure into a new kind of rock, called metamorphic
(a Greek term meaning changed).

Mountains are formed in several ways. Some are
built up as volcanoes. Molten rock is thrown up
through a weak point on the crust (generally where
two plates meet), and cools on the surface as lava.
Many islands of the Pacific and Atlantic oceans are
the tops of underwater volcanoes, most of which
are no longer active. Other mountains are built
when a section of the Earth's crust folds. If you take

a neat pile of blankets and push with one hand at
each side, you will see the layers of blanket form
great curving ridges. A similar process takes place
with rock. Mountains that are formed in this way
are called fold mountains.

A third way in which mountains are formed is
by the movement of great blocks of the Earth's
surface. Some blocks are lifted up; others sink.
If you lay a row of building blocks on the table, and
then move some slightly up and some slightly down,
you will make a series of flat-topped mountains and
flat-bottomed valleys. A mountain formed in this
way is called a block mountain. Some mountains
are made by a combination of folding and block
formation, and the original layers of rock may be
tilted at angles.

Finally, a fourth way in which mountains are
formed is due to pressure underneath forcing the
surface up in blister-like mounds. These mound
formations are called dome mountains.

The sea and the air

Less than one-third of the Earth's surface is covered by land. The rest–70·8 per cent. to be precise–is covered by the sea. The sea is made up of four great oceans–the Atlantic, the Pacific, the Indian and the Arctic oceans–and a great many smaller seas, and bays and gulfs which form part of them, such as the North Sea, the Persian Gulf, and Hudson Bay.

The seafloor is not flat and smooth, as you might think if you saw the way the tide leaves a sandy beach. Near the continents it is comparatively shallow. This is because each continent is surrounded by a continental shelf, a stretch of land which forms part of the continent but is below water level. A great many of the fish we eat are caught in the seas over the continental shelves.

Beyond the continental shelf the seafloor drops steeply away to the main ocean bottom, often called the abyss. Large stretches of the ocean bottom are flat or gently undulating plains, but these plains are interrupted by ridges and mountains. Most of the mountains are volcanic, and there are many active volcanoes under the sea. Some of these volcanoes rise above the surface of the water to form islands, and most of the islands of the Pacific

This drawing gives some idea what the Atlantic Ocean looks like under the waves, with rifts and faults (cracks). The Mohorovičić discontinuity is the 'join' between the crust and the mantle. The asthenosphere is part of the mantle which is near melting point.

are made in this way. The world's greatest mountain chain lies under the sea, and runs from north to south in the middle of the Atlantic Ocean. The second highest mountain also lies under the sea, between New Zealand and Samoa. It is only 158 metres (518 feet) lower than the highest land mountain, but its peak is 365 m. (1,197 ft) down.

There are great differences in the temperature of the sea. On the surface it can range from below freezing point towards the Poles to 30°C (86°F) in the tropics. The sea is always colder the deeper you go, because the surface is warmed by the Sun.

The sea is always moving. On the surface the wind lashes the water into great waves, and sometimes underwater earthquakes also produce waves. The winds always tend to blow in the same direction because of the rotation of the Earth, and they produce currents in the ocean. These currents move cold water south from the Arctic and north from the Antarctic, and take warm water away from the Equator. Tides–regular rising and falling of the sea–are caused by the pull of the Moon's gravity and to a lesser degree that of the Sun.

The Sun not only warms the oceans, it also evaporates some of the water, turning it into water vapour which rises into the air and forms clouds. When the clouds are cool enough the vapour turns back into water droplets and falls as rain. Rain is always fresh water because the salt in sea-water does not evaporate.

The atmosphere or layer of air around the Earth is as much a part of it as the land and sea and all that lies below them. Air consists of a mixture of

Sea level

Transform fault

Mohorovičić discontinuity

Mantle

gases: 78 per cent. nitrogen, 21 per cent. oxygen, and almost 1 per cent. argon. There are traces of at least 10 other gases, besides dust and water vapour.

The higher you go above sea level, the thinner the air becomes, and on the very highest mountains it is too thin to breathe in comfort. At the height at which modern aeroplanes fly the air pressure is so low that no one could breathe at all, so aircraft cabins have to be pressurized. Several hundred kilometres above the surface of the Earth the air ceases altogether and beyond it is space—but nobody can say for certain exactly where air stops and space begins.

Left: The restless sea is always pounding the coast.

Below: This diagram shows how water circulates all the time from sea to land and back again in a cycle.

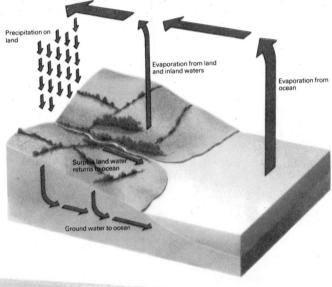

Precipitation on land

Evaporation from land and inland waters

Evaporation from ocean

Surplus land water returns to ocean

Ground water to ocean

rift

Crust (including sediments)

sphere

FINGERTIP FACTS ON THE UNIVERSE AND THE EARTH

	THE PLANETS		
Name	Diameter in kilometres/miles	Time taken to orbit Sun	Average distance from Sun in kilometres/miles
Mercury	4,990 (3,100)	88 days	58,000,000 (36,000,000)
Venus	12,400 (7,700)	224.7 days	108,000,000 (67,000,000)
Earth	12,757 (7,927)	365.26 days	150,000,000 (93,000,000)
Mars	6,790 (4,220)	686.98 days	228,000,000 (142,000,000)
Jupiter	143,000 (88,700)	11.86 years	778,000,000 (483,000,000)
Saturn	121,000 (75,100)	29.46 years	1,426,000,000 (886,000,000)
Uranus	52,000 (32,000)	84.01 years	2,869,000,000 (1,782,000,000)
Neptune	48,000 (30,000)	164.8 years	4,495,000,000 (2,792,000,000)
Pluto	5,900 (3,600)	247.7 years	5,900,000,000 (3,664,000,000)

The asteroids come between Mars and Jupiter, and they take between 643 and 5,000 days to orbit the Sun. Their size varies from 1.6 to 800 km (1 to 500 miles).

LONG DISTANCE

Stars are an incredibly long way away from us. They are so far that we cannot talk of their distance in terms of kilometres or miles. So astronomers use much bigger units of measurement. One of these measurements is the light-year, the distance light travels in one year. Since light moves at 299,793 kilometres (186,276 miles) a second, a light-year is about 9,700,000,000,000 kilometres! The nearest star, which is called Proxima Centauri, is 4.3 light-years away. In other words, the light we see from it left the star about 4 years and 3 months ago.

Other units used by astronomers are the astronomical unit, which is the distance from the Earth to the Sun, about 150,000,000 kilometres (93,000,000 miles); and the parsec, which is 3.26 light-years.

A LOOK AT THE MOON

Diameter: 3,480 km (2,160 miles)– a little less than the distance from London to Baghdad.

Distance from the Earth: The Moon's path around the Earth is an ellipse–an oval–so it is not always the same distance from us. At its closest it is 363,297 km (225,742 miles) away; at its furthest it is 405,503 km (251,968 miles) off.

Time of orbit–that is, the time it takes to go once round the Earth– is 27 days 8 hours.

Speed of rotation: The Moon turns on its axis once every time it circles the Earth–so it always keeps the same face towards us.

EARTH'S VITAL STATISTICS

Diameter through the Equator is 12,756.29 km (7,927 miles); from north to south through the Poles it is slightly less–12,713.59 km (7,900 miles).

Rotation on its axis is once every 23 hours, 56 minutes, 4.09 seconds.

Orbit around the Sun is completed once every 365 days, 6 hours, 9 minutes, 9.54 seconds.

Land Area: 152,809,290 square kilometres (57,523,000 square miles)– about 30 per cent. of the total surface.

Sea Area: 357,418,350 square kilometres (139,417,000 square miles)– about 70 per cent. of the total surface.

Circumference: Around the Equator: 40,074 kilometres (24,902 miles); north to south around the Poles: 40,004 kilometres (24,860 miles).

THE TEN LARGEST ISLANDS

Island	Area in square kilometres/ (miles)
Greenland	2,175,592 (840,000)
New Guinea	821,324 (317,115)
Borneo	746,543 (288,242)
Madagascar	595,788 (230,035)
Baffin Island (Canada)	476,066 (183,810)
Sumatra (Indonesia)	473,605 (182,860)
Honshu (Japan)	230,447 (88,976)
Great Britain	229,874 (88,755)
Ellesmere Island (Canada)	212,687 (82,119)
Victoria Island (Canada)	212,198 (81,930)

Australia looks like a huge island, but it is really a continent.

THE OCEANS

Ocean	Area (in square kilometres/miles)	Greatest depth (in metres/feet)
Arctic	14,090,000 (5,440,000)	5,466 (17,867)
Atlantic	81,662,000 (31,530,000)	9,219 (30,246) Puerto Rico Trench
Indian	73,444,000 (28,357,000)	8,047 (26,400) Diamantina Deep
Pacific	165,241,000 (63,799,000)	11,035 (36,204) Mariana Trench

THE CONTINENTS

Continent	Area (in square kilometres/miles)	Highest mountain	Lowest point
Africa	30,233,000 (11,673,000)	Kilimanjaro, 5,895 m (19,340 feet) above sea level	Qattara Depression, 133 m (436 feet) below sea level
Antarctica	13,209,000 (5,100,000)	Vinson Massif, 5,140 m (16,864 feet) above sea level	Not known
Asia	44,426,000 (17,153,000)	Everest, 8,848 m (29,029 feet) above sea level	Dead Sea, 392 m (1,286 feet) below sea level
Australia	7,695,000 (2,971,000)	Kosciusko, 2,230 m (7,316 feet) above sea level	Lake Eyre, 11.9 m (39 feet) below sea level
Europe	10,523,000 (4,063,000)	El'brus, 5,633 m (18,480 feet) above sea level	Caspian Sea, 28 m (92 feet) below sea level
North America	24,955,000 (9,635,000)	McKinley, 6,194 m (20,322 feet) above sea level	Death Valley, 86 m (282 feet) below sea level
South America	17,793,000 (6,870,000)	Aconcagua, 6,960 m (22,835 feet) above sea level	Valdés Peninsula, 40 m (131 feet) below sea level

THE TEN LONGEST RIVERS

River	Continent	Length in kilometres/miles
Nile	Africa	6,700 (4,160)
Amazon	South America	6,300 (3,900)
Yangtse	Asia	5,000 (3,100)
Zaïre	Africa	4,400 (2,700)
Missouri	North America	4,370 (2,700)
Amur	Asia	4,350 (2,700)
Hwang Ho	Asia	4,350 (2,700)
Lena	Asia	4,260 (2,600)
Mackenzie	North America	4,240 (2,600)
Mekong	Asia	4,180 (2,600)

The lengths given are approximate: geographers do not always agree on what is a main river and what is a tributary.

THE TEN HIGHEST MOUNTAINS

Peak	Height above sea level (in metres/feet)
Everest	8,848 (29,029)
Godwin Austen (K2)	8,611 (28,251)
Kanchenjunga	8,586 (28,169)
Makalu I	8,581 (28,153)
Lhotse I	8,501 (27,890)
Lhotse II	8,400 (27,559)
Cho Oyu	8,189 (26,867)
Dhaulagiri	8,172 (26,811)
Nanga Parbat	8,126 (26,660)
Manaslu	8,125 (26,657)

All these peaks are in the Himalaya range in Asia.

THE TEN LARGEST LAKES

Lake	Continent	Area in square kilometres/miles
Caspian Sea	Europe/Asia	423,400 (163,500)
Lake Superior	North America	82,300 (31,800)
Lake Victoria	Africa	74,664 (28,828)
Aral Sea	Asia	63,700 (24,600)
Lake Huron	North America	59,600 (23,000)
Lake Michigan	North America	58,000 (22,400)
Lake Tanganyika	Africa	32,900 (12,700)
Great Bear Lake	North America	31,800 (12,275)
Lake Baykal	Asia	31,460 (12,150)
Great Slave Lake	North America	28,930 (11,170)

The Caspian Sea and the Aral Sea really are lakes, in spite of their names and the fact that their waters are salty.

WEATHER EXTREMES

The hottest place on Earth is Azizia, a town in a hilly farming area of Libya. The world's record temperature was recorded there in 1922–a sizzling 57.7°C (135.83°F)! But several other places have a higher average temperature, including Death Valley in California, and parts of Western Australia. The coldest place is Antarctica, where —88.3°C (—126.94°F) has been recorded. The wettest place is on Kauai Island, Hawaii, which has more than 330 rainy days a year. Réunion Island in the Indian Ocean had the heaviest downpour ever recorded–1,870 mm (73.62 in) in 24 hours. The driest place is part of the Atacama Desert, in Chile, where little rain falls.

Plants

Plants are the basis of all life on Earth. Without them no animals could live, and the reason for this is that animals cannot manufacture their own food from simple chemicals found in air, water and the soil–but plants can. The most important plants are the green ones with leaves. They make their food by a process called photosynthesis (from Greek words meaning 'putting together of parts with light'). In this process they trap the energy in sunlight, and use it to make complex chemical compounds from the simple elements.

Many animals feed only on plants, and they in turn provide food for the meat-eating animals, such as lions. So even the meat-eaters depend on plants for their food in the long run.

In this section we look at the various kinds of green-leaved plants, the purpose of flowers, trees–the biggest of all plants–and also at some very simple forms of plant life.

The green-leaved plants

A green-leaved plant is really a kind of complex factory for making food and so building up the plant's own structure. Plants take up water from the soil through their roots, and carry it in a system of very fine tubes to the leaves. Some of the water is used to keep the plant stiff and upright. Just as a car tyre becomes firm as you pump air into it, so plants grow firm as they fill up with water.

Although plants must have water, they can even live in deserts. Some–the cacti–have reduced their leaves to spines, so they have a smaller surface through which water can evaporate. Cacti also have swollen stems in which to store water. The mesquite has deep roots to tap water 9 metres (30 feet) below the desert surface. Other desert plants have very long roots near the surface to catch as much water as possible from the brief showers. The resurrection plant, however, can survive being completely dried out. It bowls around the desert as a ball of dead-looking twigs, but after a shower of rain it puts down roots, goes green and starts to grow again. Flowering plants can also live submerged in fresh water, but very few are found in the sea.

Not all plants are strong enough to grow tall to reach light. Some straggle across others, while

A carpet of flowers covers what is normally desert in the South African veld. The seeds lie dormant then spring into life when there are heavy rains.

some, such as the runner bean, make sure of their supports by twining round them. Many plants of the pea family have leaves which have changed into tendrils – slender twining fingers. Wild roses and brambles have backward-pointing thorns to catch in other vegetation, while the honeysuckle twines its stems together to form a rope.

Some plants are parasites – that is, they depend on others for their food. The mistletoe is partly parasitic: it grows on the branches of trees, has green leaves and can make some of its own food, but instead of having roots of its own, it puts suckers through the bark into the tissues of the host, the tree on which it lives.

Other plants are completely parasitic. The dodder has almost no leaves, and is nearly colourless. Called 'the Devil's sewing thread', it twines round its host and puts suckers into the tissues to steal its food. Dodder can kill its host.

Some plants which live on trees are not parasites, and do not harm the trees. They are called 'epiphytes', and live in small pockets of dusty soil in the cracks of tree bark. The most colourful are the epiphytic orchids. The Spanish moss which drapes the trees of American woodlands covers more trees than any other epiphyte. It has no roots at all, but gets all its water from rain. Some relatives of Spanish moss form rosettes of pointed leaves on the branches of trees in tropical forests. The cup-shaped centre of the rosette is usually full of water, and this forms a home for little frogs and other water creatures, and for small water plants.

Left: This aechmea from South America is an epiphyte – it grows on a tree without damaging it.

Below: The familiar mistletoe is a parasite on trees but does little harm. Its seeds are carried by birds.

Flowering plants

Flowers are the sex organs of plants. If you look carefully at a flower, starting at the outside, you will find first a ring of small, greenish leaves, which we call sepals. Before the flower opens these little leaves protect the delicate petals inside the bud. Next come the brightly-coloured petals, and inside these, in the middle of the flower, you will find some curious structures.

Right in the centre is a long stalk with a knob on the end, or with a forked tip, called the stigma. This is joined on to a round seed-box at the bottom of the flower. At first this seed-box, which is the female part of the flower, contains just the plant eggs. These eggs later become seeds. Around it are the yellow stamens – little bags of pollen on delicate stalks.

Pollen is the yellow powder which shakes out of the flower if you pick it. It is millions of tiny spheres, each one of which is a little male plant cell.

When the pollen lands on the stigma, it grows down into the seed-box and fertilizes the egg, just as in animals the sperm and the egg join together to start a baby animal. The egg then grows into a seed.

Just as animals mate with other animals, so plant eggs have to be fertilized with pollen from other plants, or at least from other flowers. For this to happen the pollen from one plant must be transferred to another, a process called pollination. Insects do this for most plants. The flowers provide the insects with food – a sweet-scented nectar, usually produced in little cups at the base of the petals. As the insects feed, pollen rubs against them and is carried to the next flower they visit, where some will rub off on the stigma. The insects are also attracted by the colourful petals. The colours themselves are important. Insects do not see colours in the same way as we do. They also see colours that we do not see. While a red or yellow flower will look bright to us, to insects a dull violet flower may appear brighter. The ideal colour for attracting insects is thought to be a purple-blue, the colour of the Australian hovea flower. Flowers pollinated by night-flying moths are usually very

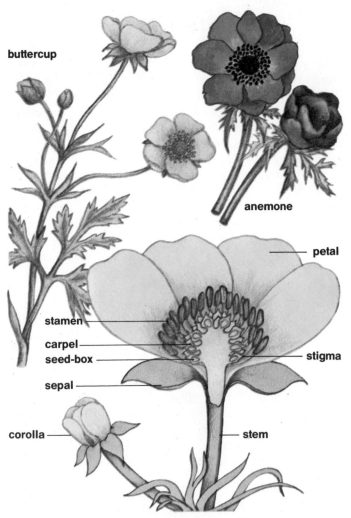

buttercup

anemone

petal

stamen

carpel

seed-box

stigma

sepal

corolla

stem

Above: This diagram of a buttercup shows the various parts of a flower. Accompanying it are a buttercup, and an anemone, which is closely related.

Left: Columbines, relatives of the buttercup.

Above: A creeper of the family which includes peas.

Below: A flame lily with its stamens clearly showing.

large and pale, such as the evening primrose, so they can be seen easily at dusk. These flowers usually open by night and close by day.

Bees and other insects are blind to red, but butterflies are not, so many butterfly-pollinated flowers are pink or red. Petals also often have guides to help the insect find the nectar: lines or bright patches leading down to the nectar cups. You can easily see them in flowers such as the pansy and the poppy.

Larger animals also pollinate flowers. The tiny humming-birds and the Australian honey-eaters feed off nectar. The birds are attracted by bright red or yellow flowers. Some bats drink nectar, too. They feed at night, so colour is not so important, and bat-pollinated flowers are usually brownish.

Flowers can be of many different shapes, sizes and colours. The largest flower family is the daisy family, where every flower head is made up of many tiny flowerlets. These produce seeds with little feathery parachutes. Some members of the pea family have petals arranged to provide platforms for insects to stand on.

The rose family includes fruit trees such as the apple, as well as roses. Flowers of the lily family always have their petals arranged in groups of three, while members of the grass family have hardly any petals at all, because the wind carries its pollen from one plant to another as a fine dust. The grasses are a very important family, including wheat, barley, oats, maize (corn), sugar-cane and rice. These plants all have long, jointed stems and narrow, ribbon-shaped leaves.

Trees

A tree is a large plant which has a main stem or trunk on which there are several leafy branches. The trunk of a tree is a much harder kind of tissue than the stems of most other plants, and is called wood. There are two main kinds of trees: conifers and broad-leaved trees.

Most conifers have leaves shaped like needles, and produce cones on which seeds are eventually formed. Nearly all conifers are evergreens–that is, they never shed all their leaves. The cones–the name conifer means 'cone-bearing'–are actually whorls of special leaves. Male cones produce pollen, which is carried by the wind to the female cones, where it fertilizes the large female spores. The spores develop into seeds.

The broad-leaved trees all bear flowers, and many of them are in the same families as small garden plants. All flowering trees bear fruits, which form and ripen when the flowers die off. The seed is hidden inside the fruit, and the kind of fruit determines how it is distributed so that plants can grow in new places. Fleshy fruits such as plums are eaten by birds, which pass the stones or seeds out with their droppings; nuts, which are woody, are carried off by mice and squirrels; while 'winged' fruits such as those of the sycamore are carried away by the wind.

Trees grow taller every year, and if they did not also grow fatter they would be very weak and spindly, and unable to withstand strong winds. They also need more food and water as they get bigger. So trees lay down extra layers of stiff water-conducting and food-conducting tissue in the stem each year. The old conducting tissues form a core of dead wood in the centre of the stem. A tree, then, is really a skeleton of dead wood (often called heart wood) surrounded by a thin shell of living tissue, the sap wood. The tree also grows more tissue round the outside of the trunk and twigs, forming a tough coat of bark.

Because trees are so big, they use a lot of water. The many thousands of leaves present a huge evaporating surface to the air, and the water has to be lifted to considerable heights. In winter in high latitudes part or all of the soil water may be frozen. This is why many trees–deciduous trees–shed their leaves in winter: by losing their leaves they lose less water. Deciduous plants also grow in countries where there is a very dry season of the year, when water evaporates quickly and there is little moisture in the soil.

Evergreen trees get round the water problem in other ways. The needle-shaped leaves of the conifers have a small surface area, while many evergreen trees and shrubs of the Mediterranean region, such as laurel and holly, have very shiny leaves with a thick waxy coating which reduces evaporation.

The other main requirements of trees are air and

The Douglas fir of North America is one of the conifers. It was discovered by Archibald Menzies, a Scottish naval surgeon, during the 1790s.

Above: The baobab tree grows in Africa, and has one of the thickest trunks of any tree. It lives to a great age. Its edible fruit is known as monkey bread.

Below: The red and silver maple trees of North America come into flower before their leaves fully open.

Above: Acorns of the Turkey oak of Turkey and southern Europe have scaly, moss-like cups.

light, which the leaves need to make food. If you lie on a forest floor and look up at the trees above, you will see that they hardly overlap one another at all. This pattern is called a leaf mosaic.

Trees develop branches in many different patterns. Some such as poplars are tall and thin, and do not take up much ground space. Others form the forest canopy, and have very tall trunks and a big crown of branches at the top. In tropical forests the canopy may be as much as 60 metres (200 feet) above ground. Under the canopy are smaller trees with bushy shapes. Many have thorns to protect them from animals.

Some trees, such as the baobab, have very fat trunks. Desert trees may look more like cacti than trees; for example the bizarre Joshua tree has fat water-storing trunks and tufts of spiky leaves at the tips of its branches.

Trees are so much bigger than men and live so much longer that there are many legends and superstitions about them. The giant sequoias of North America may live as long as seventy men.

The simple plants

There are many forms of plant life which are much more primitive than trees and flowers. Some live in the sea, some in fresh water, and some on land.

The seas are full of tiny plants so small that they can be seen only with a microscope. Some are green, and make their own food just like flowering plants. All these tiny plants are part of a mixture of plants and equally tiny animals which is called plankton, floating near the surface of the water. The plants are eaten by the animals, which in turn are eaten by larger sea-creatures, and so on, so they form the basis of all food in the sea.

Some larger sea plants are the seaweeds. They and the plankton are called algae (plural of alga), and they are simple plants without obvious stems and leaves. Some seaweeds live under water all the time. They include the bright green sea-lettuce of coastal rock pools, and the red deep-water sea-weeds. Brown seaweeds grow attached to rocks between the high and low tide levels, so that part of the day they are under water, and part of the time they are exposed to air and sunshine. Many of them have air-bladders—round gas-filled spaces—to help them float upright while they are submerged. Some kinds of algae live in fresh water, in ponds and streams.

Liverworts are strange plants which are flat green fronds (leaf-like structures) anchored to the ground by a mass of little rootlets. They are better suited to life on land than the algae because they produce spores in spore-sacs on upright stalks. The spores then blow away in the wind, which gives the liverworts a good chance of finding a new place to grow. Even so, the liverworts have to live in damp places such as the banks of streams because

Liverworts look as though they have leaves, but the 'leaf' is in fact the main body of the plants. They get their name because of their liver shape.

their thin fronds dry out very easily. Some liverwort fronds are shaped like a series of overlapping leaves, and can look similar to mosses.

The mosses range from the flat, branched feather mosses to the stiff, upright plantlets of the common hair moss, and the spongy plants of the bog mosses. Like the liverworts, they produce spores which blow away on the wind.

Ferns grow much bigger than the mosses. Their close relatives, the cycads or tree-ferns, may grow up to 9 metres (30 feet) high. Like mosses they live only in damp places. They produce their spores in little bags on stalks on the backs of the fern fronds.

Fungi also are plants. They do not make their own food; instead, some feed on dead plants and animals, or on organic matter such as the broken-down remains of leaves. Others are parasites, feeding off the living tissues of plants and animals. The brightly coloured mushrooms and toadstools we see are really the fruiting parts of fungi. From the underside of the cap of a toadstool thousands of tiny spores are produced and blow away in the wind. The main part of each fungus is in the soil – a branching mass of tiny threads which absorb food. There are other kinds of fungus, too: for example the green mould we get on bread is also a fungus.

Lichens grow where you cannot see any soil at all: on rocks, walls, roofs and trees. Lichens are found nearer to the North Pole than any other plant. They grow very, very slowly, only a few millimetres each decade, so they need very little food, and they can also stand being dried out, Lichens are really made up of two organisms, a fungus and an alga. The alga produces the food, and the fungus gives it protection from wind and water loss, so the lichen can grow where neither alga nor fungus can grow alone.

Besides the familiar mushroom, there are many kinds of fungi that can be eaten, such as this one, known as *Russula vesca*. It grows in oak woods and has a nutty flavour, but you should never eat any fungus unless a real expert tells you it is safe to do so.

FINGERTIP FACTS ABOUT PLANTS

CHOOSING A NAME

Botanists—people who study plant life–always describe individual plants by Latin names. Hundreds of years ago Latin was a form of universal language among scholars. Learned men always wrote in Latin, and so their works could be read by scholars in other countries. That is why Latin was chosen when our present system of classification, or taxonomy as it is often called, began 200 years ago.

All plants are members of the kingdom Plantae, while animals belong to the kingdom Animalia. Plants that are alike belong to the same species, and similar species are grouped together into a genus (plural, genera). Related genera form a family, and a group of families is called an order. Orders are grouped into classes, and classes together form divisions or phyla (singular, phylum) of the plant kingdom.

Normally a botanist uses only the genus and species, and these names are always printed in *italics*, with a capital letter for the genus. Often a name is 'made-up' Latin, and is based on the name of the person who first identified the plant. A good example is the blue poppy, called *Meconopsis baileyi*. *Meconopsis* actually comes from two Greek words meaning 'poppy-like', and *baileyi* is after Major Bailey who first discovered the plant.

PLANT STATISTICS

Number of Different Species: 350,000+.

Number of Flower Families: Nearly 300.

Largest Flower: *Raffelesia arnoldi*, a parasitic plant growing in Indonesia: it has a bloom that can be nearly 1 metre (3 feet) across, and smells like rotting meat.

Smallest Flower: Duckweed–the whole plant is only about 0.5 millimetre (1/50 inch) across!

Tallest Trees: The redwoods *(Sequoia)* of California, which grow more than 100 metres (330 feet) tall. (See picture above).

Oldest Trees: The bristlecone pines *(Pinus longaeva)* of Nevada, one of which is estimated to be around 4,900 years old.

THE GREEN REVOLUTION

You all know that garden plants produce finer flowers and better vegetables than wild ones. This is because they have been bred specially, by selecting and crossing the best varieties year after year. Plant breeding began in the mid-1800s, and it is the technique which is helping to save the world from famine. This improvement in plants is sometimes called the Green Revolution.

The Green Revolution really got underway in the 1940s when Mexican scientists began work on wheat. By 1967 they had produced plants which yielded crops twice as big as before. In 1968 Philippine scientists produced a variety of rice which yielded six times the crop of the old kinds. These two crops alone have solved many of the food problems in India and Pakistan.

THE MAIN GROUPS OF PLANTS

The plant kingdom is divided into four divisions–Thallophyta, Bryophyta, Pteridophyta and Spermatophyta.

Thallophytes are the simplest kinds of plants, the algae and the fungi. Bacteria are generally included in this division, and are thought to be related to fungi.

Bryophytes are green plants without flowers or roots, and we know them as mosses and liverworts.

Pteridophytes are larger than the bryophytes, and they do have roots. The main kinds of plants in this group are ferns, horsetails and club mosses.

Spermatophytes are the plants which bear seeds, and they are divided into two classes, gymnosperms and angiosperms. Gymnosperms nearly all carry their seeds in cones, and they include conifers, yews, the ginkgo or maidenhair tree, and the cycads, a small group of tropical plants which includes the 'bread palm' (which is not a true palm tree).

Angiosperms are the flowering plants, and this group includes five out of every seven known species of plants. The angiosperms are also divided into two groups. The monocotyledons have one seed leaf inside each seed, while the dicotyledons have two.

SOME STRANGE PLANTS

The Largest Leaves of any plant are possessed by a giant species of water lily, *Victoria regia*. They grow more than 1 metre (3 feet) across, and some are extremely strong.

The Candle-Tree of Panama has flowers which look like huge candles, 1.2 metres (4 feet) long. They contain a great deal of fat which is used for making lamp oil.

The Banyan Tree puts out branches from which long roots hang. These roots reach the ground and begin to grow into new stems. A really big banyan may have up to 3,000 stems, some as big round as an oak tree's trunk.

The Traveller's Tree of Madagascar grows in shape like a gigantic fan. The sheaths of its leaf-stalks hold stores of rain-water–a boon for thirsty travellers.

LIVING CALENDARS

Trees can act as living calendars. If you look at the cut end of a log, you can see a series of rings. A year's growth is represented by a pair of rings, one dark (summer growth) and one light (spring growth). Narrow rings show dry years, and wider ones years with plenty of rain.

By counting the rings you can tell a tree's age–and the weather for each year of its life also shows in the width of the rings. With the aid of long-lived species such as the bristlecone pines–some of which are more than 4,000 years old–scientists now have tree calendars going back a very long way. By matching wood from old buildings with the known tree calendars, they can say when the building was put up.

The study of tree-rings is called dendrochronology, from two Greek words meaning 'tree' and 'time'.

Right: Section through a trunk, showing the bark, the sapwood and the central dead heart wood.

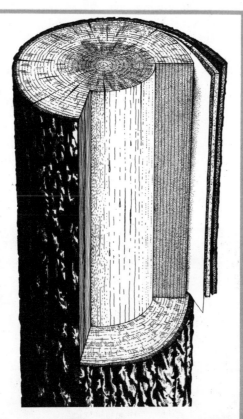

THE INSECT-EATERS

Animals, as you know, eat plants–but there are more than 400 species of plants which actually eat animals. Most of the victims are insects, but some other tiny creatures such as crustaceans are also prey to these strange plants.

There are several kinds of insectivorous plants. Pitcher plants have leaves which are shaped like small pitchers, or jugs. Nectar in the mouth of the pitcher lures the insect inside, and spines stop it getting out again. Finally it falls into the bottom of the pitcher, which is full of fluid. This fluid acts like an animal's digestive juices, and so the plant absorbs nourishment from the insect.

Venus's flytrap has a hinged leaf which opens up like the shells of an oyster. A fly landing on the leaf in search of nectar sets off the trap, and the leaf closes shut on the victim. Other insect-eating plants include sundews and butterworts, which trap insects with a sticky substance, and bladderworts, which trap tiny animals under water.

POISONOUS PLANTS

Many plants contain poisonous substances, some of which are powerful enough to kill an animal or a person eating them. In others, the poison is merely an irritant, as in the familiar stinging nettle. Poisonous plants may be divided into plants which are always poisonous, those which are sometimes poisonous, those which are poisonous to some animals and not to others, and those which have poisonous parts.

Monkshood, deadly nightshade, yew and hemlock are always poisonous. An example of a plant which is sometimes poisonous is the mayapple, which is poisonous when unripe but safe when ripe. Acorns can poison cows or horses, but will make good food for pigs, while rabbits can safely eat the death cap fungus, which can kill a person. Plants which are partly poisonous include the tomato, whose fruits are edible but whose stalks, roots and leaves are not; the potato, which has edible tubers and poisonous fruits; and rhubarb, which has edible stalks but whose leaves are deadly if cooked with salt.

Animals

If you were asked to describe the difference between a plant and an animal, you would probably say that a plant does not move about, whereas an animal can. This is true–though there are a few very simple animals which do not move about. But a much more important difference is that plants can make their own food from water and chemicals, while animals have to eat ready-made food–plants or other animals.

In the next 22 pages we describe some of the most interesting and important forms of animal life. We begin with the mammals, the largest and most familiar kinds of animals, which include cats, dogs, horses, monkeys–and even man. After that we go down the animal family tree, through birds, amphibians, reptiles, and fishes, to the small, simple creatures we call invertebrates, because they have no vertebrae, or backbones.

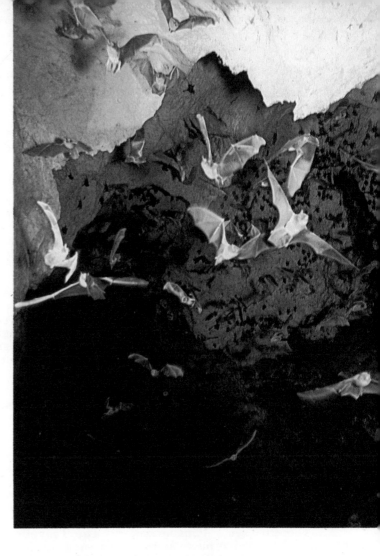

Mammals

Mammals have milk-secreting organs for suckling their young. The monotremes are mammals, yet they lay eggs. When the eggs hatch out, the young suckle from their mother through two patches of skin on her belly. Found only in Australia, the platypus is the weirdest of the group, with a bill like a duck's, fur like a seal's and webbed feet. The male has poison spurs on his hind legs.

Young marsupials are mammals that are not properly formed at birth. When they are born they grope their way to a skin pouch on the mother's belly. Here they remain as long as ten weeks, their mother's milk squirted into their mouths by a muscular device. These mammals exist mainly in Australia and New Guinea. As well as the well-known kangaroo there are marsupial wolves, moles and many others. The only other continent where marsupials are found is America, where they are represented by the opossums.

The insectivores are a large order (group) whose chief food is insects. They are fairly small and short-legged, with comparatively long snouts for snuffing out their prey. Their hearing and sense of smell are very acute but their sight is weak. Members of the order exist in many places, from the otter-shrew of West African rivers to the hedgehog of Europe.

The Chiroptera (meaning 'hand-winged') are the

Above: Bats, which are the only mammals that can fly, take to the wing in a cave in Trinidad.

Below: The duck-billed platypus of Australia makes its home in a river bank. It is a good swimmer.

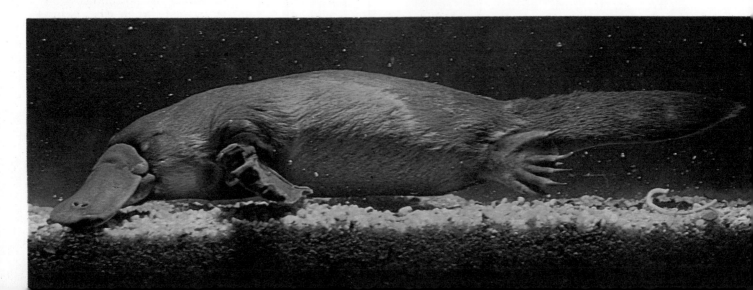

order of bats, the only mammals that can fly. A bat's wings, consisting of tough skin, stretch between body, limbs and tail. Curved claws on the hind limbs enable the bat to roost upside down. European bats hibernate. Bats are equipped with remarkable echo-location senses for their hunting at night. The new-born bat clings to its mother's body for the first week or two, even when the mother is flying. The fox bats of South-East Asia feed on fruit, and seek their food during the daytime.

The edentates get their name from a word meaning toothless. Yet only the anteaters are completely toothless. They have a long tubelike snout and an immensely long thin sticky tongue with which they pick up ants and termites after their digging-claws have broken open a nest. The 'armoured' armadillo has a large number of weak teeth unfit for biting. The sloth lives entirely in trees and is helpless on

Above: Two shrews engage in a squeaking contest. A shrew eats its own weight in food every three hours.

Left: A baby chimpanzee. Chimpanzees are the most intelligent animals, and the most like ourselves.

the ground. All the edentates live in Central America and South America.

The true rodents, which include squirrels, rats, mice and hamsters, are the most numerous and most widespread of mammals. In spite of other differences they resemble each other in their teeth: they have large and powerful front teeth with two incisors in both jaws. These teeth are coated with protective enamel on the front; the back and sides are constantly being sharpened as the animal gnaws. After the front teeth have done their work the cheek teeth crush the food.

The lagomorphs are closely related to the rodents, but for gnawing purposes have two pairs of incisor teeth in the upper jaw instead of one pair. They include the tiny pikas of Asia and North America, the more familiar rabbit and the long-legged hare, which can sprint at 70 kph (45 mph).

The primates belong to the highest order in the animal kingdom and some of its members are man's closest animal relations, especially the gorilla, the orang-utan and the chimpanzee. The chimpanzee most closely resembles us in bodily structure and is remarkably intelligent, even using branches or twigs as primitive kinds of tools. The gorilla is the largest of the man-like apes, and a male can stand nearly 2 metres (6 feet) high and weigh 300 kg (660 lb.). Modern zoologists have disproved old legends about the gorilla's ferocity and have shown it to be a placid creature in the wild. Monkeys, tarsiers, marmosets and lemurs belong to the same order as the primates.

Mammals:
the carnivores

The carnivores or flesh-eating mammals include the big cats which live mainly in hot climates, though the tiger originated in Siberia where a few remain. Lions go about in groups known as 'prides' and the females do most of the hunting. Man-eating lions and tigers are rare: they turn to human flesh because old age or injury has slowed them down for faster prey such as wild pig or antelope. In the Americas the group includes puma, jaguar and ocelot; leopards live in Asia and Africa. In Europe the only cats are the lynx of Scandinavia and Spain and the wild cat of Scotland—a true wild species, not merely a tame cat gone wild. The cheetah, which used to be tamed for hunting purposes in India and Africa, can reach a speed of 80 kph (50 mph) over short distances.

The dog was originally a scavenger and may have become domesticated through skulking round human camps long ago and gradually becoming tame. Foxes, jackals and dingoes are among the group, the most striking being the wolf of America,

Asia and Europe. Wolves hunt in pairs or packs and, unlike the cats which largely stalk their prey, chase their quarry till it drops.

Although bears are very large—the kodiak bear of Alaska can be 3 metres (10 ft) long and weigh 600 kg (1,300 lb.)—their young ones are tiny at birth, a polar bear cub being about 300 mm. (12 in.) long. The brown bear existed in Britain until about 900 years ago and is now in danger of extinction in Italy and Scandinavia. Chiefly a flesh-eater, it also consumes large quantities of wild berries and fish and becomes very fat; this enables it to survive hibernation. The polar bear of the Arctic has layers of fat under the skin which enable it to swim long distances in ice-cold waters, hunting seals, its favourite prey. Excessive hunting by man has endangered this species, too. Vastly different from other bears is the sloth bear of India and Sri Lanka. It prefers honey and termites and roots. When hunting for food the mother carries her two or three young on her back. The giant panda of China is thought to be a kind of bear.

The weasel family contains world-wide members, including the weasel itself, with a small body so slim it can follow mice into their tunnels. At the other end of the scale is the badger which digs long and complex setts in hillsides. The badger eats anything – earthworms, carrion, young rabbits and wasp grubs. It is one of the cleanest of animals; it regularly clears out its home, takes in loads of dead bracken for bedding, and has special 'lavatories' some distance from its home. One member of the weasel family, the North American skunk, defends itself by discharging a foul-smelling yellow liquid.

One group of carnivores, the raccoon family, lives mainly in trees. The raccoons have long tails for balancing: the kinkajou of South America even has a prehensile or grasping tail. The raccoon itself, of the southern United States, is a pretty animal with silver-grey fur and black and white face. It washes its food, from birds to snails, before eating it.

Many carnivores, such as dolphins, sea-lions, walruses, common seals and Atlantic seals, live in the sea. Though they seem clumsy on land, they are streamlined for life under water, swimming with immense skill and speed. When a seal dives, its nostrils and ear-holes close automatically. Some of the whales are less obviously carnivorous than others. The huge blue whale, for example, the largest living mammal, up to 30 metres (100 ft.) long (at birth its young one is about 7 metres (23 ft.), feeds on krill which are tiny shrimplike creatures. The fierce killer-whale, the swiftest swimmer of the oceans, kills porpoises and seals and even attacks much bigger whales.

Above: Lions love to take it easy, although they are fierce hunters. These three lionesses are sunning themselves in a dead acacia tree at Lake Manyara National Park, a wildlife reserve in Tanzania.

Left: The weasel is a small animal, but very fierce. It kills and eats creatures much larger than itself.

Below: The killer whale, also called the grampus, is a relentless hunter of seals, porpoises, and fish.

Mammals: the herbivores

The herbivores, a general term for several groups of mammals, are grass and plant eaters, such as the elephant, largest of living land mammals. The elephant is well-known for its size (an African male can weigh up to six tonnes), its extraordinary trunk and its tusks. These tusks are really overgrown incisor teeth and, being of ivory, have led to the slaughter of vast numbers of elephants. In India the greatest threat to the species is the destruction of its jungle habitat by men needing it for farmland.

The elephant's trunk is a remarkable tool. It can be used as a sort of periscope to test the air; as a schnorkel when crossing water; to pick up small objects with the sensitive tip; to wrench down branches for food; to squirt mud over the elephant's back as protection against insects; to draw up water which is squirted into its mouth; and as a weapon. Yet fearsome though the elephant is at times, it can be trained to do valuable work.

One of the ironies of natural history is that the

rabbit-sized hyrax is now classified in an order close to the elephants because the formation of its feet is similar. Hyraxes live in colonies in many parts of Africa. They can jump fantastically and climb vertical rocks. They leave large heaps of dung outside their dens, once valued as medicine.

Some herbivores such as the sirenians or sea-cows live in the sea. They include the manatee of the West Indies and the dugong of the Indian Ocean. Some zoologists regard these slow, clumsy, mild creatures as elephants which, over many ages, have adapted themselves to life in the water – where they graze at night on aquatic plants.

The most numerous of the herbivores are the ungulates, one of the largest groups of mammals. There are two groups, the 'odd-toed' and the 'even-toed'. The feet of animals have evolved greatly. The horse, for example, has developed from a four-toed animal into a one-toed (it is unique in this), that single toe being its one-time third toe. Vestiges of other toes can be seen on its legs in the shape of 'splint bones'. Cousins of the horse are also among the odd-toed ungulates, including the zebras and wild asses and Przewalski's horse, the only true horse still existing in a wild state. A few survive in the Mongolian desert. Another odd-toed ungulate is the rhinoceros. With its armour-plated hide and its aggressive horn, it is a doughty figure. That horn, which can measure 750 mm. (30 in.) long, is made of highly compacted stiff hair.

The even-toed ungulates are also the cloven-hoofed animals which all, with the exception of camels and llamas, walk on the tips of their toes. These even-toed ungulates are divided into two other groups. First there are the non-ruminants, such as wild pigs and hippopotamuses, which simply eat and digest their food in the normal way. Second are the ruminants or cud-chewers, including camels, giraffes, goats, deer, antelopes and cattle. The process of rumination enables them to swallow large quantities of food at a time and digest it later when they feel safe from attack. Their

stomachs are divided into four parts. When the animal begins the real process of digestion it is able to regurgitate or bring up the food, bit by bit, through the various compartments into the mouth, where it is chewed slowly and swallowed again.

One other difference exists between certain ungulates: deer shed their antlers every year and grow new ones; antelopes retain their horns throughout life. Only male deer carry antlers except in the case of reindeer; female reindeer also carry antlers. Antelopes live in many different kinds of habitats. Those that inhabit grasslands generally wander around in large herds, while antelopes in forest areas tend to live on their own.

Top left: Two zebras have a drink at a water-hole. These horse-like animals live in the wide grasslands of Africa.

Left: A baby elephant with its mother. It takes milk with its mouth, and not with its trunk.

Top right: A rhinoceros, one of the heavyweights of the grazing animals, takes no notice of two egrets strutting beside it.

Right: Two European deer. The red deer is the larger animal, and is still plentiful in the wild. The fallow deer is much smaller, and it has wide, flat antlers. Most of the remaining fallow deer live in parks.

Birds

Birds are warm-blooded creatures like mammals, but they lay eggs. Their bodies are very strong in proportion to their weight, which is why they can fly. Most mammals are far too heavy for their muscles to lift them through the air, even if they had wings. There are many different kinds of birds. Some live on or near water, spending as much time swimming as flying. Some are birds of prey, which live by hunting. A few birds cannot fly at all. The most common birds are the passerines, or perching birds, so-called because they can perch on the branches of trees, gripping with their feet.

One of the largest orders of sea and water birds contains the ducks, swans and geese, all of which have a long neck, comparatively narrow and pointed wings, webbed feet and a blunt bill. Swans, largest of waterfowl, are all white except for the black Australian swan. On land they waddle clumsily, but in water they swim gracefully. They take off ponderously but once airborne are a majestic sight.

Wild geese are smaller and more thickset, and feed much on grass. They live in flocks (the swan is more solitary) and fly fast and direct, in V-formation, uttering clanging cries. Many, such as the greylag, bean goose and white-front, breed in Arctic regions, flying south for the winter.

Ducks in general are still smaller, with shorter necks and legs. Males and females have different plumage (unlike swans and geese which are more alike in the sexes), the male being the brighter. Ducks consist of two main groups. The dabbling ducks rarely dive but feed on the surface of the water or by up-ending. They include such species as mallard, wigeon, teal and garganey. The diving ducks, such as scaup and pochard, often swim under water.

Most ducks are omnivores – they will eat anything – but the mergansers feed entirely on fish, being equipped with saw-edged bills for grasping their

Top: The herring gull lives on the sea-coasts. It hunts for food as much over land as over the water.

Left: The great northern diver is also known as the common loon. Divers can walk on land only with difficulty, and spend nearly all their time in the water. The great northern diver spends its winters in salt water, but is found in summer on rivers and lakes.

sea-eagles, including the white-tailed, largest of eagles, and not fussy as to whether it snatches fish or duck. Young dolphins and seals may also be snatched by these powerful birds.

Not all birds of prey hunt over water. The golden eagle sweeps across the hillsides at near 200 kph (125 mph.) to seize hare or grouse. The kestrel hovers over the fields watching for voles. In the Philippines the monkey-eating eagle lives up to its name.

The largest living bird, the ostrich of Africa, makes up for its flightless state by being able to run as fast as a horse. Equally, those other flightless birds, the numerous penguins of Antarctica and some other areas of the southern hemisphere, are compensated by being expert underwater swimmers.

Left: The hen harrier – called the marsh hawk in North America – is a bird of prey with long wings and a long tail. It glides low over the ground.

Below: Penguins are flightless birds that have made their home in the sea. They use their short wings as paddles for swimming. They go ashore in Antarctica and nearby islands to lay their eggs and raise chicks.

prey. Some ducks are notable for their nesting habits. Shelducks often live in old rabbit-burrows. The female eider plucks down from her breast to line her nest. Mallard sometimes nest in trees.

Some birds such as the storm petrel – scarcely bigger than a robin – spend all but a few weeks of the year at sea, coming to land only to lay their eggs. The stately gannet, a very large bird, also spends much time at sea. It is a spectacular bird because of its magnificent diving skill, plunging into the sea from as much as 30 metres (100 ft.) to snatch a fish. Another formidable fisherman is the pelican, whose best known feature is the extendable pouch on the lower bill which it can fill to capacity.

The many other kinds of water birds range from the wandering albatross of southern seas, with a wing-span of nearly 4 metres (12 ft.), to the tiny dabchick of freshwater lakes; from the handsome great northern diver of Alaska and Iceland to the comic-looking puffin with its gaudily-striped bill. The families of gulls, kittiwakes, terns and waders throng the shores in their thousands.

Some birds of prey seek their food in fresh or salt water. Notable among these is the osprey which soars over lake or river, then plunges down to seize large fish. Even more majestic are the

Below: Emus live in the great deserts in the middle of Australia. They are very large birds, as tall as a man. They cannot fly, but they can run very fast. The females lay as many as 16 huge, dark green eggs.

Perching birds

There are over 5,000 species of the passerines or perching birds, more than all the rest of the bird orders together. For the most part they are small or medium-sized, distributed all over the world except Antarctica. The most colourful and most numerous live in tropical regions. They include such brilliant specimens as the paradise whydah which, only 150 mm. (6 in.) long in the body, has a tail over twice that length; the three-coloured tanager of Brazil; and the black-naped monarch flycatcher.

Some passerines are much bigger, such as the raven which reaches a length of 660 mm. (26 in.) or the equally big Indian blue pie. Some have strange characteristics: a colony of buffalo weaver birds builds a large communal nest, each pair of birds having its own room. The long-tailed tit uses perhaps 2,000 feathers, as well as other material, to make its snug oval nest, into which a dozen fledglings are crammed. As for food, this varies from the nectar which the fairy-like hummingbirds sip to the nuts preferred by the nutcrackers of northern Europe and North America.

Practically all birds have a form of song, the main purpose of which is to assert the male bird's claim to his territory. For bird-watchers, song is often the most important way of identifying a bird, which may remain unseen.

Many passerines are 'resident', that is to say they remain in the same region all the year, such as the robin and wren. Others are migratory, living part of the year in one place and part in another. Swallows, warblers, golden orioles and flycatchers are all migrants. Some birds even make a round trip of 30,000 km. (18,000 mi.) in the year, seeking better feeding according to the seasons. Nobody has completely unravelled the wonderful means by which birds find their way: in some cases young birds migrate after their parents have left.

Another colourful order of birds is the parrot family, with more than 300 species. They all live in the tropics, ranging from the handsome metre-long macaw of South America to the tiny but equally lovely blue-crowned hanging parakeet of Indonesia, which sleeps upside down. Parrots use their powerful hooked beaks for cracking hard food such as nuts, and also as an extra claw to help them climb. For centuries they have been notorious for their ability to talk, though this is only mimicry. That

Top left: The song thrush lives in Europe. It is one of the finest songsters in the bird world.

Below: A tiny broad-billed hummingbird hovering, ready to insert its long, thin beak into a flower. Its wings move 60 times a second, making the hum.

favourite cage-bird, the budgerigar, is a member of the Australian parrot family.

Beautiful colours are not confined to the parrots. The bee-eaters and hoopoes are equally beautiful, as are some of the kingfishers. The kingfishers are an interesting group, for while some of them simply sit on a branch and fly down to earth after insects, others have evolved into skilled fishermen, such as the turquoise-hued kingfisher itself, which can sometimes be seen flashing along European rivers like a feathered jewel. From a branch it dives down at a small fish, flies back, flips its catch in the air and swallows it head first.

Like the kingfishers, the woodpeckers are another family that specialises, and they live up to their name. They have long sticky barbed tongues that pick up the ants and grubs they prise out of the bark of trees. The pigeon family thrives almost everywhere, except in polar regions. The young 'squabs' are fed on so-called pigeon's milk, a thick semi-liquid formed in the parents' crops. The most famous member of the family used to be the American passenger pigeon, so numerous that when the birds migrated they darkened the sky; when they roosted, branches broke under the weight of the flocks. Yet now these birds are extinct, shot in their millions by hunters during the 1800s.

These gaudy macaws live in the tropical forests of South America. They are members of the parrot family.

Reptiles and amphibians

Reptiles and amphibians are cold-blooded animals whose blood-heat rises or falls with the temperature of their surroundings. There are 6,000 species altogether. Reptiles include the legless snakes, but many have four legs, such as the crocodiles and their various cousins, caymans and alligators. These crocodilians all have large heads, long, powerful jaws, thick 'armoured' hide, and long, strong tails with which they swim. Most members of the group live in fresh water, feeding on fish and carrion (animals already dead).

The Nile crocodile, a very large beast indeed, seizes animals drinking at a river, and many humans have also been killed in this way. One of its methods of hunting is to deal a sweeping blow with the tail, knocking the victim within range of its jaws. Often a crocodile glides along submerged, for a kind of fleshy valve prevents water entering its lungs. The female lays large numbers of eggs, some in sand-holes, others in nests of vegetation.

Other four-legged reptiles are the turtles and tortoises. Like the crocodilians they live mainly in the tropics. Their backs are protected by a firm carapace, a rounded shield under which they can withdraw neck and legs. One of the biggest is the now rare Galápagos giant tortoise, nearly 1·5 metres (5 ft.) long. One of the smallest (also one of the few European specimens) is the pond tortoise, only about 150 mm. (6 in.) long. The lizards, too, are numbered among the reptiles. Perhaps the weirdest lizard is the stump-tailed skink of Australia, which can move backwards as fast as it can forwards. It is often called the shingleback.

There are nearly 2,500 species of snakes. Their bodies are covered with scales that not only protect them but help their locomotion, which is carried out through the movement of their many ribs. All snakes slough (discard) their skins several times a year. Some 600 poisonous species of snakes exist, and the poison of well over 100 kinds can kill a

Above: The garter snake is one of nearly 2,000 kinds of snakes which are not poisonous. Garter snakes are often found in town parks and gardens. Unlike most snakes, they bear live young.

Left: The salt-water or estuarine crocodile lives near coasts in northern Australia and the islands of south-eastern Asia. It spends a large part of its time in the sea and can swim long distances.

Right: The wood turtle of the eastern United States lives near swamps and woodland streams. It is surprisingly intelligent.

human being. Two types of poison exist; one affects the victim's nervous system, the other the blood. The tongue of the snake does not sting. It is an instrument of touch and an aid to the sense of smell. The snake bites its prey, poison being carried from sacs or glands in the upper jaw through grooved fangs. Some of the deadliest snakes are Russell's viper of India, the tiger snake of Australia and the hamadryad or king cobra of Asia, longest of poisonous snakes, measuring up to 5 metres.

One well-known family of snakes, the constrictors, kills its victims by suffocation, not by poison. Biggest of all is the reticulate python of south-eastern Asia, which has been known to reach a length of 10 metres (33 ft.). These snakes can swallow wild pig and leopards. The jaws of all snakes are only loosely connected, enabling them to expand greatly and thus swallow large prey.

The amphibians take their name from Greek words meaning creatures that are equally at home in water or on land. The best known are the toads and frogs, most of which feed on insects and worms. The much bigger bullfrogs of Africa, America and India even hunt mice and fledglings. The other amphibians, the newts and salamanders, live mainly in the temperate parts of the northern hemisphere, unlike the toads and frogs, which are found in the tropics as well. The amphibians lay spawn, a mass of eggs. The eggs hatch out as tadpoles, which live in the water until they are fully developed.

In the colder parts of the northern hemisphere reptiles and amphibians such as the viper, grass snake, frog and toad hibernate during winter. The African bullfrog buries itself in the ground to avoid the heat of the day.

Above: The green tree frog of the southern United States is one of more than 300 kinds of frogs which live in trees. The green tree frog changes colour: in cool weather it is grey, and at night, calling to its mate, it becomes a golden yellow.

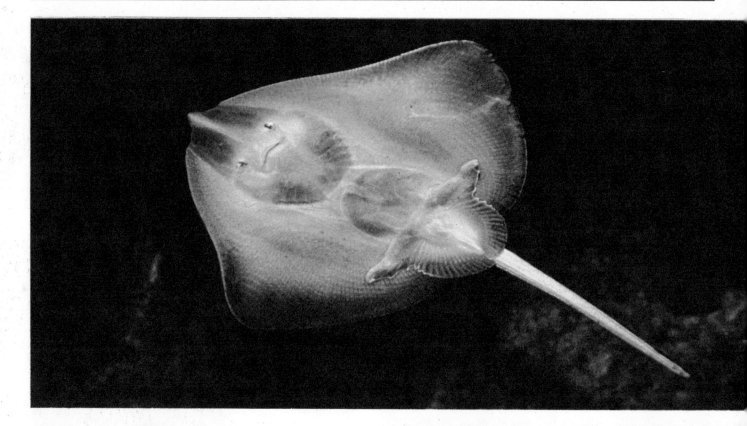

Fishes

Scientists believe that all life on Earth began in the sea, and there are a great many animals still living there. The most important of these are the fishes. They are vertebrates – that is, they have backbones, like mammals, birds, reptiles and amphibians. But unlike the other animals mentioned, almost all fishes can live only in water. They cannot breathe air, and they do not have lungs. Instead they breathe through organs called gills, which extract the oxygen from water just as lungs take it from air.

There are two main groups of fishes: the bony fishes, that is, those which have bone in their skeletons; and the cartilaginous fishes, which do not have bone but have a flexible substance called cartilage, or gristle. The soft ridge on the lower part of your nose is cartilage.

The cartilaginous fishes include some of the largest and fiercest of all – the sharks. Unlike the other giants of the ocean, the whales, the sharks are not mammals, but most of them do give birth to live young. Only a few sharks lay eggs as other fishes do.

Some members of the shark group are more familiar to us than we realise: the so-called 'rock salmon' on sale at fishmongers is often the dog-fish. Some dog-fish have been called scavengers of the sea, grabbing what they can where they can.

Rays and skates are also related to the sharks. One of these, the sting-ray, is equipped with a long, sharp saw-toothed spine in the tail which can deal out a serious wound. The electric ray can deliver a considerable shock, to knock out its prey or in self-defence. The common skate is highly prized for

the table. Like some of its cousins its body is flattened, extending on either side like wings, which can measure nearly three metres from side to side. Rays and skates swim by moving their wings up and down, almost 'flying' through the sea.

Many of the real sharks have a fearsome reputation which is not always deserved. For example, one of the commonest and biggest North Atlantic specimens is the basking shark: although it sometimes attains a length of 10 metres (30 ft.), it is harmless—and gets its name from its habit of lying on the surface of the sea, enjoying a spell of fine weather. But the man-eating sharks of Australian and South African waters can indeed be dangerous characters and frequently live up to their name.

A shark constantly sheds its teeth, which are replaced by a succession of new teeth. However, the biggest of all the family, the so-called whale-

Left: An underside view of a young ray, showing its slit-like mouth. Rays move by flapping their large, wing-like fins, and mostly swim close to the seafloor.

Below: A great white shark, the world's largest flesh-eating fish, entangled in a net used to guard an Australian bathing beach. It is comparatively rare.

shark, 13 metres (42 ft.) long, has feeble teeth. One of the strangest sharks is the hammerhead, unique among fishes: as its name suggests, its head sticks out on either side of the body, the eyes being situated on the ends.

Of the bony fishes, the cod has been one of the most important for fishermen since early times, its value greatly increased by its oil-containing liver. Cod live mainly in the Atlantic, in regions off Iceland, the Lofoten Islands and the Newfoundland Banks. The cod can reach a weight of 40 kg (90 lb.). The female produces between three million and seven million eggs; only a tiny minority of these hatch out, let alone reach maturity, for fish in general have many natural enemies, quite apart from man. The adult cod itself feeds on other fish, molluscs and crustaceans. One of its most unpleasant enemies is the hagfish, an eel-like creature which bores its way into the stomach cavity of its victim, living and feeding inside the fish.

Usually a particular kind of fish can only survive in particular conditions: for example a cod cannot live in fresh water; a gudgeon would not survive in salt water. But there are certain species that pass part of their lives at different times in the

oceans and the rivers. The salmon, found in temperate and Arctic regions of the northern hemisphere, is an anadromous fish: a long word, but it gives the clue to the salmon's way of life, for it means 'ascending rivers to spawn'.

Some scientists regard the salmon as a seafish, only becoming a freshwater fish at spawning or breeding-time. It spends the third year of its life in the waters south of Greenland, growing strong and fat. Then a grilse, as it is now called, it feels the mating-urge and makes its way across hundreds of kilometres of ocean. The strange but marvellous thing is that it always returns to the river where it hatched out, whether in Britain, Norway, Iceland or North America. Its passage up-river is difficult and spectacular, for it has to leap weirs and cascades, sometimes having to attempt a jump several times. But it persists and swims on and on even into streams little bigger than ditches. At the chosen spot, the female makes a redd, or shallow trough, by violently wiggling her body to and fro. She lays her eggs and the male salmon fertilizes them with his milt.

The young salmon – parr – live in the river for two years, at the end of which they are called smolt. Those few that survive make their way down river and out into the open sea. There they stay for a year or so until they in turn are mature enough to breed, when they return – again, always to the distant river of their birth.

The eel, too (snakelike in appearance but a true fish) spends part of its life at sea and part in fresh water. It ranges from the Mediterranean sea lands to Scandinavia and also exists in North America. Unlike the salmon, eels hatch at sea, the main

breeding ground being in the western Atlantic. After breeding, the adult eels die. The young eels, or elvers as they become, spend more than two years drifting back towards Europe, growing all the time. North American eels have a shorter journey. In the spring of each year huge numbers of eels ascend the rivers, feeding on worms and crayfish, though when really big they will even eat frogs and water-voles.

They remain in the rivers for about two years, when they feel the strange urge that draws them back to the sea – and nothing will stop them. This happens in autumn. So determined are the eels to return to the sea that they will even make their way across land from one piece of water to another. Eels have been known to travel 1,200 km. (750 mi.) in three months.

There are many strange creatures among the fish tribe. One of the strangest (which sometimes gets stranded on European shores) is the angler-fish. Its head is very wide and much bigger than its body, and its mouth is extremely large – which gives it its other name of frog-fish. Its most interesting feature is a long dorsal or back-fin, resembling a bent rod at the end of which hangs a flap of skin. This the angler-fish dangles above its mouth as a kind of bait. A passing fish cannot resist this, grabs at it and is at once pulled downwards into the angler's mouth, which bristles with teeth.

Some fish have poison-stings, notably the weever family, while the moray or muraena possesses poison-glands and its bite can be dangerous. Yet the Romans considered this fish a delicacy. One famous Roman was even said to keep a moray as a pet – and feed it on the flesh of slaves.

Left: A female sockeye salmon using her tail to dig a nest site in the bed of the Adams River in British Columbia. Gravel is spurting out behind her as she works.

Right: The angler-fish gets its name because it has a long, rod-like projection on the front of its snout, with a flap on the tip. The angler-fish waves the rod to and fro like a fishing rod to lure small fish to it, so that it can catch them for food. This particular angler-fish has a transparent body, and its lure gives off light.

Below: Elvers (young eels) swimming up a river in Britain after their long journey from the western Atlantic. The eels spend up to two years in their river homes before going back to sea.

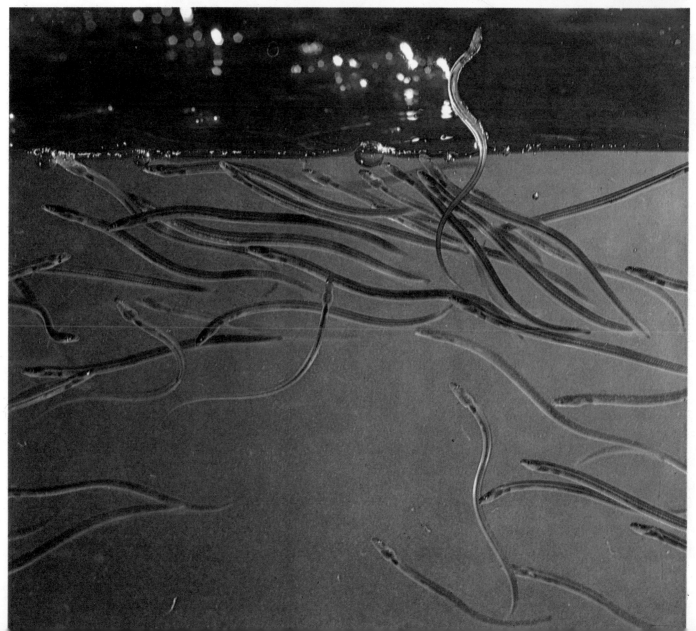

Above: A garden spider spins its web, a trap to catch flying insects. Not all spiders spin webs.

Below: This shield bug is a member of the insect group known as the Hemiptera – the true bugs.

Invertebrates: the arthropods

All the animals we have described on the past few pages – mammals, birds, reptiles, amphibians and fishes – are vertebrates: that is, they have backbones. Now we come to much the largest group of animals, the invertebrates, which have no backbones. A backbone gives an animal's body strength, so it is not surprising that most of the invertebrates are small creatures, such as insects and worms.

A very important group of the invertebrates is that known as the arthropods. Arthropods get their name from two Greek words meaning that their limbs are divided by joints into a series of movable segments. They include spiders, all the insects, and crustaceans such as crabs.

Spiders look a bit like insects, but they are in an order on their own, the arachnids. They differ from insects in various ways: they do not have wings; they do not possess antennae or feelers as the butterflies do; and they have eight legs instead of six. We usually think of spiders and webs. A web is a beautiful piece of work – but it is actually a trap for catching the insects on which the spider feeds. When an insect is snared in the web, the waiting spider rushes up, paralyses its victim with its poisonous bite, and sucks out its life-juices.

Not all spiders make webs. In South America the bird-eating spider, which can be almost as big as a rat, sometimes lives up to its name, though usually it simply seizes insects. The name of the trap-door spider also gives an idea of its tactics, for it lurks in a burrow underground with a hinged lid at the surface. The jumping spider uses other methods: it stalks its prey – then jumps on it. Although a spider's poison can kill an insect, only that of a very few spiders has any effect on man, and only the black widow of North America has been known to kill.

Also numbered among the arachnids are the scorpions, which have a pair of grabbing claws rather like those of a lobster. The scorpion's most powerful weapon is hidden in the tail, secreting a paralysing poison, though this is not as fearful as was once believed. The young are born live and in some cases the mother runs around with them on her back while they are very young.

Crabs are among the best-known crustaceans. Crabs range from the large edible crab which often ends up on the tea-table, to the strange hermit crab which, unlike other crabs, is not properly armoured, so it takes up residence in empty mollusc shells for protection. Crabs generally live in water, but one species, the land crab of India, spends much time on land, migrating back to the sea to breed. Other crustaceans include such varied creatures as lobsters, shrimps, barnacles – and even woodlice. All are protected by a hard, close-fitting kind of shell or crust, which acts as an external skeleton.

Insects form the largest group of arthropods, and indeed the largest group of all animals. There are more than 1,000,000 known species, and more are being found every year.

An adult insect's body is divided into three separate parts – the head, thorax, and abdomen. Usually it has one or two pairs of wings. A few very simple insects, such as silverfish, have no wings, and some others lose their wings in later life. It is only adult insects which ever have wings.

Nearly all insects lay eggs. In some species the

Butterflies and moths are members of the same group of insects. The differences between butterflies and moths are small, but most butterflies rest with their wings closed, like this one, while moths keep their wings out.

newly-hatched young are very like their parents in form, such as the grasshopper. Most young insects, however, are completely different from the adults and go through various changes before they finally become like them. From the egg the larva (called a caterpillar in butterflies) emerges. It eats and grows steadily. In due course the larva bursts its skin and turns into a pupa or chrysalid. In this form it does not eat but lies unmoving, dormant, while the young insect grows into the likeness of its parents. Presently the pupa skin breaks open and the perfect adult insect comes forth.

This scarlet prawn is a typical example of a crustacean. It lives in deep water, where the light of the Sun barely penetrates, and has a hard, close shell.

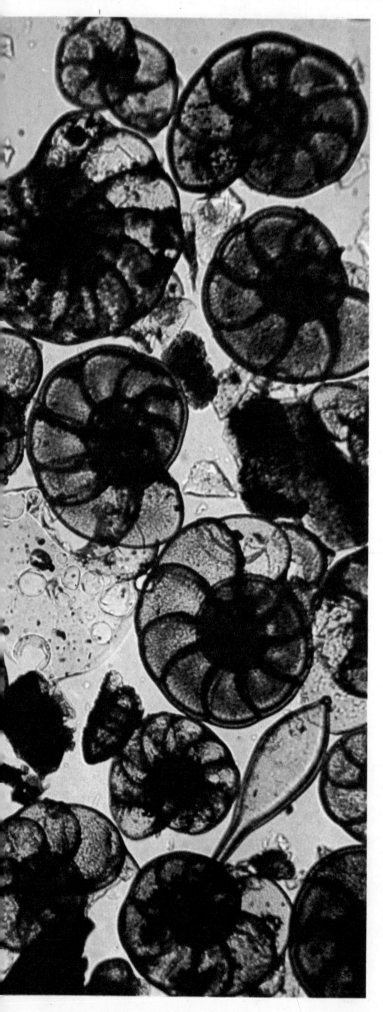

The other invertebrates

Besides the arthropods there are 21 other groups of invertebrate animals. Some of them are the simplest forms of animal life. They are the protozoa, which are believed to represent the first animal life to appear on Earth. The amoeba is one of the simplest of all, and it consists of just a single cell, the basic building-brick of life (most animals contain a great many cells, generally millions upon millions of them, and of more than one kind).

The amoeba reproduces itself just by dividing in two. It feeds on organisms even tinier than itself by flowing over them, and thus taking them into its body. It moves by oozing its way onward. Insignificant though the amoeba is, this creature is scientifically extremely important, for it contains all the qualities that we can see in all living animals: it can reproduce itself; it can move about; it can feed; and it takes in oxygen from the water in which it lives. From single-celled creatures of this kind all the other animals have evolved, over a period of several hundred million years.

Perhaps to the surprise of many people, sponges are now classed as animals. They are made up of vast numbers of cells held together by an outer 'skeleton' of a threadlike substance called spongin. Through a complicated system of minute canals the sponge draws in water from which it gets oxygen and food. Large varieties exist, mostly in salt water. Some, such as the blood-red pomegranate sponge or the romantically named mermaid's glove, are extremely beautiful—very different from the bath sponge some people use to wash themselves.

The group of animals called coelenterates includes the sea-anemones, corals and jellyfish. Though they are such lowly creatures coelenterates are often astonishingly beautiful. Corals are best known for their colourful limestone homes, which build up the Great Barrier Reef of Australia. Most of the coelenterates have one thing in common—their ability to sting in self-defence. Perhaps the best-known example of this is the jellyfish, whose 'tentacles' are armed with poisonous hairs. Another marine creature you may come across at the seaside is the starfish, belonging to a group called echinoderms, and related to the sea urchin, the brittle-star and the sea cucumber.

Molluscs are soft-bodied animals, usually protected by a hard shell. They have eyes of a sort and a nervous system, but no real brain. Although they can move about many of them stay fixed to the same

Left: Tiny, one-celled creatures known as Foraminifera live in the sea. They have shells, some of them no bigger than a pin-head, and many are found in rocks.

Right: The garden snail carries its spiral-shaped shell on its back. It moves by stretching and contracting its single, broad foot, on a carpet of slime.

spot all their lives–limpets and dog-whelks, for example. But the garden snail, another mollusc, moves around, and so does its cousin the slug. Many molluscs such as oysters and mussels are highly prized as food.

More spectacular is the eight-limbed octopus, which sometimes reaches a great size and has been the subject of many an old salt's yarns. Another mollusc, the shipworm, with razor-sharp teeth in its head, used to be a fearful menace in the days of wooden ships. In their hundreds, shipworms battened on to a hull, eating away until the woodwork was riddled through and through. More fine ships went to the bottom because of the shipworm's attacks than because of enemy cannon-balls.

Another worm of a different family and one of

Above left : The crown-of-thorns starfish is an example of the group of animals called echinoderms, which are symmetrical in shape. It lives in tropical seas.

Above right : The earthworm helps to break up the soil.

the lowliest forms of animal life is also one of the most important: the earthworm. It is vitally useful to agriculture, for it feeds on the soil, breaking this up finely as it does so. As it tunnels through the ground an earthworm actually 'digs' the soil, bringing up subsoil from below and taking leaf-mould down into the ground from the surface. One hectare of farmland may contain as many as 7,500,000 earthworms, and in a year's digging they bring 45 tonnes of soil to the surface!

FINGERTIP FACTS ABOUT ANIMAL LIFE

GROUP NAMES

There are special names for groups of animals when they are together, such as a herd of deer or a pack of hounds. Here are some of them:

An army of frogs

A charm of finches

A chattering of starlings

A congregation of birds

A covey of grouse

A field of racehorses

A gaggle of geese when they are swimming, or a skein of geese when they are flying

A herd of seals

A kennel of dogs

A nest of mice

A pride of lions

A school of fishes or whales

A shoal of fishes, especially herrings and mackerel

A siege of bitterns

A sounder of swine

A team of ducks

A troop of kangaroos

A wedge of swans

WHAT'S IN A NAME?

We saw on pages 30–31 how botanists use Latin names to identify plants—many of which have no common name, or share the same name. Zoologists, the scientists who study animals, use a similar code. This is very necessary when people who speak different languages are talking about the same animal. An Englishman says 'The dog'; a Frenchman says 'Le chien'; a German says 'Der Hund'; a Spaniard says 'El perro'; and an Italian says 'Il cane'. Zoologists may not understand each others' languages, but they would all know the scientific name for the animal, *Canis familiaris*.

There is even more confusion when people who talk the same language use one name for two different animals. For example, an American, an Australian and an Englishman each use the word 'robin'—but they are talking about three different birds!

Animals all belong to the kingdom Animalia, just as plants all belong to the kingdom Plantae. The animal kingdom is divided into several phyla (singular, phylum), groups of roughly similar creatures. Each phylum is split into classes, and each class into orders. Within each order are families, groups of animals which are very similar, such as all the big and little cats. A genus is a small group of animals within a family, while a species is a group of animals which are all the same, such as lions or tigers. If a family is very big it may be split up into two or more sub-families.

THE DOG

This is how a zoologist would give a complete scientific classification of a dog:

Kingdom: Animalia

Phylum: Chordata

Subphylum: Vertebrata

Class: Mammalia

Order: Carnivora

Family: Canidae

Genus: *Canis*

Species: *familiaris*

If the zoologist were writing about the animal, he would use only the genus and species. They are always printed in *italic type*, like this, *Canis familiaris*; the genus always begins with a capital letter, and the species is always written in small letters. The family and other group names are given in Roman type.

YOUNG ANIMALS

There are many special names for the young of animals. Here are just a few:

Name of animal	Name of young
Bear	Cub
Beaver	Pup
Cat	Kitten
Cow	Calf
Deer	Fawn
Dog	Puppy
Elephant	Calf
Goose	Gosling
Horse	Foal
Kangaroo	Joey
Pig	Piglet
Rabbit	Kindle
Sheep	Lamb
Turkey	Poult

KEEPING OUT OF SIGHT

Animals that are likely to be pounced on and eaten by other animals have developed means of keeping themselves safe. Many of these ways involve some form of disguise. Very few animals disguise themselves deliberately: as a rule, they are born either with the right colouring to keep them safe, or with an instinct which leads them to take protective action automatically.

The simplest form of disguise is what we call *protective colouration*. The animal is coloured to look like its background. For instance, a polar bear and an Arctic fox both have white coats that do not show up on snow. The blotchy coat of a giraffe and the spots on a leopard make them hard to see in undergrowth where there are patches of shadow and brilliant sunshine. *Protective resemblance* is the term used when the shape of an animal matches its background.

The familiar stick insect looks just like a twig, and other insects

Above: A sea anemone stings a victim with its tentacles, then slowly digests it.

THE ANIMAL KINGDOM

The animal kingdom is divided into 23 major sub-divisions called phyla. Of these phyla, 22 are invertebrates – animals without backbones, generally very small.

Protozoa are one-celled animals, which are found in water, the soil, or the bodies of other animals.

Porifera are sponges. Their bodies have many cells, but they have no real digestive systems.

Mesozoa are tiny, worm-like parasites, living inside other small animals.

Coelenterata are jelly-like animals such as sea anemones, jellyfish and corals.

Ctenophora, or comb-jellies, are also tiny jelly-like animals.

Platyhelminthes, flatworms, are parasites.

Nemertinea are ribbonworms, mostly living in the sea.

Entoprocta are flower-like animals living in water.

Ectoprocta are called moss animals because they live in colonies that look like moss. They cannot move about.

Aschelminthes are worm-like animals living in water.

Acanthocephala are spiny-headed worms which are parasites in other animals' bodies.

Phoronidea are worm-like animals living in mud.

Pogonophora are also worm-like animals which live in the sea. They are called 'beard worms' because of their beard-like mass of tentacles.

Brachiopoda, or lamp shells, also live in the sea.

Echinodermata are sea animals with hard plates. Many, such as starfish, have five 'arms'.

Chaetognatha, or arrow-worms, are very tiny sea animals with transparent bodies.

Mollusca, the molluscs, have soft bodies, many protected by a shell. They include slugs, snails, limpets and clams; some live in the sea, some on land.

Annelida, or segmented worms, have long bodies divided into many sections. They include the familiar earthworm.

Sipunculoidea are worm-like animals which burrow into the sand of the seashore.

Priapuloidea are also worm-like creatures which live in mud just off the seashore.

Echiuroidea are bag-shaped animals which live in burrows in mud, sand or rock on the seashore.

Arthropoda, joint-footed animals, are the largest group of animals, including spiders, crustaceans, insects, centipedes and millipedes.

Chordata are animals with backbones. There are a few simple worm-like animals among them, but otherwise they include all the large and important animals – fishes, amphibians, reptiles, birds and mammals.

resemble leaves or stones.

Mimicry is the term used when one animal looks like another. It is most common in insects and is also found in the snake world. For example, some insects which are dangerous or unpleasant to eat, such as wasps, have markings of black and yellow. Many of the harmless – and edible – hoverflies are also coloured black and yellow, and for this reason birds leave them alone.

ANIMAL RECORDS

Largest animal is the blue whale, which can grow up to 30 metres (100 feet) in length.

Smallest animals are the protozoa, which can be seen only under a microscope.

Largest land animal is the African elephant, which can be as much as 3.5 metres (11½ feet) tall.

Longest-living animals are some bacteria, which can live for hundreds of years. Of larger animals, the giant tortoise holds the record with 177 years.

MIGRATION

Some animals move from one place to another according to the seasons of the year. In the northern hemisphere a great many birds spend the spring and summer in northern parts of Europe, America and Asia, where there are plenty of insects for them to feed their babies on. When the colder weather comes the birds fly south where the Sun is hot and there are further supplies of food. When the weather down south becomes too hot, they fly north again to lay their eggs.

Animals larger and smaller than birds also migrate every year in search of food. Herds of caribou in Canada and Alaska move north in the summer and south again in the winter, though only a few hundreds of kilometres. Birds migrate for great distances: the record is held by the Arctic tern, which leaves its northern haunts as the long Arctic summer ends and flies to the Antarctic to spend a second summer there – an annual round trip of 36,000 kilometres (22,400 miles). One of the smallest migrants also covers long distances. It is the monarch butterfly of North America, which flies from Hudson Bay to Florida and back – an 8,000-kilometre (5,000-mile) journey.

Lands of the world

The world as we know it today is a home for more than 4,300,000,000 people, who have cut down and cleared the wild forests which once covered much of the land and made towns and roads and farms.

The natural division of the world is into its continents, the large land-masses. There are seven of them – Africa. Asia, North America, South America, Antarctica, Australia and Europe. People live in all but one continent – Antarctica is too cold for everyday life.

Country	Km²	Sq. miles	Capital	Population	Money unit
Anguilla	90	35	—	6,500	Dollar
Antigua and Barbuda	440	170	St. John's	74,000	Dollar
Bahamas	14,400	5,400	Nassau	225,000	Dollar
Barbados	430	166	Bridgetown	265,000	Dollar
Belize	23,000	8,900	Belmopan	153,000	Dollar
Bermuda	54	21	Hamilton	58,000	Dollar
Canada	9,220,000	3,560,000	Ottawa	23,499,000	Dollar
Cayman Islands	260	100	George Town	12,000	Dollar
Costa Rica	50,900	19,700	San José	2,111,000	Colón
Cuba	114,000	44,000	Havana	9,728,000	Peso
Dominica	750	290	Roseau	81,000	Dollar
Dominican Republic	50,000	19,300	Santo Domingo	5,121,000	Peso
El Salvador	19,900	7,700	San Salvador	4,354,000	Colón
Greenland	2,176,000	840,000	Godthaab	51,000	Krone
Grenada	344	133	St. George's	97,000	Dollar
Guadeloupe	1,782	688	Pointe à Pitre	330,000	Franc
Guatemala	109,000	42,000	Guatemala	6,621,000	Quetzal
Haiti	28,000	10,700	Port au Prince	4,833,000	Gourde
Honduras	111,000	43,000	Tegucigalpa	3,439,000	Lempira
Jamaica	11,000	4,400	Kingston	2,133,000	Dollar
Martinique	1,040	400	Fort de France	325,000	Franc
Mexico	1,973,000	762,000	Mexico City	66,994,000	Peso
Montserrat	101	39	Plymouth	13,000	Dollar
Netherlands Antilles	1,020	394	Willemstad	246,000	Guilder
Nicaragua	148,000	57,000	Managua	2,395,000	Córdoba
Panama	82,600	31,900	Panama City	1,826,000	Balboa
Panama Canal Zone	1,676	647	Balboa Heights	45,000	Dollar
Puerto Rico	8,800	3,400	San Juan	3,317,000	Dollar
St. Kitts-Nevis	262	101	Basseterre	67,000	Dollar
St. Lucia	616	238	Castries	113,000	Dollar
St. Pierre and Miquelon	241	93	St. Pierre	6,000	Franc
St. Vincent	390	150	Kingstown	96,000	Dollar
Trinidad and Tobago	5,130	1,980	Port of Spain	1,133,000	Dollar
Turks and Caicos Islands	500	193	Grand Turk	6,000	Dollar
United States of America	9,160,000	3,537,000	Washington, D.C.	218,059,000	Dollar
Virgin Islands, British	153	59	Road Town	12,000	Dollar
Virgin Islands, U.S.	344	133	Charlotte Amalie	104,000	Dollar

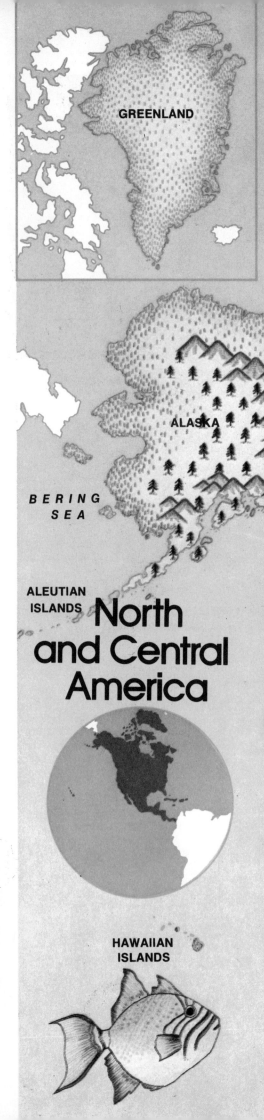

GREENLAND

ALASKA

BERING SEA

ALEUTIAN ISLANDS

North and Central America

HAWAIIAN ISLANDS

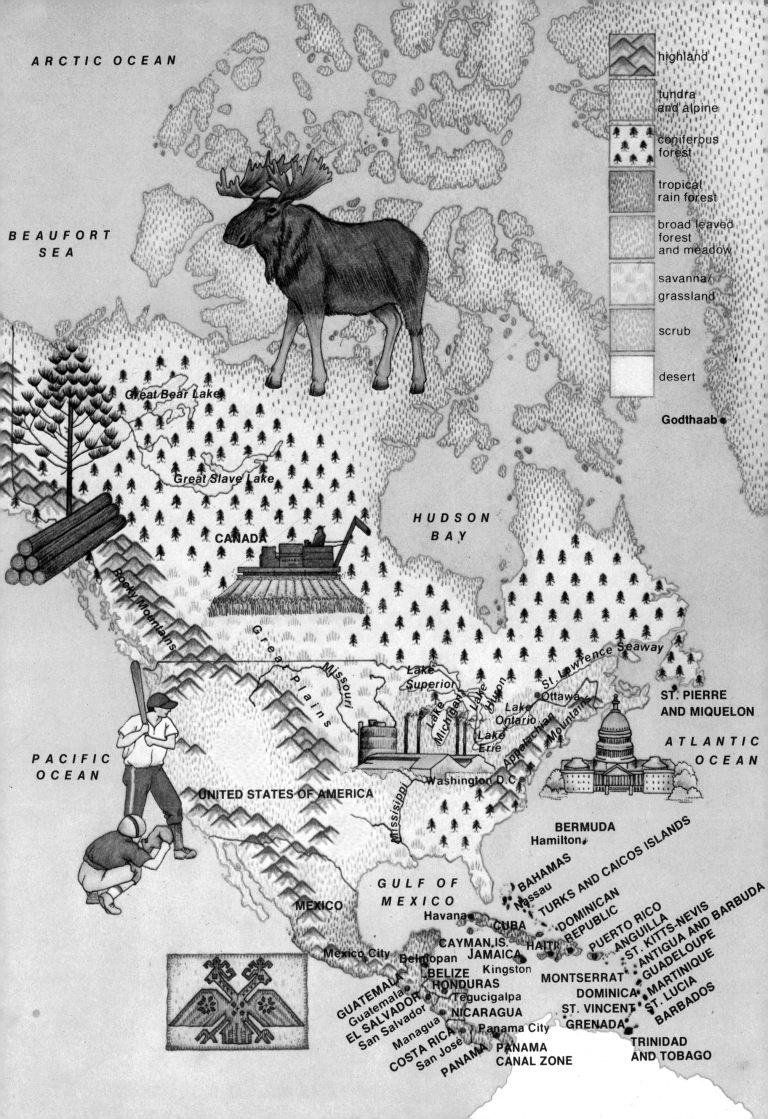

ARCTIC OCEAN

BEAUFORT SEA

highland

tundra and alpine

coniferous forest

tropical rain forest

broad leaved forest and meadow

savanna/grassland

scrub

desert

Godthaab

Great Bear Lake

Great Slave Lake

CANADA

HUDSON BAY

Rocky Mountains

Great Plains

Missouri

Lake Superior

Lake Michigan

Lake Huron

Lake Ontario

Lake Erie

St. Lawrence Seaway

Ottawa

ST. PIERRE AND MIQUELON

Appalachian Mountains

ATLANTIC OCEAN

PACIFIC OCEAN

UNITED STATES OF AMERICA

Mississippi

Washington D.C.

BERMUDA
Hamilton

GULF OF MEXICO

BAHAMAS
Nassau

TURKS AND CAICOS ISLANDS

MEXICO

Havana

CUBA

DOMINICAN REPUBLIC

PUERTO RICO

ANGUILLA

ST. KITTS-NEVIS

ANTIGUA AND BARBUDA

Mexico City

CAYMAN IS.

JAMAICA

HAITI

GUADELOUPE

Belmopan

Kingston

MONTSERRAT

MARTINIQUE

GUATEMALA

BELIZE

DOMINICA

ST. LUCIA

Guatemala

HONDURAS

BARBADOS

EL SALVADOR

Tegucigalpa

ST. VINCENT

San Salvador

NICARAGUA

GRENADA

Managua

Panama City

COSTA RICA

PANAMA

TRINIDAD AND TOBAGO

San José

PANAMA

CANAL ZONE

North America

Most of North America is made up of just two huge countries, the United States and Canada. The United States of America, the richest, most powerful, and fourth largest country in the world in area and population, is more a continent than a country. It ranges from the icy wastes of Alaska to the sunny almost tropical beaches of California and Florida; and from the burning deserts of the south-west to the green forests of the north east.

The Rocky Mountains, high and jagged, run down the western part of the country like the teeth of some gigantic saw. East of them are the Great Plains—a gentle region, flat and mostly treeless. The plains merge with the Central Lowlands, which extend to the Canadian border in the north. In the south they reach Texas, and to the east they stretch as far as the Appalachian Highlands. The Appalachians are a range of mountains that runs southwards from the Gulf of St. Lawrence to Alabama. These mountains are lower, less jagged and much older than the Rockies.

Two states, Alaska and Hawaii, are separate from the others. Alaska is separated by Canada, and Hawaii is a group of islands in the Pacific.

The American people, English-speaking but

Lakes by the St. Lawrence Seaway, the longest navigable waterway in the world. The Great Lakes themselves, together with a never-failing tourist attraction, the Niagara Falls, lie between Canada and the United States.

The 23 million Canadians are almost swallowed up in the vastness of their country, and seven out of ten of them live in the towns and cities near the U.S. border. Their main source of income is grain, especially wheat, which Canada exports to much of the rest of the world.

The British and the French fought over Canada in the early years of its history. Today the battle looks like starting again, politically this time, over the strong demands by the French-speaking people of Quebec for a measure of self-government.

To the north-east of Canada lies Greenland, the largest island in the world, not counting Australia. It belongs to the kingdom of Denmark. More than four-fifths of the land is covered by ice. It was given its misleading name by a Viking explorer, Eric the Red, who wanted to lure other Vikings to colonize it. Greenlanders of today, some Eskimos but mostly European settlers, make their living from fishing and hunting. Greenland also has important weather forecasting stations, and defence installations belonging to the North Atlantic Treaty Organization, including radar posts.

Below: Baffin Island, in northern Canada, is covered by snow and ice, with glaciers – great ice rivers. Although it is the fifth largest island in the world, it is too cold for more than a few people to live there.

Above: A combine harvester at work on a farm in the United States. The Great Plains region of North America, where this photograph was taken, is one of the world's greatest wheat-growing areas.

Left: The lights of Manhattan, heart of New York City.

combining the values and traditions of many different lands, are vigorous, inventive, and optimistic. They usually have more money and more to spend it on than most other people. Their farms produce more food than the Americans need, so they are able to export it to other countries. Their factories stock half the world with goods of all kinds and among their best known exports are Hollywood films.

Canada, the second largest country in the world after the Soviet Union, takes as its motto 'From Sea to Sea' because it stretches all the way from the Atlantic to the Pacific. It is a country of huge forests and enormous treeless prairies; of thousands of rivers and lakes and rugged mountains; of bottomless swamps and vast, icy wastes.

In the north a huge inland sea, Hudson Bay, cuts deep into the heart of the country. In the south-east the mighty St. Lawrence River is linked to the Great

Mexico and the Caribbean

Hundreds of years ago Hernán Cortés, the great Spanish adventurer, threw a piece of crumpled parchment on the table. 'That', he said, 'is what the map of Mexico looks like!' It was a fair description of the towering volcanoes, blank deserts, dark smudges of jungles, and swamps oozing out to sea that make up the Mexican scene.

Most Mexicans live on the high stretch of level land that nestles among the mountains in the centre of the country. In contrast, a part called Yucatán, far to the south, is almost empty save for the ruins of mysterious cities buried in the jungle.

Mexicans love singing and dancing and feasting. They dress up in colourful costumes as bands march through the gaily decorated streets during special

Patiently waiting for customers, two traders sit beside their net-covered baskets in the market at Mérida, capital of the Mexican state of Yucatán.

holidays called fiestas. They also love eating and drinking. The tortilla, a large thin pancake of ground maize, is a favourite dish. Tequila, an alcoholic drink made from cactus, is also popular.

However, life is not all fun, especially for the million pure-bred Indians. Many Mexicans struggle merely to exist. The gap between the few very rich and the many very poor is wide, but today it is gradually narrowing. Those who have land are being made to share it with those who have none.

Central America, a narrow, twisting land bridge, links Mexico with Colombia in South America. About 20 million people live in the seven countries that make up the region. Most of them are of mixed Spanish and Indian blood, and are known as mestizos. Most of them are also farmers. Coffee, bananas, and cotton are the main crops. A backbone of fearsome volcanoes runs down the middle of Central America. Some of these erupt from time to time and cause great damage, but the lava and ash that they throw out help to enrich the soil.

Every country in Central America, except for El Salvador and Belize, has coasts on both the Caribbean Sea and the Pacific Ocean. The lowlands are

generally heavily forested and hot, and as a result most of the people live in the highlands where the air is cooler. The Panama Canal, a man-made waterway opened in 1914, links the Atlantic and Pacific oceans and saves ships a long and dangerous journey around Cape Horn.

A huge necklace of islands, sparkling like green jewels in the blue waters of the Caribbean, stretches from the tip of Florida in the north to the coast of South America in the south. The islands are known as the West Indies. They are actually the peaks of drowned mountains poking out of the water. Most of them were formed by volcanoes, but others are made of coral. The weather is generally sunny and hot, and wealthy people from many parts of the world like to spend their winter holidays there.

Most crops grow well in the islands but the main ones are sugarcane, fruit and tobacco. Most of the people are black. Their ancestors were brought to the West Indies from Africa as slaves to work on the sugar plantations. Good-natured and easy going by nature, many have become increasingly bitter because of overcrowding, lack of employment, and the uncertainties of the tourist trade. Most of the islands are independent nations, though some are still controlled by other countries.

Left: Banana-growing is an important occupation in Central America, particularly in Honduras and Panama.

Below: It was to palm-fringed beaches washed by surf, like this one at Blanchisseuse on the northern coast of Trinidad, that the earliest Europeans came in the late 1400s and early 1500s. They thought at first they had found the Spice Islands of southern Asia.

SOUTH AMERICA

Country	Km²	Sq. miles	Capital	Population	Money unit
Argentina	2,797,000	1,080,000	Buenos Aires	25,719,000	Peso
Bolivia	1,075,000	415,000	La Paz	4,688,000	Peso
Brazil	8,518,000	3,289,000	Brasília	109,181,000	Cruzeiro
Chile	751,000	290,000	Santiago	10,454,000	Peso
Colombia	1,140,000	440,000	Bogotá	24,372,000	Peso
Ecuador	585,000	226,000	Quito	7,305,000	Sucre
Falkland Islands	12,200	4,700	Stanley	2,000	Pound
French Guiana	91,000	35,000	Cayenne	55,125	Franc
Guyana	215,000	83,000	Georgetown	783,000	Dollar
Paraguay	407,000	157,000	Asunción	2,724,000	Guarani
Peru	1,375,000	531,000	Lima	16,090,000	Sol
Surinam	140,000	54,000	Paramaribo	435,000	Guilder
Uruguay	186,000	72,000	Montevideo	3,101,000	Peso
Venezuela	917,000	354,000	Caracas	12,361,000	Bolivar

A Peruvian Indian clad in a poncho playing a flute in the traditional 'Fête of the Sun'.

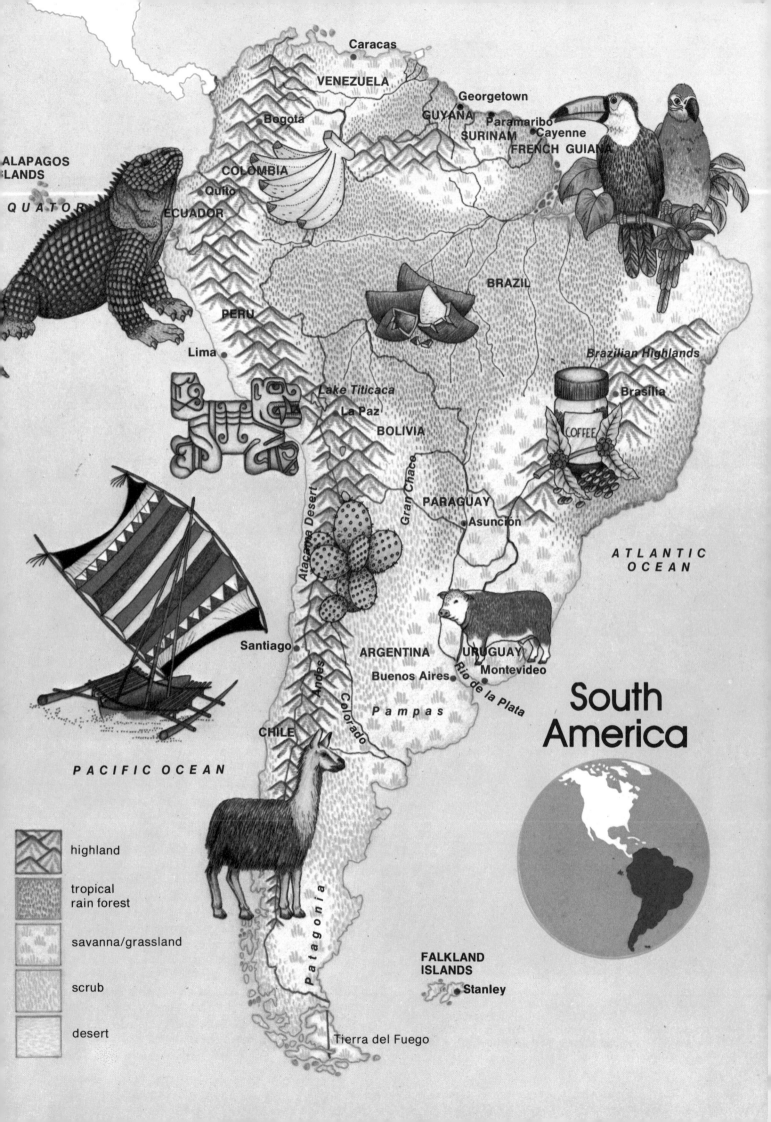

GALAPAGOS ISLANDS

EQUATOR

VENEZUELA
Caracas

Bogotá

Georgetown
GUYANA
Paramaribo
SURINAM Cayenne
FRENCH GUIANA

COLOMBIA

Quito
ECUADOR

BRAZIL

PERU

Brazilian Highlands

Lima

Brasília

Lake Titicaca
La Paz
BOLIVIA

COFFEE

Gran Chaco

PARAGUAY

Asunción

Atacama Desert

ATLANTIC OCEAN

Santiago

ARGENTINA
URUGUAY

Buenos Aires
Montevideo

Pampas
Río de la Plata

Andes
Colorado

South
America

CHILE

PACIFIC OCEAN

highland

tropical
rain forest

savanna/grassland

scrub

desert

Patagonia

**FALKLAND
ISLANDS**

Stanley

Tierra del Fuego

Brazil and its neighbours

South America is a triangular-shaped continent of great contrasts. It contains many modern, sophisticated cities and booming industries, supported by mines producing valuable metals, and oil-wells. It also has regions of great poverty, where people barely manage to grow enough food for their own needs. A great deal of the land is hot, steaming forest, but many people live in cool areas high up among jagged mountains.

The largest country in South America is Brazil, which is the fifth largest country in the world. Brazil covers nearly half the continent and is full of undiscovered riches. It ranges from the hot, wet coastal plain in the north-east and the steaming Amazon River valley in the north, to the rolling temperate grasslands of the south. There, cattle-rearing is the main industry.

The heart of the country lies in the east-central region. Gold, diamonds and iron ore are abundant there. Typical of this wealth is Rio de Janeiro, a beautiful city fringed by sparkling beaches. Farther

The National Congress Building towers over the wide roads and open spaces of Brasília, the new capital of Brazil. Work began on this city only in the 1950s. It became the capital in 1960, just 460 years after the European discovery of Brazil.

south, in the middle of the coffee-growing region with its rich, red earth, stands São Paulo, the fastest growing city anywhere south of the equator.

Brasília, the nation's new capital, has been built only in the past 20 years. Designed with boldness and imagination, it is shaped like a drawn bow and arrow and is full of fine buildings.

The first people to settle in Brazil were Portuguese, and that is the official language. Three-quarters of the people have white ancestors, but there are also many Negroes, American Indians and people who are a mixture of races. Brazilians love festivals, and among the many they celebrate the most famous is Carnival. It lasts for three days before the start of Lent. During this time the people put on fancy dress, eat and drink, and dance and sing through the streets, especially in Rio.

The Guianas are three small countries in the north-east corner of South America. They are

French Guiana, Surinam (once Dutch Guiana), and Guyana (once British Guiana). The word 'Guyana' means 'land of many waters', and many slow rivers flow northwards through the jungles into the Atlantic Ocean.

Most of the people live on the hot, swampy, coastal plain, and much of their income comes from the export of bauxite (aluminium ore). The people themselves are made up of a wide variety of races. Descendants of escaped Negro slaves, Arawak and Carib Indians, and European settlers rub shoulders with Indians, Chinese, Lebanese and a host of other peoples from Asia.

Next to the Guianas lies Venezuela, which means 'little Venice'. It was so named by the Spaniards who first landed there because it reminded them of Venice. The most northerly of the South American republics, Venezuela is also the richest, being one of the world's great producers and exporters of oil.

Wax palms tower over the steaming jungle in Colombia. Many parts of South America still look like this.

Its wide range of scenery embraces the snow-capped peaks of the Andes Mountains, windswept plains, sunny beaches, and dense jungles.

The people in the cities are mostly young, with plenty of money and a great interest in education, but many of the peasants in the country areas are poor and can neither read nor write.

Colombia, on the north-west coast of South America, is the only country of that continent with coastlines on both the Atlantic and Pacific oceans. It is a land of jagged mountains, high valleys, and jungle lowlands.

The people, mostly with a mixture of Indian and white blood, are passionately fond of learning. There are 28 universities, and the nation has produced many talented writers.

The pampas and the Andes

Argentina, which is Spanish for 'Land of Silver', stretches from the tropics in the north to the southern tip of South America in the south – well on the way to the Antarctic. Much of the country is made up of vast areas of grasslands, called the *pampas*. This region supports great cattle ranches, and cattle provide a great part of the wealth of Argentina.

A cooler area to the south, called Patagonia, is the great sheep-rearing region. The same region is also rich in oil. The huge Andes Mountains to the west separate Argentina from its not always friendly neighbour Chile. Some hundreds of kilometres to the east, in the South Atlantic, lie the British Falkland Islands. Argentina has laid claim to these islands for many years, calling them Las Islas Malvinas, but the people are of British stock.

About 97 out of every 100 Argentinians are of European blood. The colourful *gaucho*, whom Argentina shares with its northern neighbour, Uruguay, is the rugged independent cowboy of the pampas. His favourite drink is called *maté* (it rhymes with 'patty'). This is a bitter, green, herb tea, sucked from a hollow gourd with a silver tube.

Chile is long and thin and looks like a shoestring squeezed in between the Pacific Ocean and the Andes Mountains. Most of Chile is desert, but that is where an important product, sodium nitrate, is found. Most of the people live in the central valley, but there, as elsewhere in the country, they are subject to frequent earthquakes. The people are proud and independent, and much of their recent violent history has resulted from a national spirit that will not be put down.

Bolivia is one of the highest countries in the world, and La Paz, perched high in the Andes, is the highest capital city in the world. Lake Titicaca is the world's highest navigable lake. Like its neighbour Paraguay, Bolivia has no seacoast. It is the most American-Indian of all South American nations, but most of the Indians are very poor and their life is hard.

Paraguay is one of two landlocked countries in South America (Bolivia is the other). The land is divided into quite different halves by the River

Paraguay. To the east are fertile grasslands with a forested high plain; to the west lies the unfriendly Chaco—jungle, scrub, and swamp. There are many pure-blooded American Indians in Paraguay, called Guaranís, and the Guaraní language, along with Spanish, is one of the two official languages.

Ecuador is a small country of huge volcanoes, high valleys, and swampy coastlands. The country is named for the Equator, which runs through it. The Galápagos Islands, far out in the Pacific, are also part of Ecuador. Many unusual animals and plants live on these islands.

Peru, the third largest country after Brazil and Argentina, has a narrow desert plain backed by a range of high mountains. These fall away eastwards in jungle-covered slopes. Half the population is made up of Indians, and most of them are extremely poor, with barely enough food to live on.

Uruguay, one of the smallest and for many years one of the most enlightened of the South American republics, faces its neighbour Argentina across the Río de la Plata estuary. The land is an extension of the Argentine pampas, and the Uruguayan gaucho is no less hardy and patriotic than his Argentine counterpart. riding to round up his cattle.

Left: Gauchos, the cowboys of the pampas, guide cattle into a corral in Argentina. Cattle-raising provides much of that country's wealth.

Below: Andean Indians in brilliant costumes perform a traditional dance in honour of the Christian Feast of Corpus Christi. The Indians of South America kept many of their ancient customs when they adopted the Christian religion.

Europe and the Soviet Union

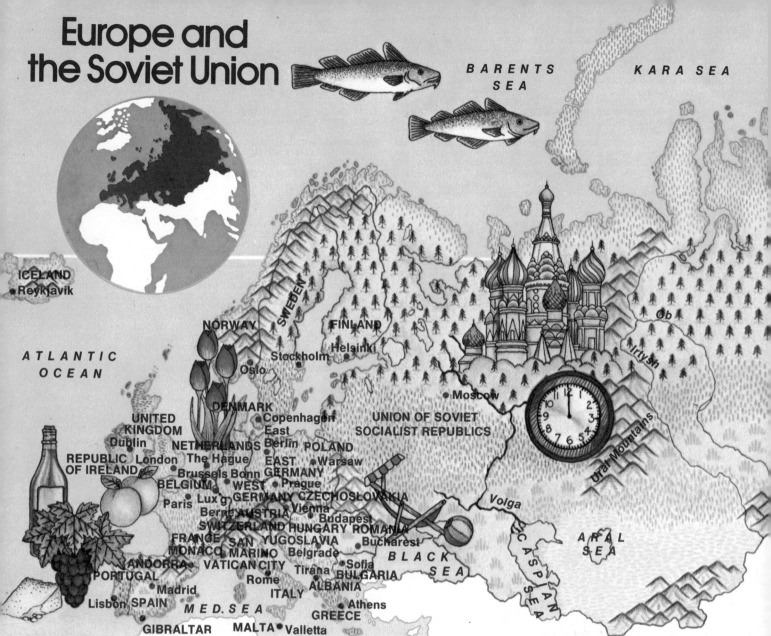

Country	Km²	Sq. miles	Capital	Population	Money unit
Albania	27,700	10,700	Tirana	2,608,000	Lek
Andorra	466	180	Andorra La Vella	30,000	Franc and Peseta
Austria	83,800	32,300	Vienna	7,508,000	Schilling
Belgium	30,600	11,800	Brussels	9,840,000	Franc
Bulgaria	111,000	43,000	Sofia	8,814,000	Lev
Czechoslovakia	128,000	49,400	Prague	15,138,000	Koruna
Denmark	44,000	17,000	Copenhagen	5,104,000	Krone
Finland	337,000	130,000	Helsinki	4,752,000	Markka
France	552,000	213,000	Paris	53,278,000	Franc
Germany, East	108,000	42,000	East Berlin	16,756,000	Mark
Germany, West	249,000	96,000	Bonn	61,310,000	Deutsche Mark
Gibraltar	5.2	2	—	29,000	Pound
Greece	132,600	51,200	Athens	9,360,000	Drachma
Hungary	93,000	36,000	Budapest	10,685,000	Forint
Iceland	104,900	40,500	Reykjavik	224,000	Króna
Ireland, Republic of	68,900	26,600	Dublin	3,236,000	Pound
Italy	339,000	131,000	Rome	56,697,000	Lira
Liechtenstein	168	65	Vaduz	25,000	Franc
Luxembourg	2,600	1,000	Luxembourg	356,000	Franc

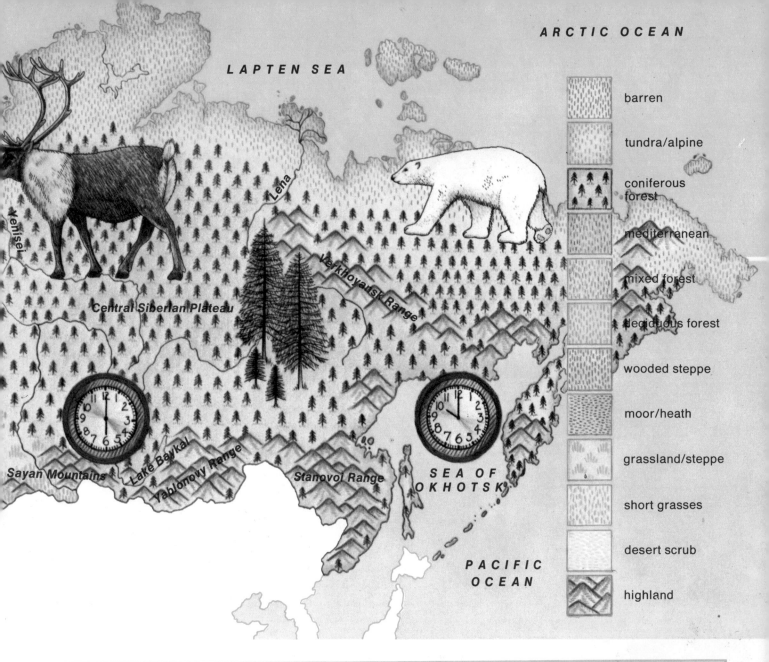

Country	Km²	Sq. miles	Capital	Population	Money unit
Malta	313	121	Valletta	340,000	Pound
Monaco	1.73	0.66	—	26,000	Franc
Netherlands	35,000	13,500	The Hague / Amsterdam	13,986,000	Florin
Norway	386,000	149,000	Oslo	4,059,000	Krone
Poland	313,000	121,000	Warsaw	35,010,000	Zloty
Portugal	89,400	34,500	Lisbon	9,798,000	Escudo
Romania	237,200	91,600	Bucharest	21,855,000	Leu
San Marino	60	23	—	21,000	Lira
Spain	510,000	197,000	Madrid	36,780,000	Peseta
Sweden	448,000	173,000	Stockholm	8,278,000	Krona
Switzerland	41,500	16,000	Berne	6,337,000	Franc
Turkey see Asia map index page 77					
United Kingdom	241,000	93,000	London	55,822,000	Pound
Union of Soviet Socialist Republics*	22,328,000	8,621,000	Moscow	261,569,000	Rouble
Vatican City State	0.441	0.17	—	1,000	Lira
Yugoslavia	256,500	99,000	Belgrade	21,914,000	Dinar

*Including part of the USSR which is in Asia

North-Western Europe

Europe is a peninsula extending westwards from Asia. From this main peninsula other smaller peninsulas jut outwards, penetrating the Atlantic Ocean to the west, the North Sea and the Baltic Sea to the north, and the Mediterranean Sea to the south. Because of its shape Europe has a relatively long coastline, so that many parts of it have easy access to ocean highways and sea trade. Thanks to a generally temperate climate in which it is easy to work, a large area of rich agricultural land, and great mineral wealth, Europe has become one of the most important areas in the world.

Separated from the mainland on the north-west by the narrow Strait of Dover and the English Channel is the British Isles archipelago, comprising the two large islands of Great Britain and Ireland and more than 5,000 smaller islands. The highest ground in these islands is in the north in Scotland, in the Pennine range running north-south through northern England and in most of Wales. The heavy rain in these high areas gives rise to many rivers which flow down through the rich farmland lying between the mountains and the sea. Ireland is like a shallow basin with a central lowland area and high ground on the coastal fringes.

England and Wales are densely populated, Scotland and Ireland less so, but the distribution of the population is very uneven. Most people live in conurbations, or built-up areas, on the lower ground near which great industrial centres have been built up.

North-west of the British Isles is Iceland, which in area is a little larger than Ireland. This volcanic island is noted for its hot thermal springs and geysers, many of which have been harnessed to heat people's homes. The island is poor in natural resources, and most people are employed in the fishing industry, for the island is surrounded by rich fishing grounds.

Most Icelanders are descended from the Norwegians whose country, Norway, forms with Sweden the Scandinavian peninsula. The northern part of the peninsula and adjoining Finland, known as Lapland, lies within the Arctic Circle. In winter it is covered with ice and snow and sees no sunshine. On the west the land is almost entirely mountainous with a coastline broken by many inlets of the sea known as fjords. Most people there earn their living from fishing, for there is little land suitable for growing crops. To the east the land slopes away to sea level at the Gulf of Bothnia – which in winter is iced over – and the Baltic Sea. On this lower ground forests provide abundant timber while rivers are harnessed for hydro-electric power.

Most of the Scandinavian people live and work in the central and southern lowlands, where there is greater industrial development and the soil is better. They are of the Nordic race, pale-skinned and generally with light hair and eyes.

Along the western seaboard of Europe are France and the Benelux countries of the Netherlands, Belgium and Luxembourg. The land is very different from that of Scandinavia and changes quickly from mountain and high plateau to wide, low plateaus and river valleys, and some lowland areas even below sea-level. A changeable and generally mild

Left: The calm, rolling landscape of the Eden river valley in northern England is typical of much of the countryside in north-western Europe

Right, above: Housewives bargain with fishermen for freshly-landed fish in the quayside market of the Old Port at Marseille, in France. In the background loom modern hotels and other buildings.

and damp climate helps the growth of heavy crops of foodstuffs. It also encourages the growth of rich grass on which cattle and sheep feed.

Abundant supplies of coal and iron ore have led to prosperous industrial development in north-western Europe. Recent and increasing discoveries of natural gas and oil deposits in the lowland areas, and particularly in the North Sea, are increasing the wealth of this part of Europe. The general standard of living of the people, already higher than in many other parts of the world, is continually improving, and will continue to do so as long as their natural resources last out against the increasingly heavy demands of industrial societies.

Central Europe

Central Europe lies between the Baltic Sea in the north, and the great mountain chain of the Alps in the south. It extends to the south-east into the Balkan Peninsula. This very large region can be divided into two distinct parts. In the north are Germany (East and West), Poland, Czechoslovakia, Austria and Switzerland, while in the south-east are the Danube River valley countries of Hungary, Romania, Yugoslavia and Bulgaria.

Across the north runs the North European Plain, the world's largest lowland area, which extends from Belgium and the Netherlands in the west to the Ural Mountains of Russia in the east (described on pages 74–75). The Alps, in the south, form Europe's largest mountain range, and many important rivers have their beginnings there. A lower mountain chain, the Dinaric Alps, continues south-eastwards through Yugoslavia into the Balkans.

Central Europe has a varied climate, which has affected its history and the way of life of the people who live there. In the north the weather is influenced by the sea, with summers that are not too hot and winters that are not too cold. In Austria, Czechoslovakia and the countries to the south-east summers are warm or hot and the winters are very cold.

Hundreds of years ago forests covered almost all of the North European Plain, where the soil is rich. Nearly all this area has now been cleared for farming, with wide fields of waving corn and, near the rivers, rich grasslands with herds of grazing cattle. To the south of the plain are huge coalfields, and big industrial towns have grown up in this region, in Czechoslovakia and southern Germany and Poland. In the Alps much of the land is too rugged for farming or for industry, and most people in Switzerland and Austria live and work in the lands at the foot of the high mountains. Tourists flock to the Alps for winter sports and for mountaineering in summer.

Europe's longest river, the Danube, flows from the Alps south-east to the Black Sea. It not only provides a main highway for travel and for carrying goods, but the rich lands on its banks make splendid farming country, particularly in the Hungarian Plain. There, farmers grow large quantities of wheat and maize, and raise cattle, pigs and horses. Unfortunately the lower reaches of the river, forming the boundary between Bulgaria and Romania, pass through marshland and swamps, and the land is unsuitable either for farming or for building factories.

The countries of south-eastern Europe were at one time among the poorest and most backward.

They depended largely on farming, which was inefficiently carried on. Since the end of World War II in 1945 there has been a considerable improvement, with more efficient farming and a steady growth of industry. These countries all have mineral resources, and mining is increasing all the time. Romania has valuable deposits of oil and natural gas.

Many of the people of south-eastern Europe are descended from the Magyars, a wandering race who came into Europe hundreds of years ago from Asia. Most of them have broad heads, with medium brown hair, and their eyes are varying shades of brown. In the north of Central Europe many people are related to the Nordic peoples of Scandinavia, with fair hair and blue eyes. However, there is a great mixture of types of people in all parts of Europe, and with the increase of travel people are becoming more mixed. Today the main differences among Europeans are in the languages they speak and the historical traditions of their own countries. In spite of serious political rivalry between the countries of western Europe and the Communist-dominated lands of eastern Europe, travel, television, radio and other forms of communications are gradually breaking down old barriers and Europe is slowly becoming one great unified community, helped also by the gradual growth of the European Economic Community (EEC). The EEC forms a common market with no tariffs or trade controls within it. It has both a Common External Tariff and a Common Agricultural Policy. Much of the Community budget is used for agricultural support. The agreed exchange rate between the English pound and the other Community currencies when calculating contributions to the Budget is the Green Pound.

Left: Dominating the skyline of Prague, the capital of Czechoslovakia, is the famous Hradcany castle. Prague is a city of great historic interest and lies in Bohemia, the western part of the country.

Below: The jumble of tiled roofs that makes up the ancient city of Dubrovnik in Yugoslavia—one of the few remaining walled cities left in Europe.

THE EUROPEAN COMMUNITY

1958	Treaty of Rome Members: Belgium, France, Holland, Italy, Luxembourg, West Germany
1973	Britain, Eire, Denmark entered
1981	Greece joined EEC

Southern Europe

Southern Europe is a region of hot, dry summers, and mild winters during which there is rain. Almost all the countries border the Mediterranean Sea, and pleasant climates of this sort the world over are known as 'Mediterranean climates'. It is one of the best for holidays, and millions of people from other countries flock to the Mediterranean lands every year to relax.

Southern Europe includes three large peninsulas. They are the Iberian Peninsula (Spain and Portugal), Italy and the Balkan Peninsula, which includes Greece. There are several large islands, such as Corsica, Sardinia and Sicily, and hundreds of smaller ones. The small islands are mainly in the Adriatic, Ionian and Aegean seas, which are arms of the Mediterranean.

The countries of the Mediterranean are mountainous, and there is only a narrow strip of lowland between the mountains and the sea. It is very difficult to farm the land, except for the wide Lombardy Plain of northern Italy and a few similar areas. In many places farmers have built low stone walls to form terraces and so hold the soil on the steep hillsides. In Malta, where the land is rocky though not mountainous, soil is so precious that if you build a house you must remove all the topsoil before you start and move it somewhere else where it can grow crops.

The chief southern European crop is fruit, and there is a lush harvest of oranges, lemons, peaches, grapes and olives. In some places farmers contrive to grow a little wheat and barley. Keeping livestock is difficult because the long, dry summers mean that there is very little grass available for grazing. Goats and sheep, which can browse on very scrubby vegetation, are the main animals, and the few cows may indeed be kept indoors in the hot weather and given special foodstuffs.

The people of southern Europe tend to be dark-eyed and dark-haired, and those who live outdoor lives are often deeply tanned by the hot Sun that blazes down day after day from clear blue skies. Many of the houses have comparatively small doors and windows, and flat roofs which provide a place to relax in the cool of the evening. A feature of life in many Mediterranean towns is the *corso*, when in the evening people stroll about the streets in their hundreds, to meet their friends, have a gossip, or sit at one of the many pavement cafés to sip wine and coffee.

None of the Mediterranean countries is rich in natural resources. There is some iron ore, but little coal or oil, and so industry has grown only slowly. Northern Italy, however, has a number of busy manufacturing cities, which rely on electricity generated by hydro-electric power stations on the

swift rivers that rush down from the Alps. This region is also a rich farming country, and its climate is more like that of central Europe than the Mediterranean. The western part of southern Italy is also very fertile.

Portugal faces the Atlantic Ocean, and also has a different climate, with cool, rain-bearing winds sweeping in from the sea. Spain, on the other hand,

is a high plateau land, much of it very dry and barren.

Greece is a country of rugged mountains and many scattered islands. Only a small part of the land is suitable for growing crops, and the farmers make the most of it, producing citrus fruits, cotton, currants, grapes, olives, olive oil and tobacco for export. Most of the factories are concerned with processing food and other farm produce. For

An historical regatta of gondolas and barges in Venice, the ancient Italian seaport where the main streets are canals, and taxis are boats.

hundreds of years the Greeks have looked to the sea for their living, and today Greece has a large merchant fleet. Many of its ships carry goods for other countries, such as oil.

The Soviet Union

The Soviet Union is the biggest country in the world. It covers more than half of Europe and over one third of Asia, stretching from the Baltic and Black seas in the west to the Pacific Ocean in the east. As you cross from one end to the other of this huge country you have to alter your watch 11 times as you pass through different time zones. When day dawns in the lands bordering the Pacific the European part is just in darkness. The country's official name is the Union of Soviet Socialist Republics, but it is often called 'Russia', its old name and still the name of a large part of it. The Asian part is often called Siberia.

The country is a vast plain, with the Ural Mountains separating the European part from the Asian part. There are more mountains to the south and east. More than three-quarters of the people live in the European part of the Soviet Union, and if you look at the other parts this is not so surprising. Part of the country lies inside the Arctic Circle, and in this area the soil just beneath the surface is frozen all the time. North-eastern

Siberia has some of the coldest temperatures ever recorded. In the south, in central Asia, there are deserts where high temperatures make life unpleasant and difficult.

The wide plains in the European part of the Soviet Union are the most fertile, and great areas are under cultivation. The country leads the world in producing wheat, barley, oats and rye, though bad weather can sometimes wreck a year's harvest. The country also grows more potatoes than any other and produces the most milk and butter. In the warmer parts of central Asia farmers grow cotton, and other major crops include tea, tobacco and flax (for making linen). Thanks to the use of tractors and other machines, only about two of every ten workers is needed to farm.

Industry absorbs four out of every ten workers, mainly processing raw materials and making machinery. The Russians tend to be short of con-

Red Square lies in the very heart of Moscow, capital city of the Soviet Union. On the left is the 400-year-old St. Basil's Church, now a museum. On the right are the grim walls of the Kremlin, an ancient fortress which now houses the Russian government. Centre is the tomb of Communist leader Vladimir Lenin.

sumer goods—that is, the sort of things ordinary people buy such as motor-cars, refrigerators, and washing-machines; but production of such items is increasing, and more people have them.

As might be expected in such a huge country, many different peoples live there. Three out of every four are Slavs, and they form most of the European part of the population. Near the border with Finland are people who are closely related to the Finns, while in the south-west part of Asian Russia there is a large group related to the Turks. One group living in the Caucasus Mountains of the Republic of Georgia is renowned for living a very long time—many of the inhabitants claim to be well over 100 years old. Siberia has many different peoples living in it, some following traditional ways of life.

Before the Russian Revolution in 1917 the country was ruled as one. It is now divided into 15 republics, of which the Russian Soviet Federal Socialist Republic (RSFSR for short) is by far the biggest and covers the bulk of the country. The Communist Party dominates the government and decides on policy, both for the central government and for the republics' own governments.

For many people in Russia life was very hard. Their homes were simple and small, and tended to be crowded as sometimes two or more families shared a home. Life has improved with Communist rule, although harsh winters with extreme cold still make life difficult in many parts of the country.

The wrinkled, rugged face of a farmer from Georgia, a Soviet republic in the Caucasus Mountains. The farmlands lie close to the Black Sea, and there people grow grapes, lemons, oranges, tea and tobacco.

Farmers and their families from a collective farm in the Kara Kum desert of Turkmenistan, one of the Soviet republics which lies just north of Iran.

The Soviet people are proud of their culture. Their writers include world-famous men such as Leo Tolstoy and Alexandr Pushkin, and Petr Tchaikovsky and Dmitri Shostakovich are among their composers. Russian ballet is among the world's best. Russians also excel in sports, especially athletics, and win many gold medals at international events such as the Olympic Games.

Asia

BLACK SEA

• Ankara
TURKEY
Nicosia
CYPRUS
SYRIA
LEBANON Beirut IRAQ
ISRAEL Damascus
Jerusalem Amman
JORDAN

• Tehran
Baghdad
IRAN
Kabul
AFGHANISTAN
KUWAIT

BAHRAIN
Al Manamah
QATAR Doha
Riyadh UNITED
SAUDI ARAB
ARABIA EMIRATES

• Muscat

YEMEN
San'a'
YEMEN

RED SEA

OMAN

Madinat
ash Sha'b

ARABIAN SEA

Islamabad

PAKISTAN

New Delhi

INDIA

Himalaya

NEPAL
Kathmandu
BHUTAN
BANGLADESH
Dacca

CHINA

Thimbu

BURMA
Rangoon •

BAY OF
BENGAL

Bangkok •

LAOS
Vientiane •

THAILAND

KAMPUCHEA

Phnom Penh

Hanoi •

VIETNAM

MACAU
HONGKONG

Ulan Bator •

MONGOLIA

SRI LANKA
Colombo •

• Malé

INDIAN OCEAN

MALDWE
ISLANDS

Kuala Lumpur •

BRUNE

MALAYSIA

SINGAPORE

Djakarta

coniferous
forest

tropical
rain forest

mediterranean

temperate
rain forest

deciduous
forest

grassland

scrub

desert

highland

Country	Km²	Sq. miles	Capital	Population	Money unit
Afghanistan	647,500	250,000	Kabul	15,490,000	Afghani
Bahrain	598	231	Al Manamah	345,000	Dinar
Bangladesh	142,780	55,126	Dacca	86,640,000	Taka
Bhutan	46,600	18,000	Thimbu	1,240,000	Ngultrum
Brunei	5,765	2,226	Bandar Seri Begawan	210,000	Dollar
Burma	678,600	262,000	Rangoon	32,910,000	Kyat
China	9,583,000	3,700,000	Peking	970,000,000	Yuan
Cyprus	9,000	3,500	Nicosia	616,000	Pound
Hongkong	1,046	404	Victoria	4,900,000	Dollar
India	3,269,000	1,262,000	New Delhi	650,980,000	Rupee
Indonesia	1,904,000	735,000	Djakarta	138,100,000	Rupiah
Iran	1,627,000	628,000	Tehran	36,650,000	Rial
Iraq	445,000	172,000	Baghdad	12,327,000	Dinar
Israel	20,700	8,000	Jerusalem	3,689,000	Pound
Japan	370,000	143,000	Tokyo	115,810,000	Yen
Jordan	97,600	37,700	Amman	2,984,000	Dinar
Kampuchea (Cambodia)	181,000	70,000	Phnom Penh	8,720,000	Riel
Korea, North	124,000	48,000	Pyongyang	17,072,000	Won
Korea, South	100,000	38,500	Seoul	37,600,000	Won
Kuwait	19,500	7,500	—	1,199,000	Dinar
Laos	233,000	90,000	Vientiane	3,630,000	Kip
Lebanon	11,000	4,300	Beirut	3,012,000	Pound
Macau	13	5	—	276,000	Pataca
Malaysia	332,000	128,000	Kuala Lumpur	10,760,000	Dollar
Maldwe Islands	298	115	Malé	141,000	Rupee
Mongolia	1,554,000	600,000	Ulan Bator	1,590,000	Tugrik
Nepal	140,000	54,000	Kathmandu	13,710,000	Rupee
Oman	311,000	120,000	Muscat	839,000	Rial Saidi
Pakistan	803,940	310,403	Islamabad	79,080,000	Rupee
Philippines	298,000	115,000	Quezon City	47,180,000	Peso
Qatar	10,300	4,000	Doha	201,000	Riyal
Saudi Arabia	2,401,000	927,000	Riyadh	7,866,000	Riyal
Singapore	585	226	—	2,360,000	Dollar
Sri Lanka	65,600	25,332	Colombo	14,470,000	Rupee
Syria	184,000	71,000	Damascus	8,808,000	Pound
Taiwan (Formosa)	35,800	13,800	T'ai-pei	16,508,000	Dollar
Thailand	513,000	198,000	Bangkok	46,490,000	Baht
Turkey*	762,000	294,200	Ankara	43,210,000	Lira
United Arab Emirates	82,900	32,000	—	711,000	Dirham
USSR see Europe map index page 67					
Vietnam	334,000	129,000	Hanoi	51,080,000	Dong
Yemen (Aden)	466,000	180,000	Aden	1,853,000	Dinar
Yemen (San'a')	194,000	75,000	San'a'	5,642,000	Riyal

*Including part of Turkey which is in Europe

Eastern Asia

China is the main country of eastern Asia. It is the third largest country in the world and covers more than one-fifth of the whole of Asia. For hundreds of years its people have cut themselves off from the rest of the world because of a deep distrust of things non-Chinese, and this secrecy continues even to-day. As a result, comparatively little is known of the land or its people.

This huge land ranges from empty deserts to dizzy, snow-capped mountains; and from fertile plains to cities that are bursting at the seams. For China also has more people than any other country –over 960,000,000– and the birthrate and the population are rapidly increasing.

The Chinese people have traditionally a great respect for learning, religion and the arts. They also have a keen eye for beauty. In spite of the handicap of a variety of spoken languages and a written language made up of 40,000 word-pictures, they have also, under their post-war Communist government, become an efficient, industrialized nation. The peasants, who not long ago were starving, now have an ample if uninteresting diet based mainly on rice, which they eat with chop-sticks. China is an amazing contrast of old-fashioned ways and advanced technology: agriculture, building, and similar occupations are carried on almost entirely by hand, but Chinese scientists have already exploded more than one hydrogen bomb.

To the east of China lies Japan. The Land of the Rising Sun, as the Japanese call their country, is made up of four main mountainous islands and hundreds of smaller islets. They form a huge arc in the Pacific off the eastern coast of the Asian mainland, across the Sea of Japan.

The scenery is beautiful, with towering mountains, placid lakes, and hundreds of short, swift streams, but there is the ever-present menace of 200 volcanoes and almost daily earthquakes.

The Japanese are tough, inventive and hard-working, and these qualities have lifted their nation from ruin after World War II to become one of the leading industrial countries of the world.

The peninsula of Korea juts out from the northeastern coast of the Asian mainland between China and Japan. In 1945, after being freed from Japanese

Members of a commune in China building a small dam to stop flooding and provide water for irrigation. China is short of machinery but has plenty of people, so much work which in the west would be done by machine is carried out by human labour.

Japan is one of the most highly industrialized countries in Asia. It has few natural resources, so it has to depend on the work and skill of its people. They have made it a very rich country.

rule, it was divided into North Korea and South Korea. War broke out between these two countries in 1950 and lasted for three years. Today there is still much tension.

Korea is so mountainous that very little of the land can be farmed. Winters can be unbearably cold and summers brutally hot. Koreans love tradition and sports. Tradition is strongest in food, clothes and arranged marriages.

The Philippines are made up of about 7,100 islands of breathtaking beauty located in the Pacific Ocean off the south-east coast of Asia. The people are mostly Malays, but Chinese, Spaniards, Americans and Pygmy blacks also live there.

Mongolia is a bleak, barren, unforgiving, mountainous land lying in the heart of eastern Asia between the Soviet Union and China. There are more Mongolians outside the country than in it. Those within are largely farmers, but some are wanderers, roaming the country with their livestock from pasture to pasture as their ancestors did for many hundreds of years past.

Above: The Ganges is regarded as a sacred river by many people in India. Every year thousands of Hindus bathe in it, hoping to be cured of illnesses.
Left: Rice is the staple diet of millions of people in southern Asia. It is cultivated in fields called paddy fields, surrounded by dirt walls. These fields are flooded when the plants are young because rice needs a constant supply of water to grow properly.

Southern Asia

The Indian sub-continent is a huge peninsula largely cut off from the rest of Asia by high mountain ranges. It includes India, Pakistan, Bangladesh, the Maldive Islands, and the Himalayan kingdoms of Bhutan and Nepal. The whole area forms an enormous area of land with its point jutting out into the Indian Ocean.

India is easily the largest of all these countries, and it has more people than any other nation except China. In the north, the Himalayas form the world's highest mountain range, and include Mount Everest, the world's tallest peak. A second mountain chain, the Vindhya Range, cuts across the middle of the country. A third range is split into two: the Eastern and Western Ghats, which run down the eastern and western flanks, respectively, of southern India.

Some of the country's great rivers are regarded as sacred by Indians. They include the Ganges and the Brahmaputra. Many of the people are farmers and live on the plains. They depend on rain-bearing winds called monsoons, which blow every year. If the monsoons are seriously delayed, crops fail and thousands of people may die of starvation. India's cities are generally badly overcrowded and in Calcutta, for example, hundreds of people sleep and live on the pavements.

Pakistan came into being only in 1947, when India was split into two countries, India and Pakistan. Pakistan was itself broken up in 1971 when East Pakistan separated to become the new nation of Bangladesh.

Most of Pakistan is steeply mountainous, with the ranges of the Himalayas and the Hindu Kush occupying the north-east and the north-west respectively. Many Pakistanis, almost all of whom are Muslims, live off the land, but there are several cities with more than 100,000 people, of which Karachi is the largest.

Bangladesh lies at the head of the Bay of Bengal, and its name means 'Land of the Bengalis'. It is a tropical country made up mainly of low plains crossed by rivers. It is open to fierce storms that sweep up the bay and send huge tidal waves roaring inland with heavy loss of life.

Lying just off the south-east tip of India is Sri Lanka, formerly Ceylon, a beautiful pear-shaped island. Its climate is hot and wet, and its dense forests are rich in rare animal and plant life. Most of the people are Buddhists.

East of India is Burma, a gentle, tropical country

famous for its many pagodas—temples in the shape of a tower. Lying on the north-east of the Bay of Bengal, it is a land of hills, rivers and forests. Almost all the Burmese are Buddhists. They enjoy many festivals, a feature of which are their kite-flying games.

South-East Asia consists of a long peninsula and thousands of islands. It is a region of hot, humid tropical forests, from which the people have cleared large areas to build their towns and villages and grow crops. The countries are Vietnam, Laos, Kampuchea—better known as Cambodia—Thailand, Malaysia, Singapore, Indonesia and Papua New Guinea. Malaysia is divided into two parts, one on the mainland and the other on the island of Borneo. Singapore, once part of Malaysia, is a tiny island off the tip of the Malay Peninsula.

New Guinea, the second largest island in the world, is split in two. The eastern half is occupied by Papua New Guinea; the western half forms part of Indonesia, a land of about 3,000 islands, including part of Borneo. Most Indonesians live on Java, the fourth largest of the Indonesian islands.

The Temple of the Dawn is one of 300 Buddhist temples in Bangkok, the capital of Thailand. Their brightly-tiled roofs and spires glisten in the brilliant Sun.

Western Asia

Western Asia is generally a much bleaker region than southern and eastern Asia. In this it is more like some parts of northern Asia – Siberia – which is described on pages 74-75. The countries of western Asia include Afghanistan, Iran, Turkey, Cyprus, Syria, Lebanon, Israel, Iraq, Jordan, Saudi Arabia, and a number of smaller Arab states on the Arabian peninsula. The area is sometimes loosely referred to as the Middle East.

Afghanistan, a landlocked country, served as a buffer between Pakistan, Soviet Union and Iran. Once known as the Forbidden Kingdom, it came under Soviet Union influence in 1980. Two thirds of the country suffer intense summer heat and severe winter cold. The Afghans are noted for their carpets and woollens, as well as for their fierce and hardfought independence.

The former kingdom of Iran, once known as Persia, is now an Islamic republic. Previously a valuable trading post between East and West, the revolution of 1979 has closed the country to outside influences. The country itself is made up of two harsh deserts, with blazing summers and freezing winters. These deserts are almost entirely surrounded by bleak mountains. Many of the people are desert wanderers or farmers. Oil is one of Iran's greatest natural resources, although since the revolution exports have decreased dramatically.

Turkey sits astride two continents, Europe and

A brilliantly-domed mosque dominates the city of Yazd in central Iran. The towers, called *badgir*, **take air, cooled underground, into buildings.**

Asia. Once a vast, powerful empire dominating south-east Europe, it is today a comparatively small republic. Because of its geographical position it is most important to the peace of the Middle East and the world. Asian Turkey is sometimes called Asia Minor, and European Turkey is known as Thrace. They are separated by the Dardanelles Strait, the Sea of Marmara and the Bosporus Strait. Asian Turkey is a land of mountains and high plains. European Turkey is a small area of plains, low hills, and a coastline cut up into many bays. Most Turks are Muslims and are Asian in their language and traditions. They have always been renowned as tough fighters.

The island-state of Cyprus in the eastern Mediterranean is a beautiful land torn by battles between its Turkish and Greek communities. It has a fertile plain lying between two forested mountain ranges. Most Cypriots are farmers, growing mainly olives, wine grapes and citrus fruits.

South-western Asia is a series of Arab kingdoms and republics, some of them very poor, others with great wealth earned by selling petroleum. Set among them is Israel, the modern Jewish homeland founded in 1948 in the ancient land of Palestine. Israel is a narrow strip at the eastern end of the

The new way of life: pipelines in Kuwait carry the oil that has brought wealth to many Asian countries.

The old way of life: drying grain in the traditional method in a village of eastern Turkey. Many ancient farming methods persist in western Asia.

Mediterranean, with the huge Negev desert covering more than half the country. For much of their short history Israel's hard-working people have been at war with their Arab neighbours. In spite of this their vigorous *kibbutzim* (farming settlements) have prospered.

Saudi Arabia is the largest of the Arab states, but a great deal of it is bleak desert. Syria and Jordan, Israel's close neighbours, are also largely deserts and mountains. Lebanon, north of Israel, is a much more fertile land and was once a favourite place for visitors and international trade, but a series of fierce civil wars in the 1970s put an end to the tourist trade for the time being.

Iraq, between Iran and Saudi Arabia, was the home of the earliest civilizations, in the triangle of land between the Tigris and Euphrates rivers known as Mesopotamia. People still live and grow crops in this region. Money from petroleum is paying for irrigation schemes, which bring water to desert lands so that they can be turned into farms. Of the several small countries around the Arabian peninsula the richest is Kuwait, which has a small population and earns huge sums from petroleum. It was one of the world's poorest countries until oil sales began in the 1950s.

Country	Km²	Sq. miles	Capital	Population	Money unit
Algeria	2,215,000	855,200	Algiers	18,520,000	Dinar
Angola	1,264,000	488,000	Luanda	6,730,000	Kwanza
Benin	121,700	47,000	Porto Novo	3,340,000	Franc
Botswana	569,800	220,000	Gaborone	726,000	Pula
Burundi	27,700	10,700	Bujumbura	4,256,000	Franc
Cameroon	474,955	183,381	Yaoundé	7,000,000	Franc
Cape Verde	3,926	1,516	Praia	314,000	Escudo
Central African Republic	606,000	234,000	Bangui	3,200,000	Franc
Chad	1,264,000	488,000	Ndjaména	4,309,000	Franc
Comoros	2,170	838	Moroni	207,000	Franc
Congo	336,600	129,960	Brazzaville	1,459,000	Franc
Djibouti	23,300	9,000	Djibouti	113,000	Franc
Egypt	997,150	385,000	Cairo	39,636,000	Pound
Equatorial Guinea	28,500	11,000	Malabo	346,000	Ekuele
Ethiopia	1,036,000	400,000	Addis Ababa	29,705,000	Dollar
Gabon	262,650	101,400	Libreville	538,000	Franc
Gambia	10,360	4,000	Banjul	569,000	Dalasi
Ghana	238,550	92,100	Accra	10,969,000	Cedi
Guinea	251,250	97,000	Conakry	4,763,000	Syli
Guinea-Bissau	36,250	14,000	Bissau	553,000	Escudo
Ivory Coast	329,000	127,000	Abidjan	7,613,000	Franc
Kenya	582,750	225,000	Nairobi	14,856,000	Shilling
Lesotho	30,300	11,700	Maseru	1,279,000	Rand
Liberia	111,400	43,000	Monrovia	1,742,000	Dollar
Libya	2,097,900	810,000	Tripoli/Benghazi	2,748,000	Dinar
Malagasy Republic	590,500	228,000	Tananarive	8,289,000	Franc
Malawi	118,500	45,750	Lilongwe	5,669,000	Kwacha
Mali	1,204,400	465,000	Bamako	6,290,000	Franc
Mauritania	1,085,200	419,000	Nouakchott	1,544,000	Ouguiya
Mauritius	2,085	805	Port Louis	924,000	Rupee
Morocco	466,200	180,000	Rabat	18,906,000	Dirham
Mozambique	772,000	298,000	Maputo	9,935,000	Escudo
Namibia	824,000	318,000	Windhoek	883,000	Rand
Niger	1,189,000	459,000	Niamey	4,994,000	Franc
Nigeria	925,000	357,000	Lagos	72,217,000	Naira
Rhodesia see Zimbabwe					
Rwanda	26,340	10,170	Kigali	4,508,000	Franc
São Tomé and Príncipe	963	372	São Tomé	83,000	Escudo
Senegal	202,000	78,000	Dakar	5,381,000	Franc
Seychelles	443	171	Victoria	62,000	Rupee
Sierra Leone	72,500	28,000	Freetown	3,292,000	Leone
Somalia	637,000	246,000	Mogadishu	13,443,000	Shilling
South Africa	1,180,040	455,616	Pretoria Cape Town	27,700,000	Rand
Sudan	2,506,000	967,500	Khartoum	17,736,000	Pound
Swaziland	17,350	6,700	Mbabane	544,000	Lilangeni
Tanzania	940,200	363,000	Dar-es-Salaam	16,553,000	Shilling
Togo	54,400	21,000	Lomé	2,400,000	Franc
Tunisia	165,150	63,380	Tunis	6,079,000	Dinar
Uganda	235,700	91,000	Kampala	12,708,000	Shilling
Upper Volta	259,000	100,000	Ouagadougou	6,558,000	Franc
Zaïre	2,345,450	905,582	Kinshasa	27,745,000	Zaïre
Zambia	753,700	291,000	Lusaka	4,696,000	Kwacha
Zimbabwe	391,100	151,000	Salisbury	6,310,000	Dollar

ATLANTIC OCEAN

GULF OF GUINEA

Africa

tropical rain forest

mediterranean

thorn forest

dry open woodland

savanna/grassland

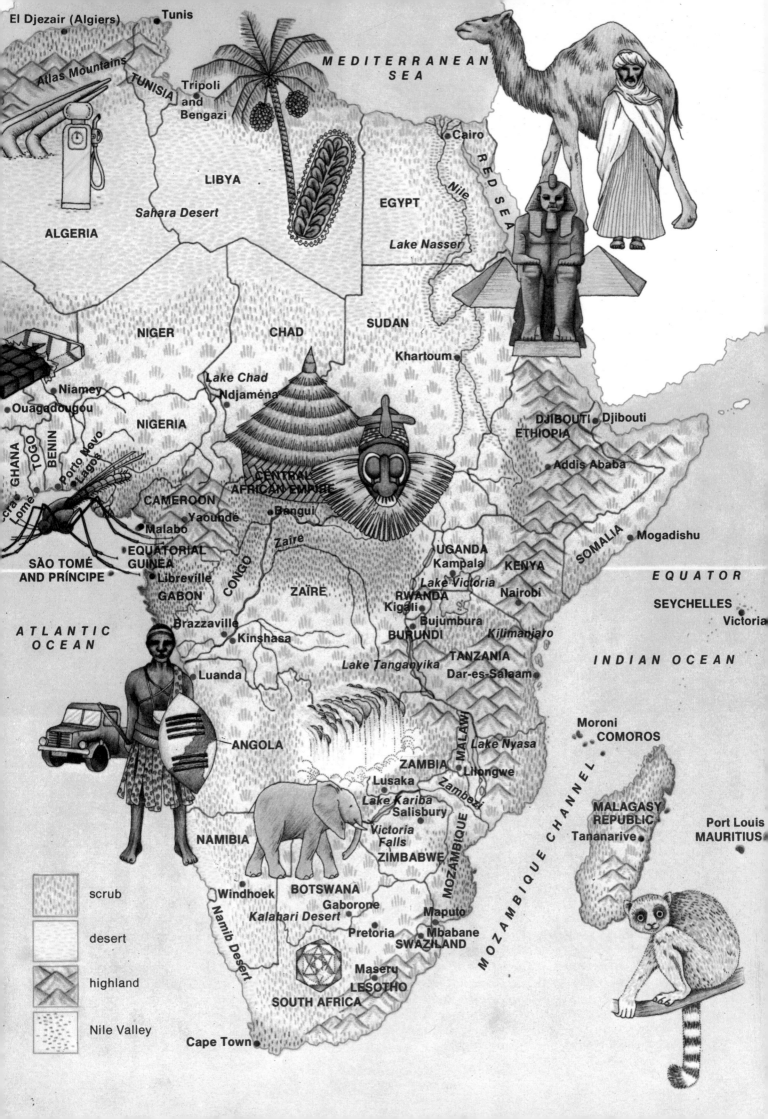

El Djezair (Algiers)
Tunis

Atlas Mountains
TUNISIA
Tripoli and Bengazi

MEDITERRANEAN SEA

Cairo

RED SEA

LIBYA

Sahara Desert

Nile

EGYPT

ALGERIA

Lake Nasser

NIGER

CHAD

SUDAN

Lake Chad
Ndjaména

Khartoum

Niamey

Ouagadougou

NIGERIA

DJIBOUTI Djibouti
ETHIOPIA

GHANA
TOGO
BENIN
Porto Novo
Lagos
Lomé
cra

Addis Ababa

CENTRAL AFRICAN EMPIRE

CAMEROON
Yaoundé

Bangui

Malabo

SÃO TOMÉ AND PRÍNCIPE

EQUATORIAL GUINEA

Zaïre

CONGO

Libreville

GABON

ZAÏRE

UGANDA
Kampala

SOMALIA

Mogadishu

KENYA

Lake Victoria

Nairobi

EQUATOR

SEYCHELLES

Victoria

RWANDA
Kigali

Brazzaville

Kinshasa

BURUNDI
Bujumbura

Kilimanjaro

ATLANTIC OCEAN

Luanda

Lake Tanganyika

TANZANIA
Dar-es-Salaam

INDIAN OCEAN

ANGOLA

MALAWI
Lake Nyasa

Moroni
COMOROS

ZAMBIA
Lusaka

Litongwe

Lake Kariba
Salisbury

Zambezi

MOZAMBIQUE

MALAGASY REPUBLIC
Tananarive

Port Louis
MAURITIUS

NAMIBIA

Victoria Falls

ZIMBABWE

Windhoek

BOTSWANA
Gaborone

Kalahari Desert

Maputo

MOZAMBIQUE CHANNEL

Namib Desert

Pretoria

Mbabane
SWAZILAND

Maseru
LESOTHO

SOUTH AFRICA

Cape Town

scrub

desert

highland

Nile Valley

Northern Africa

People often say there are two Africas because the northern part of this great continent differs so much from the southern half. The two halves of Africa are separated by the Sahara, a burning-hot desert. South of the Sahara most of the people are Negroes; in the north they are mostly Arabs or people closely related to Arabs.

The Sahara itself contains some areas of wind-swept sand dunes, while other parts include bare, rocky volcanic mountains and gravelly plains. In this bleak landscape are a number of oases, places where water comes to the surface and plants can grow. Many dates are grown in the oases, and people live there; but generally only a few wandering herdsmen can live in the Sahara. Underneath the dry surface of the desert, however, is hidden wealth –petroleum and natural gas. These fuels are the

chief source of income for the people of Algeria and Libya. Tunisia also has some petroleum.

Otherwise, people in North Africa live in a comparatively narrow strip of green and fertile land along the coast of the Mediterranean Sea, in the north-western corner, and in the valley of the River Nile. The greatest number of people in northern Africa are crowded into the Nile valley. The Nile is the world's longest river. It rises in eastern Africa and flows northward through Sudan and Egypt. Along its banks are farms, and the land is green where water has been carried from the river through canals and ditches for irrigation. The green vegetation extends for only 10 km. (6 mi.) or less either side for much of the Nile's length. Then, as if a giant hand had ruled a line, it stops, and the yellow sand and rock begin. The Egyptians have built a huge dam across the Nile at Aswan, creating an artificial lake, Lake Nasser. The lake provides water to extend the fertile area, while generators

Above: The waters of the River Nile, and the rich silt they bring down, provide a narrow strip of fertile land in the middle of the dry desert.

Left: Cairo, Egypt's capital, is a flourishing city where modern buildings contrast with ancient mosques.

at the dam provide power for Egypt's factories. Egypt is Africa's second-biggest industrial country, South Africa being the first.

Libya, to the west of Egypt, has a narrow strip of fertile land along the coast, but in north-western Africa the desert ends at the high Atlas mountains of Tunisia, Algeria and Morocco. Between the mountains and the sea is a region of hot, dry summers–which attract tourists–and rainy winters, which enable farmers to grow crops. Many people live in this area, and there are pastures for camels, cattle, goats and sheep.

Nearly all the people living north of the Sahara follow the Islamic religion, which was founded by the prophet Muhammad in the AD 600s. These North African Muslims have introduced Islam to the Black people living immediately south of the Sahara, although some of those people are Christians while others follow traditional religions.

The countries south of the great desert are Mali, Upper Volta, Niger, Chad and Sudan. The northern parts of most of these lands are dry, but there is more rain further south. As a result the desert gradually merges into savannah–tropical grasslands with scattered trees. The drier, northern parts of the savannah are called the Sahel. In rainy years the Sahel has enough grass and water for the large herds of animals that live there. But sometimes practically no rain falls for several years, and the grass withers, wells and water-holes dry up and

A camel for sale in the market at Nabuel, in Tunisia. Camels are ideal for travel in the desert because they can go for long periods without food or water.

millions of animals may die. The people, who depend on these animals for their livelihood, then starve, and many may also die.

Most people in the lands just south of the Sahara are extremely poor. In the east the mountainous land of Ethiopia has enough rainfall for farming, but parts of Ethiopia and most of neighbouring Djibouti and Somalia are desert.

West Africa

West Africa is a vast area, running from the dry grasslands south of the Sahara to the hot, moist lands along the coast of the Gulf of Guinea, which is part of the Atlantic Ocean. There are large forests near the coast, on land which will grow crops well when it is cleared. Inland there are few forests, except near the banks of the Niger, West Africa's longest river, and other smaller rivers. Away from the coast the land is covered by savannah, grassland with trees, where the rain falls mostly in the summer and the winters are dry and cool.

Most of the people of West Africa are poor and have to work very hard to make any kind of living. Because they do not always eat properly and there are many tropical diseases, people tend not to live very long. In Ghana, for instance, the average length of life is only about 48 years, and in Guinea it is about 30 years – less than half that of people in North America or Europe.

There are 13 countries in West Africa, ranging from Senegal in the west to the Central African Republic – the only one with no coastline. The richest is Nigeria, which not only grows large crops for export – it sells cocoa beans, vegetable oil and rubber – but also has petroleum. It is now using

'Peanut power' in action: this West African mill grinds up peanuts (groundnuts) to make meal, and burns the waste part, the shells, to raise steam which provides power for the mill. Groundnuts are important products in many African countries.

Smoked fish is one of the main products sold in this market in Sierra Leone. Open-air markets like this are common in most of Africa.

money from oil sales to build new factories and roads, and raise the standard of living.

Another relatively wealthy country is Ivory Coast, which sells coffee, cocoa beans and timber. It also has many factories, which help to give it a balanced economy, one where there is a variety of ways of earning money. Many other countries in West Africa depend largely on growing and selling one crop, such as the groundnuts which provide nearly all Gambia's income. If plant diseases or bad weather ruin the harvest, the country's income is greatly reduced, and people go short of food.

Most of the wealth of West Africa lies in the rich lands of the coastal region, but inland people make a living by raising cattle in the grasslands.

East Africa

People use the phrase 'East Africa' to describe five countries: Kenya, Tanzania, Uganda and the two tiny republics of Rwanda and Burundi. To the north and slightly to the east three countries make up what is called the 'Horn of Africa', that part of the continent which points eastward at Asia. These three countries are Ethiopia, Somalia, and the small country of Djibouti which lies on the coast between them.

East Africa proper has one of the pleasantest climates in Africa. The lands along the coast are very hot and humid, but away from the sea is a high tableland where the climate is cool and frequently very dry. Rising above the tableland are some of Africa's highest mountains, and the highest peak, Kilimanjaro, is always capped with snow even though it lies very close to the Equator.

Shortage of rain—or, even worse, uncertainty whether there will be enough rain or not—is one of East Africa's main problems. However, there is enough suitable land to grow good crops. The dry grasslands were formerly home for millions of grazing animals, such as antelope and zebra, and the lions which hunted them. Many have been shot, but sizable herds survive in game reserves.

The Horn of Africa is cut off from the rest of the continent by arid plains to the north-west and south-west, and the very steep slopes of the Ethiopian Highlands to the west. The rainy season is in winter. The people of the region have more in common with the Arabs and Berbers of North Africa than with the Negro peoples to the south. Many of them lead a life untouched by modern ways.

A herd of buffalo wanders across the wide plains of Kenya in East Africa. Behind looms the peak of Kilimanjaro, snow-covered although it is very close to the Equator. Kenya has many wild animals.

Central and Southern Africa

Central Africa and Southern Africa consist of a vast tableland, the edges of which slope sharply down to narrow lowlands around the coasts. The lowlands are widest in Mozambique. There are few real mountains, but rivers such as the Zambezi slice their way through the tableland, leaving deep gorges. The Zaïre River flows in a big loop through the country of Zaïre, and with the rivers that run into it makes a large, saucer-shaped depression in the tableland.

The climate and the plant life depend on how near the Equator they are, and how high above sea level. The Equator runs through Gabon, Congo and Zaïre in Central Africa, and these countries are mostly hot and wet, with vast, dense forests. Tribes of tiny pygmies live and hunt in those forests. South of the forests lies an enormous region of lush grassland with scattered trees, and the further south you go the fewer the trees. In the south-west the grass becomes gradually scantier until you are in the Kalahari semi-desert of Botswana, and the bleak Namib desert of Namibia (South-West Africa).

In South Africa, the southernmost country, the plateau is largely dry, but because it lies higher it is also cooler. Around Cape Town and other southern parts the climate is much more like that of lands bordering the Mediterranean Sea.

Most of the people of Southern and Central Africa are Black Africans, people of Negro stock who speak the many languages of the Bantu language group. Southern Africa also has the largest number of people of European origin, mostly living in South Africa and Zimbabwe (Rhodesia). Before the Bantu-speakers and the Europeans arrived there were Bushmen and Hottentots, and a few of these original inhabitants of the land still live in the south-west. The Bushmen wander about, hunting, while the Hottentots rear cattle.

Most of the people in Central and Southern Africa live at subsistence level—that is, they grow only enough food for their families, and have nothing left over to sell so that they can buy other things. Some countries have valuable minerals: for example, Zambia produces copper, and Zaïre can sell copper, diamonds and other minerals.

The wealthiest country is South Africa, which has rich deposits of asbestos, coal, copper, diamonds, iron ore and uranium, and leads the world in gold production. South Africa is the best-developed

A group of Bushmen performs a traditional dance in the Kalahari Desert of southern Africa. The Bushmen used to roam all over southern Africa, but over the years they were gradually driven away from the best lands by the stronger Bantu-speaking tribes.

Above: Bantu huts made of sun-dried bricks thatched with straw form a typical *kraal* (village). Africans have lived in huts like these for hundreds of years.

Left: The face of modern Africa is similar to that of big cities everywhere. Johannesburg is South Africa's largest and wealthiest city. Europeans live in the city centre, but there are many Africans, 'Coloureds' and Asians in the suburbs.

country, too, but it faces problems because it has a mixed population. Seven out of every 10 persons are Bantu-speaking Africans, two are whites of European origin, and the rest are either Asian or so-called 'Coloureds'–people of mixed race. The white South African government pursues a policy of *apartheid*–separate development for each racial group–which is opposed by many people outside South Africa as well as by most of the Bantu-speakers and Coloureds. The Europeans control the country's economy, and under their rule farming and mining are efficient, and there are many manufacturing industries. Many Bantu-speakers from other countries such as Swaziland and Botswana go to South Africa in search of work because there is not enough in their own lands.

Off the coast of Africa, in the Indian Ocean, lies the world's fifth largest island, Madagascar. Like mainland Africa, Madagascar consists of a table-land with coastal plains. Most of the west coast is swampy, and there are few natural harbours. Most of the island is covered with poor soil and rough grassland. There are many animals which are found nowhere else, including lemurs, close re-latives of chimpanzees. The people, too, are different from those of the mainland, being a mixture of Indonesians, from Asia, and Africans.

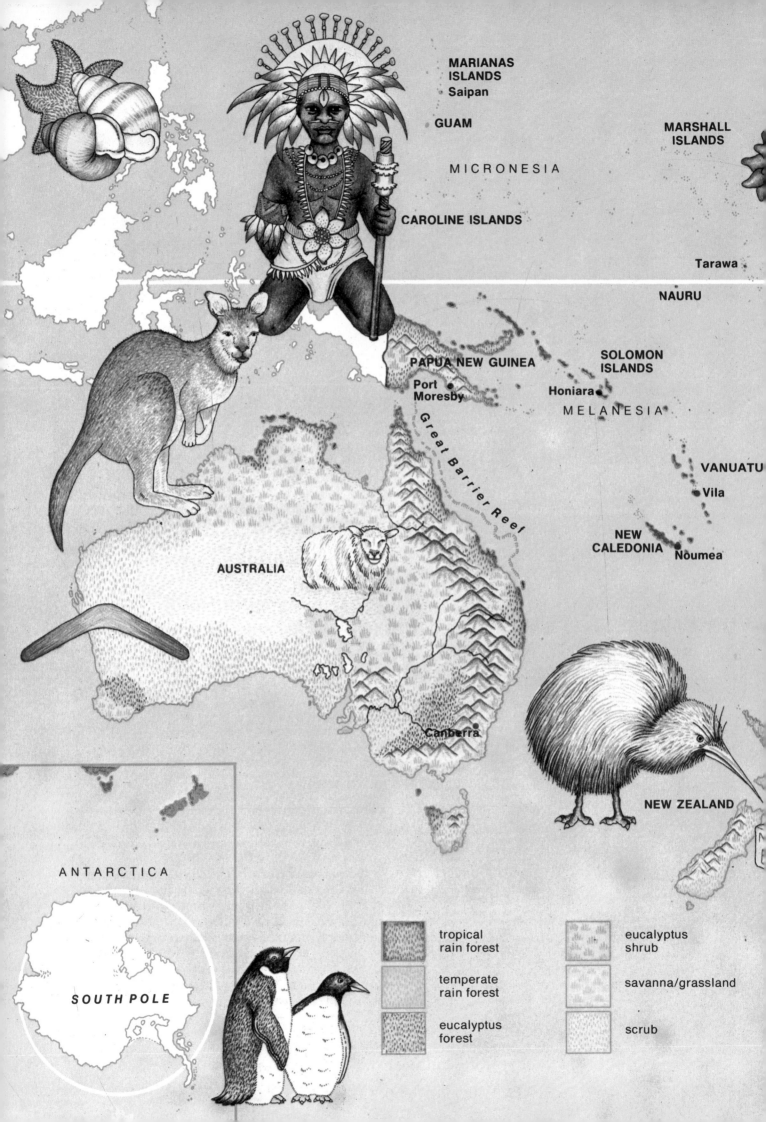

MARIANAS ISLANDS
Saipan

GUAM

MARSHALL ISLANDS

MICRONESIA

CAROLINE ISLANDS

Tarawa

NAURU

PAPUA NEW GUINEA
Port Moresby

SOLOMON ISLANDS
Honiara

MELANESIA

VANUATU
Vila

Great Barrier Reef

NEW CALEDONIA
Noumea

AUSTRALIA

Canberra

NEW ZEALAND

ANTARCTICA

SOUTH POLE

tropical rain forest	eucalyptus shrub
temperate rain forest	savanna/grassland
eucalyptus forest	scrub

Oceania

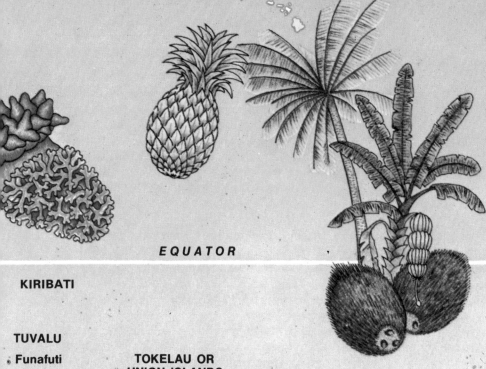

EQUATOR

KIRIBATI

TUVALU
Funafuti

TOKELAU OR
UNION ISLANDS

WESTERN Apia
SAMOA   Pago Pago
FIJI   AMERICAN
          SAMOA
Suva   TONGA

POLYNESIA

COOK ISLANDS

Papeete

FRENCH POLYNESIA

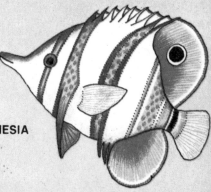

Nuku'alofa

PACIFIC OCEAN

llington

highland

desert

ice pack

Country	Km²	Sq. miles	Capital	Population	Money unit
American Samoa	197	76	Pago Pago	30,000	Dollar
Australia	7,687,000	2,968,000	Canberra	14,420,000	Dollar
Caroline and Marshall Islands	1,340	517	—	92,000	Dollar
Fiji	18,400	7,100	Suva	820,000	Dollar
French Polynesia	6,500	2,500	Papeete	146,000	Franc
Guam	541	209	Agaña	113,000	Dollar
Kiribati	684	264	Tarawa	63,000	Dollar
Marianas	477	184	Saipan	14,000	Dollar
Nauru	21	8	Nauru	8,000	Dollar
New Caledonia	18,700	7,200	Noumea	144,000	Franc
New Zealand	269,000	104,000	Wellington	3,107,000	Dollar
Papua New Guinea	462,000	178,300	Port Moresby	3,080,000	Kina
Solomon Islands	29,800	11,500	Honiara	22,000	Dollar
Tonga	700	270	Nuku'alofa	90,000	Pa'anga
Tuvalu (Ellice Islands)	26	10	Funafuti	7,900	Dollar
Vanuatu	14,800	5,700	Vila	104,000	Franc
Western Samoa	2,800	1,090	Apia	154,000	Tala

The Ocean Islands

Oceania is the vast region that lies between Asia and America. It contains the Pacific Ocean and more than 20,000 islands. The Pacific itself is large enough to swallow up all the rest of the world's oceans. Despite its name, which means 'peaceful', great storms often lash its waters into fury.

The islands of Oceania range from tiny coral atolls formed from the dead bodies of minute sea animals to huge landmasses such as Australia. It is a volcanic region where earthquakes at great depths under the ocean can unleash destructive tidal waves. Such waves can send a wall of water many metres high crashing on to the shore.

The islands of Oceania belong to three groups:

Most of the people of Fiji make their living from farming or from catching fish. This young islander is selling ornamental seashells. A hundred years ago the Fijians were cannibals, but most of them became Christians during 96 years of British rule.

Melanesia, Micronesia and Polynesia. Melanesia lies to the north and north-east of Australia. It includes Fiji, the Vanuatu and the Solomon Islands. The name means 'black islands', and most of the inhabitants are of Negroid stock, with dark skins and woolly hair.

Micronesia, which means 'small islands', comprises such islands as the Carolines, the Marianas and the Kiribati. The inhabitants are of Mongoloid origin, and are thought to have settled in the region from Asia in ancient times.

Polynesia is the most scattered of the island groups. The islands include Tonga, Samoa, the Hawaiian Islands and New Zealand. The people are tall and graceful, and lighter-skinned than in other parts of Oceania. The name 'Polynesia' means 'many islands'.

The sea plays a great part in the islanders' lives, and many people in the smaller islands live by fishing. In the larger islands of Melanesia more people are farmers.

The tropical warmth, the blue ocean, the palm-fringed beaches and the gentle pace of life have always made the region very attractive to visitors,

and tourism is a very important source of income. Situated at the south-west of Oceania is Australia, a continent consisting mainly of a hot, dry plateau. Australia is one of the most isolated and ancient of the landmasses. The oldness and the isolation can be seen in its unusual animals, which have become extinct elsewhere. These include the marsupials like the kangaroo, which have pouches for their young, and the duck-billed platypus which has

Above: Mustering sheep on a farm at Swan Hill, in Victoria, Australia. The country has nearly 14 times as many sheep as there are people living there!

Left: Antarctica is a bleak and inhospitable part of the world. It is covered with thick ice, in places more than 4 km. (2½ mi.) deep.

webbed feet and fur, lays eggs like a reptile but suckles its young like a mammal.

Most of Australia's modern inhabitants came from Britain in the early 1800s, some as convicts to work on penal settlements. Since the end of World War II other Europeans have settled there, including Italians, Dutch, Poles and Greeks. A few of the original inhabitants, the Aborigines, still lead their tough and primitive life in the interior.

Australia is rich in many minerals such as uranium, copper and zinc. It is a rich farming country, especially in livestock such as cattle and sheep. It exports a great deal of meat and wool.

New Zealand lies about 1,900 kilometres (1,200 miles) east of Australia. It also has a population of mainly British origin, although one person in ten is a Maori, one of the original inhabitants.

New Zealand is a beautiful country of meadows, forests, snow-capped mountains and hot volcanic springs. Its wealth comes mainly from farming, and breeding cattle and sheep for meat, wool and dairy produce, most of which is exported.

At the southernmost end of Oceania is Antarctica, the coldest and bleakest of the continents. The lowest temperature ever recorded on Earth, $-88\cdot3°C$ ($126\cdot9°F$), was registered near the South Pole. Temperatures never rise above freezing point, and though the seas round the coast abound with life, the land is permanently locked in ice, and harsh gales constantly blast it.

Antarctica is thought to have deposits of coal and oil. Its only human inhabitants are scientists living in carefully protected bases set up by the Soviet Union and the United States. The continent belongs to no nation but territorial claims to parts of it have been made by Argentina, Australia, Britain, Chile, France, Norway and New Zealand.

FINGERTIP FACTS ABOUT COUNTRIES

THE UNITED NATIONS

The United Nations is an organization designed to keep peace in the world. Nearly all the world's countries belong to it. The United Nations was founded in 1945 with 50 members. Now nearly three times as many countries belong to it.

The United Nations has its headquarters in New York City. All the countries belong to the UN General Assembly, which meets once a year. Fifteen countries belong to the Security Council, which meets every month. The Security Council has the main task of keeping peace. Five countries are permanent members of the council–China, France, the United Kingdom (Britain), the United States of America, and the Union of Soviet Socialist Republics. The other ten members are elected by the General Assembly, and serve for two years.

The Secretariat is the 'civil service' of the United Nations. It is headed by a Secretary-General, who is appointed for five years at a time.

Disputes between members are settled by the International Court of Justice. Problems concerning health and money are dealt with by the Economic and Social Council. The Trusteeship Council looks after some lands which the UN allows other countries to govern for it. There are also 17 agencies looking after food, health, education and other matters.

COUNTRIES IN THE UNITED NATIONS

Afghanistan
Albania
Algeria
Angola
Argentina
Australia*
Austria

Bahamas*
Bahrain
Bangladesh*
Barbados*
Belgium
Benin
Bhutan
Bolivia
Botswana*
Brazil
Bulgaria
Burma
Burundi
Byelorussia

Cameroon
Canada*
Cape Verde
Central African
    Republic
Chad
Chile
China
Colombia
Comoros
Congo
Costa Rica
Cuba
Cyprus*
Czechoslovakia

Denmark
Djibouti
Dominican Republic
Dominica*

Ecuador
Egypt
El Salvador
Equatorial Guinea
Ethiopia

Fiji*
Finland
France

Gabon
Gambia*
Germany, East
Germany, West
Ghana*
Greece
Grenada*

Guatemala
Guinea
Guinea-Bissau
Guyana*

Haiti
Honduras
Hungary

Iceland
India*
Indonesia
Iran
Iraq
Ireland, Republic of
Israel
Italy
Ivory Coast

Jamaica*
Japan
Jordan

Kampuchea
    (Cambodia)
Kenya*
Kuwait

Laos
Lebanon
Lesotho*
Liberia
Libya
Luxembourg

Malagasy Republic
Malawi*
Malaysia*
Maldive Islands
Mali
Malta*
Mauritania
Mauritius*
Mexico
Mongolia
Morocco
Mozambique

Nepal
Netherlands
New Zealand*
Nicaragua
Niger
Nigeria*
Norway

Oman

Pakistan
Panama
Papua New Guinea*
Paraguay

Peru
Philippines
Poland
Portugal

Qatar

Romania
Rwanda

St Lucia*
St Vincent and
    the Grenadines*
São Thomé and
    Príncipe
Saudi Arabia
Senegal
Seychelles*
Sierra Leone*
Singapore*
Solomon Islands*
Somalia
South Africa
Spain
Sri Lanka*
Sudan
Surinam
Swaziland*
Sweden
Syria

Tanzania*
Thailand
Togo
Trinidad and
    Tobago*
Tunisia
Turkey

Uganda*
Ukraine
Union of Soviet
    Socialist Republics
United Arab
    Emirates
United Kingdom
    (Britain)*
USA
Upper Volta
Uruguay

Venezuela
Vietnam

Western Samoa*

Yemen (Aden)
Yemen (Sǎn 'a')
Yugoslavia

Zaïre
Zambia*
Zimbabwe

*Commonwealth members.

UNITED NATIONS AGENCIES

International Labour Organization deals with problems of unemployment and working conditions.

Food and Agricultural Organization deals with farming and food distribution.

International Atomic Energy Agency advises on nuclear power planning.

UNESCO (the UN Educational, Scientific and Cultural Organization) helps countries to help each other in science, education, and communications.

World Health Organization deals with the fight against disease.

United Nations Children's Fund meets the emergency needs of children in times of disaster.

International Bank for Reconstruction and Development (also called the **World Bank**), lends money to countries to help them build roads, factories and other big projects.

International Development Association also helps countries to improve their transport, farms, and industries.

FORMER NAMES OF COUNTRIES

Many countries have changed their names in recent years. You will sometimes find the old names in books or on maps. Here is a list of most of the important changes.

AFRICA

Old name	Now
Abyssinia	Ethiopia
Afars and Issars, Territory of the	Djibouti
Basutoland	Lesotho
Bechuanaland	Botswana
Belgian Congo	Zaïre
British East Africa	Kenya
Dahomey	Benin
German East Africa	Tanzania (part)
Gold Coast	Ghana
Kamerun	Cameroon (part)
Madagascar	Malagasy Republic
Middle Congo	Congo
Nyasaland	Malawi
Portuguese Guinea	Guinea-Bissau
Rhodesia, Northern	Zambia
Rhodesia, Southern	Zimbabwe (Rhodesia)
Rio de Oro	Part of Morocco and Mauritania
Ruanda-Urundi	Rwanda and Burundi
Spanish Guinea	Equatorial Guinea
Somaliland, British	Somalia (part)
Somaliland, French	Djibouti
Somaliland, Italian	Somalia (part)
South-West Africa	Namibia

Old name	Now
Sudan, Anglo-Egyptian	Sudan
Sudan, French	Mali
Tanganyika	Tanzania (part)
Togoland	Togo
Ubangi-Shari	Central African Empire
Zanzibar	Tanzania (part)

THE AMERICAS

British Guiana	Guyana
British Honduras	Belize
Dutch Guiana	Surinam
Dutch West Indies	Netherlands Antilles

ASIA

Aden	Part of Yemen (Aden)
Cambodia	Kampuchea
Ceylon	Sri Lanka
Chosen	Korea
Dutch East Indies	Indonesia
East Pakistan	Bangladesh
French Indo-China	Kampuchea, Laos and Vietnam
Hejaz and Nedj	Saudi Arabia
Indian Empire	Bangladesh, India, Pakistan
Khmer Republic	Kampuchea
Malay States	Part of Malaysia
Palestine	Israel and Jordan
Persia	Iran
Siam	Thailand
Tibet	Part of China
Transjordan	Jordan
Trucial States	United Arab Emirates
West Pakistan	Pakistan

EUROPE

Bohemia	Part of Czechoslovakia
Estonia	Part of the USSR

Old name	Now
Irish Free State	Republic of Ireland (Eire)
Latvia	Part of the USSR
Lithuania	Part of the USSR
Montenegro	Part of Yugoslavia
Ottoman Empire	Turkey
Papal States	Part of Italy
Prussia	Part of East Germany and Poland
Russia	Union of Soviet Socialist Republics
Serbia	Part of Yugoslavia
White Russia	Byelorussia (USSR)

THE COMMONWEALTH

The Commonwealth is a group of countries which used to be part of the British Empire. The British began acquiring their empire in the 1600s. By 1900 it covered one fifth of the world's land, and contained a quarter of all the people.

The empire was renamed the Commonwealth in the 1930s. By then, several countries in it were independent. Most of the rest have become independent since World War II ended in 1945. The Commonwealth today contains 43 independent countries, plus some small islands. The majority of the 43 countries are members of the United Nations, and are marked with a star (*) in the list on page 96.

Several countries that were in the old British Empire have chosen not to be in the Commonwealth. They include Burma, Pakistan and South Africa.

Most Commonwealth countries have their own heads of state (kings or presidents). Britain's queen, Elizabeth II, is head of state of the others, and also head of the Commonwealth.

International Finance Corporation helps the World Bank in its work for poorer countries.

International Monetary Fund provides loans to all countries to help trade.

International Civil Aviation Organization keeps an eye on all flying, and makes safety rules.

Universal Postal Union makes sure that postal services between countries work smoothly.

International Telecommunication Union keeps the world's radio and telephone services working properly.

World Meteorological Organization helps weather forecasters in all countries.

Inter-Governmental Maritime Consultative Organization looks after safety at sea.

General Agreement on Tariffs and Trade is designed to make trading easier between members.

UN High Commissioner for Refugees deals with refugees' problems by repatriation and resettlement.

The arts

We use the term 'art' in two ways. Sometimes we use it to mean pictures, which artists paint or draw. We can also use it for all the forms of art, which include sculpture, writing, music, the theatre, the cinema, photography, dancing, and also radio and television. Together, these activities are known as 'the arts'.

Sometimes we use the word 'art' as an opposite to the word 'craft'. We call making something that is beautiful rather than useful an art, and making something that is useful more than beautiful a craft. This difference is not really important, because useful things can be beautiful if they are well made, and many beautiful things are useful too. The great thing about art is that it enables us to express ideas. We can express ideas not only by writing a poem or a story, but also by painting a picture, carving a statue, or writing a piece of music. In the next 22 pages we can look at some of the ways people do all these things.

Painting and drawing

Drawing and painting were the two main ways of making flat pictures until photography was invented (see pages 114–115).

Drawing is usually done on paper, using pencil, pen and ink, or charcoal. The idea is to 'trace' the outline of what you see. Drawing has always been considered very good practice for artists because it makes you concentrate on the use of line. Shading can also be used to make drawings more lifelike and realistic. Some of the world's best-known drawings are by the Italian artist Leonardo da Vinci (1452–1519). He drew everything from animals and birds to ideas for flying machines.

Another way of making pictures which also concentrates on line is engraving. This is a bit like making lino-cuts, except that wood or copper is used instead of lino. Using a sharp tool, the artist cuts his picture into a flat piece of wood or a copper plate. The wood or plate is then inked and pressed on to paper. In this way you can make as many copies of a picture as you want, until the plate wears out. One of the greatest engravers of all time was the German artist Albrecht Dürer (1471–1528).

Etching is a development of engraving. A copper or zinc plate is covered with a 'ground'–a smooth coating of wax mixed with pitch and amber. The artist scratches the picture into the ground and puts the plate in acid, which 'eats' the picture into the plate. The ground is scraped off and the plate is then used to print the picture, as in engraving.

The other main way to make pictures is by painting in colour. The colour is usually put on with a brush. The Stone Age artists, who made the earliest paintings we know on the walls of caves in Spain and France, blew powdered colour on to the

Above: European cavemen made this drawing of a mammoth about 20,000 years ago. It proves that this animal, now extinct, was still around in those days.

Left: This colourful picture of St. George and the Dragon was painted in the 1400s. It is an icon, a religious picture of the Russian Orthodox Church.

Above: Albrecht Dürer made this engraving, 'Melencolia' (Melancholy) in 1514. He is renowned for engravings.

Above: Leonardo da Vinci painted 'The Virgin of the Rocks' in the late 1400s. It is one of two versions.

Right: A self-portrait by Rembrandt van Rijn, the Dutch artist who lived from 1606 to 1669. It is one of about 60 pictures he painted of himself.

walls through bone tubes. To make the colour stay on they put a kind of glue on the wall.

From Stone Age times right up to about AD 1400, murals – wall paintings – continued to be one of the main kinds of art. In Europe in the late Middle Ages artists used a technique called fresco (Italian for 'fresh'). The wall was plastered and the paint was put on while the plaster was still damp ('fresh'). The colours were mixed with white-of-egg and vinegar to make them stick to the plaster.

One trouble with this way of binding colour (called tempera) was that the paintings did not last very well, and eventually turned greenish. Oil paints, with the colour mixed with linseed oil, last much better and look brighter. They were invented by two Flemish artists, the brothers Huybrecht and Jan van Eyck (1366–1426 and 1370–1440). After the invention of oil painting artists mostly used canvas to paint on. Before, they used wooden panels.

Brush painting is not done only with oil paints. Pictures can be made with brush and ink and also with water-colours. The Chinese and Japanese use brush and ink both for writing and painting. With just a few brush strokes Chinese artists can suggest complete landscapes. Water colour is also good for landscape painting, particularly for capturing the gentle colours of the English countryside.

Throughout history and in different countries there have been so many pictures in so many styles and by so many different artists, some little known, others famous, that it would be impossible to describe them all. But most pictures of the past and present fit into one or another of these groups: 1, realistic pictures; 2, non-realistic pictures; 3, pictures with some immediate use or purpose; and 4, pictures with a less direct use or purpose.

Until the 1900s most of the world's pictures were realistic or figurative–that is, they were recognisable pictures of things or people. The earliest cave paintings, made about 20,000 years ago, are lifelike pictures of the animals which Stone Age people hunted. These paintings had a definite use because they taught people which animals to look out for and how to hunt them. The Stone Age

Above: Jean Ingres's portrait of Madame Moitessier shows the more formal style of the early 1800s.

Top right: Auguste Renoir painted 'La Loge' (The Box at the Theatre) in 1874. It is an example of Impressionism, a less detailed and more sketchy way of painting.

artists probably believed that imitating the animals in pictures worked magic on the animals.

The ancient Egyptians covered the walls of their temples and palaces with pictures that showed every aspect of their lives, with much realistic detail. However, Egyptian paintings had a flat effect with no feeling of depth. The Greeks and Romans did realistic wall paintings, but not many survive.

In Europe in the Middle Ages pictures were mainly of saints and other religious subjects. Like Egyptian art long before, medieval Western paintings looked flat.

Also in the Middle Ages the Arabs developed one of the world's first great styles of non-realistic art, based on geometrical shapes. This was because their religion, Islam, discouraged pictures of living things. European artists used the geometry they learned from the Arabs to make pictures more realistic by using perspective, that is, drawing things that are further off smaller than those near by. Perspective was one of the most important changes in art which happened during the Renaissance period (about 1400 to 1600). Renaissance means 'rebirth', and at that time there was in Europe a rebirth of interest in Greek and Roman art.

As in the Middle Ages much Renaissance art was religious. Renaissance artists painted many other subjects too, such as battle scenes and portraits of princes and nobles.

After the Renaissance European painters continued to paint realistic pictures, scenes of every-day life and ordinary people. Dutch painters produced indoor scenes, known as 'Dutch interiors', which were almost like photographs. Landscape painting became popular for the next 300 years. However, when the camera was invented, artists realised that it was not necessary to see things as the camera did. The first move away from the older kind of realism was called the Impressionist style. It began in France in the 1870s, when a group of young painters set out to capture the 'impression' made by the way light shines on things. The next step was called Cubism. This style developed when painters began to interpret what they saw as built up from simple shapes such as cubes, cones and circles. Along with this went a new interest in non-European art, such as African sculpture.

Finally, many Western artists developed a new style of completely non-realistic or abstract art, using shapes which they made up.

Above: 'The Three Dancers' by Pablo Picasso (1881–1973) shows the essence of Cubism – an interest in basic shapes rather than a realistic view of things.

Right: 'Fall' by the modern British artist Bridget Riley is an example of 'Op Art', in which artists try to create an optical illusion of movement.

Below: 'Whaam', painted by the American Roy Lichtenstein in 1963, is an example of Pop Art, which is inspired by subjects such as strip cartoons.

Sculpture

Carving and modelling are the ways in which artists make beautiful things out of any material that is plastic – which means 'can be shaped'. We sometimes call this 'plastic art'. The materials we now call 'plastics' got their name because they can be shaped easily in factories.

Modelling is usually done in clay, which can be made hard by baking it. Articles made of clay in this way are called ceramics, from a Greek word meaning pottery. Carvings, sometimes called sculptures, are generally made from wood, or stone. When you model something in clay, you generally build it up. When you carve, you cut away the waste material you do not want. In modelling with clay, you can use your hands directly, because clay when damp is soft enough to be shaped just with the fingers. Wood and stone have to be cut with saws and chisels, or bored with drills.

Metals can also be used for making sculpture. Soft metals such as copper and gold can be beaten into shape. Harder ones such as bronze, which is a mixture of copper and tin, can be filed or sawn to

shape. But shaping metal by these means is a slow job, so large metal sculptures are generally cast – the metal is melted and poured into a mould.

Ceramics began as a strictly useful occupation when Stone Age people discovered how to make clay pots. They made some of their earliest pots by a method a bit like basket weaving. Some people still make simple pots in this way. You begin by rolling out the clay in a long 'snake', which you then coil round and round to build up your pot. People found it quicker and easier to make pots after the invention of the potter's wheel 5,000 years ago. Modern mass-produced pottery is made by pressing the clay into a mould.

By mixing special clay with other substances, potters make hard china, used for cups, jars, vases and dishes. Some of the world's most beautiful pottery was made in China at the time of the Ming emperors (1368–1644).

Carving wood and stone to make sculpture also began in the Stone Age. Even today many people, particularly tribesmen in Africa and the American Indians, prefer wood to stone for their carvings.

Top left: This Greek sculpture of one of the Muses playing a lyre is a relief – the figure is shown attached to its background. It was made 2,000 years ago and is a good example of the clean, beautiful lines of what is called 'classical' sculpture.

Above: Giovanni Lorenzo Bernini completed his 'Four Rivers' fountain in the Piazza Navona, Rome, in 1651. It is in the Baroque style, which combines classical human forms with more elaborate decoration. This fountain is Bernini's most spectacular work.

Some Africans make wooden masks, which they paint in bright colours. A mask is just the face, and if you add the rest of the head you have a carving which is called a bust. Many busts are carved in stone, or cast in metal.

One method of making metal castings is called the 'lost wax' process. The artist begins by making a rough model in clay. Then he covers the model with wax, and finishes his modelling in the wax. He next covers the wax with more clay, and lets it all harden. Then he heats the model. The wax melts and runs out, leaving a space between the two lots of clay. Into this space the artist pours hot metal. He breaks away the clay, and there is his sculpture reproduced in metal. Rough parts are then filed off.

The ancient Greeks made some of the world's most beautiful sculptures. They liked to carve them in marble, a hard stone which takes a good polish. The Romans copied the Greeks. After the Romans, more than a thousand years went by before another sculptor as good as the ancient Greeks came along. His name was Michelangelo Buonarroti, and he lived and worked in Italy in the 1500s.

Like the ancient Greeks and Romans, Michelangelo made statues of men and women. Today sculptors make sculptures in many shapes and a wide variety of materials. A great many of these sculptors make figures of people which are highly simplified, or are distorted, perhaps with big heads and very long legs. Other artists make shapes to express ideas. Some make sculptures that move about, so that they are always changing shape as the wind blows them.

The modern British sculptor Henry Moore likes his statues to reflect the type of stone or wood in which they are carved. His 'Madonna and Child' is at St. Matthew's Church, Northampton, England.

Above: This bronze plaque from Benin (now in Nigeria) was made more than 300 years ago. It shows the country's ruler, the Oba, as a god.

Right: A great deal of modern sculpture consists of interesting shapes that do not represent any special object. Tim Scott made this one in 1966 using wood and steel tubes. It is called 'Quantic of Meidum'.

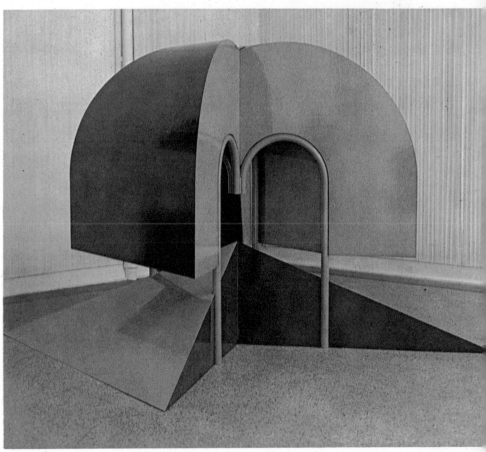

Above: The Parthenon at Athens in Greece was built more than 2,400 years ago as a temple to the goddess Athene. It was ruined during the 1600s.

Architecture

Architecture began when early people started to build their own shelters rather than relying on ready-made ones such as trees, overhangs and caves. Before the art of growing food was discovered most people were nomadic (wandering) hunters. They followed herds of animals as they moved around, and so used movable shelters–in other words, what we call tents and what American Indians called tepees or wigwams. Fishing peoples tended to settle in one place, by seashores or river-banks and so built more fixed shelters out of branches and leaves, or with slabs of turf.

When farming started people began to live in permanent villages. In hot, dry regions, such as the deserts of North America, baked mud was often used for walls. When people started living in cities, they built in brick and stone as well, and the skills of the bricklayer and mason (stone cutter) became important. It also became necessary to have architects to specialize in planning and designing the larger and more important buildings, such as palaces, temples and tombs. The first architect we know by name, Imhotep of Egypt, was also a doctor, a statesman and a priest. He lived about 4,700 years ago, and designed the first pyramid.

Egyptian and Greek architecture was mostly flat-roofed. The arch, which was invented in Babylonia and taken over by the Etruscans and Romans, made it possible to have vaulted (curved) roofs. A circular vault made a dome. Vaulted stone roofs are heavier than flat roofs, and they weigh more heavily on the walls that hold them up. To prevent the walls from buckling outwards, supports called buttresses are sometimes used.

Vaults and buttresses were leading features

Left: The church of Aulnay in France is a masterpiece of Romanesque architecture. It was built in the AD 1100s, and is covered with rich carvings.

of the churches and cathedrals built in Europe during the Romanesque, Gothic and Renaissance periods–roughly 1000–1600. Builders in the Romanesque period used round-headed arches. In the later Middle Ages the Gothic style appeared, with pointed instead of round arches. This gave Gothic churches a 'tall' look known as the perpendicular style. A massive effort was needed to plan and organize the building of a medieval cathedral, as complicated in its way as building a Concorde jet-liner today. Big cathedrals, often richly decorated with stone carvings and stained-glass windows, often took more than a hundred years to finish, and employed generations of masons and other craftsmen.

During the Renaissance (see pages 104–105) architects rediscovered the principles of classical (ancient Greek and Roman) building. Italian designers–particularly Leon Battista Alberti and Andrea Palladio–used musical ideas to work out the dimensions of their buildings. For instance, if you have a stretched string tuned to the note C,

Above: The towering might of the Royal Bank building at Toronto in Canada is typical of today's city skyscrapers. Buildings like this have been made possible by the use of steel framing and concrete.

Left: St. Paul's Cathedral in London is a fine example of Renaissance architecture. It was designed in the late 1600s by Sir Christopher Wren to replace an earlier building destroyed in the Fire of London.

and you shorten it to 4/5ths of its length, you get the note E, which makes a pleasant harmony with C. In the same way a Renaissance architect might make the two shorter walls of an oblong room 4/5ths the length of the longer walls, so that the two sets of walls were 'in harmony'. No wonder the German poet Johann von Goethe later called architecture 'frozen music'.

In the 17th century a style of building developed which was called baroque, from a Portuguese word for 'irregular pearl'. Baroque buildings have many twisting and turning decorations which seem 'irregular' compared with the balanced form of Renaissance structures. In the 18th century baroque

was followed by an even more decorative style of building called rococo. The 19th century brought various styles of architecture. In England the Neo-Gothic style developed for public buildings. This was influenced by the Gothic style of medieval building, but tended to be more formal and less spontaneous in appearance.

Modern architecture owes a great deal to the use of steel framing to support structures–an extension of the wooden-framed houses of the 1500s which we call 'half-timbered'. Steel girders combined with reinforced concrete make it possible to use shapes and span wide areas in a way impossible with older materials and methods. Walls are often 'curtain walls'–that is, they fill in the gaps between the framework, and are not weight-carrying parts of the building.

Partly because of the high cost of decorative work, such as carving, the emphasis in present-day architecture is on function rather than appearance. One of the most influential of 20th century architects, Le Corbusier (a Swiss whose real name was Charles Jeanneret), once described a house as 'a machine for living', and this emphasis on the mechanical aspects of buildings is very evident in much of today's construction, be it housing, offices, factories or public buildings. Only occasionally is appearance put before function, as in the Sydney Opera House with its series of shell-shaped half-domes, looking like sails.

Literature

There is no exact dividing line between writing things down because people need information, and writing to give pleasure or entertainment. Prose and poetry, the two main kinds of written art (that is, literature) both inform and entertain.

Prose is usually written in periods or sentences which are arranged in groups called paragraphs. This way of writing is normally used to explain things clearly, for instance in an encyclopedia. Prose is also used in newspapers and letters. Sometimes, letters come to be works of art in themselves. Lord Chesterfield's **Letters to his Son**, written by an 18th-century English nobleman, are famous for their clear style as well as for the good advice they contain.

A more artistic use of prose is fiction. This is basically story-telling in written form. The events

Below: This beautiful page of a book is from a manuscript copy of 'The Canterbury Tales' by Geoffrey Chaucer. It shows the start of 'The Tale of Melibeus', illustrated with a picture of Chaucer himself.

Below: Caleb Plummer and his blind daughter Bertha in Charles Dickens's 'The Cricket on the Hearth'.

described in fiction may come from real life, but the writer usually rearranges and develops them according to his or her imagination.

The main kinds of fiction are short stories and novels. A novel (the word just means 'something new') is a work of fiction occupying a whole book. Most novels have several stories or plots. Each one may be about a character or a group of characters. The writer weaves the various plots together, much as a composer may weave several tunes together in writing a piece of music.

In historical novels the writer gives you the 'feel' of life during a particular time of history. Then there are novels set in or near to the writer's own times. An example is **War and Peace**, written by the Russian, Leo Tolstoy, in the 1860s. In Tolstoy's time Napoleon Bonaparte's invasion of Russia in 1812 was remembered by people still living, and Tolstoy used this war as the background of his novel. The greatness of **War and Peace** is in the way that Tolstoy weaves this background together with the personal lives of his characters.

Novels set in the future are usually called science fiction, or just 'sci-fi'. Sci-fi looks at the way people might behave in a possible future which scientific progress, such as space travel, has made very different from the present. Some sci-fi books are pure fantasy but others may be a disguised comment on the way things seem to be going now. A famous example was **Brave New World**, written in the early 1930s by the English novelist Aldous Huxley.

Much poetry is written so that the words are in regular rhythms and arranged in lines of regular lengths. Often, too, rhyme is used. Poetry is the most artistic way of expressing thoughts and feelings in writing, and there are as many types of it as there are of prose.

A very concentrated form of poetry is the Japanese *haiku*. The haiku poet uses only 17 syllables to get his idea across. The sonnet is a form which has been used by many European poets, such as William Wordsworth and Petrarch. Haiku and sonnet are examples of forms or shapes of poetry.

Poems also vary in style and content. For instance, lyric poetry is song-like. The earliest poetry of this kind was sung by ancient Greek bards.

Before writing was invented all literature was oral – that is, it consisted of stories and myths which were memorized and passed by word of mouth from generation to generation. Oral literature is still very important in tribal societies, whose languages have only recently been written down.

The first written literature was stories about heroes and gods. The oldest example is **The Epic of Gilgamesh**, written in Mesopotamia about 4,000 years ago. The next oldest works are the **Iliad** and the **Odyssey**, written by the Greek poet Homer probably about 2,800 years ago.

The ancient tradition of telling stories by word of mouth is carried on today by these storytellers in the market-place at Marrakesh, in southern Morocco.

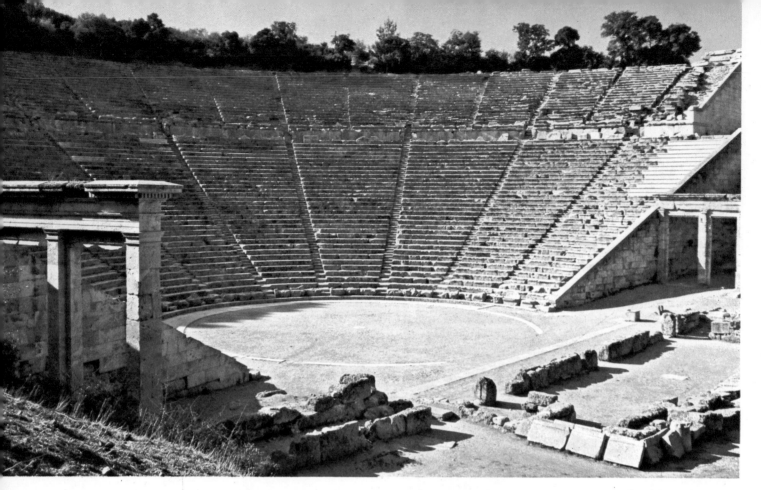

Theatre

Drama is an art-form in which the performers act a story to the audience. If it is done by actions and expressions, but without speech, the drama is called mime. In most drama, however, the actors speak as well. Drama is usually acted on a stage in a theatre–and for this reason it is often called 'theatre'. A piece of drama (usually called a play) is generally written by a dramatist or playwright, though it can be improvised (made up) by the actors. Most plays have several sections or acts, and each act may be divided into several scenes. To make a play more realistic the actors generally wear costumes and make-up. Stage scenery and special lighting are usually used as well.

Drama is a combination of different arts. Like dance, drama uses movement. Actors do not necessarily move in the same way as dancers, but they move for much the same reason, to express feelings and ideas. The words in drama are 'spoken literature'. Many dramatists have written their plays in a form of poetry. The Elizabethan dramatists such as Christopher Marlowe and William Shakespeare used a form called blank verse, with regular rhythm but no rhymes. Many plays have a bit of music here and there, called incidental music. When there is a lot of music, and the actors mostly sing instead of talking, the result is called opera. The actors' costumes and the stage scenery also make drama into a spectacle, in other words a visual art like painting.

Stone Age hunters performed the earliest drama by copying the actions and sounds of the animals they hunted. As with their paintings of animals, they thought this would magically bring the animals within their power. This sort of 'hunting drama' became part of early religious worship. In ancient Greece drama began as the worship of the god of wine, Dionysus. From this, classical Greek drama developed, written by poets and musicians such as Aeschylus and Sophocles.

More than 3,000 years ago in China a kind of play was performed when the seasons changed. Young men and women from different villages met at places where rivers joined, and sang, danced and acted in praise of the gods. To this day Chinese theatre includes much music, and for this reason it is often called 'opera'. In Japan a type of drama called *Nō* (meaning 'talent') grew from temple dancing in the 14th century, and has kept its musical beginnings in its rhythm. All through a *Nō* play, a steady beat is felt (in groups of 8 or 16), and the words fit into this beat.

The earliest Indian plays that still survive date from about AD 100. Touring theatre companies went from town to town hundreds of years before the same thing happened in Europe.

In the Middle Ages European drama grew out of short Bible stories acted as part of the Christian Mass. These stories developed into the popular mystery, miracle and morality plays. In the 16th century a popular style of theatre called *Commedia dell'arte* grew up in Italian cities. Its characters included Pulcinella, the 'ancestor' of Mr. Punch in puppet Punch-and-Judy shows. In England the

Elizabethan and Jacobean period produced Shakespeare, perhaps the greatest dramatist of all time. Since then some of the leading Western dramatists have included Molière (1622–1673) in France; Lope de Vega (1562–1635) in Spain; Johann von Goethe (1749–1832) in Germany; Henrik Ibsen (1828–1906) and August Strindberg (1849–1912) in Scandinavia; Anton Chekhov (1860–1904) in Russia; George Bernard Shaw (1856–1950) in Britain; Eugene O'Neill (1888–1953) in the United States; and Bertholt Brecht (1898–1956) in Germany.

Puppet drama has existed as long as drama using full-sized actors, and it can have an enchanted, magical effect of its own. The main kinds of puppet are glove puppets, which the puppeteer puts over his hand; string puppets or marionettes, worked from above by strings; and flat shadow puppets which are worked by rods. Shadow puppet theatre is an important art-form in Asian countries such as Indonesia and China.

Left: 'Once more unto the breach, dear friends . . .' the actor Alan Howard delivers Henry V's famous speech in the Shakespeare play of that name. This production was by the Royal Shakespeare Company at Stratford-upon-Avon, where the playwright was born.

Below: Grotesque masks are a feature of Chinese drama. This one is worn by an actor in a theatre in Singapore, which has a mostly Chinese population.

Musicians of the
late 1700s, seen
by the French artist
Jean Honoré Fragonard

Music

Music is the art of making sounds into patterns which express how we feel and give pleasure to people who hear them. We can make music either by singing or by playing musical instruments, or both. A musical sound is called a note. Notes usually have certain lengths of time. The simplest time length is called a beat. Played one after another, beats give music a steady speed or tempo. Beats are grouped in twos, threes, fours and so on to make bars or measures. The time of a beat can also be divided into two, four, eight and so on, to make shorter notes. The patterns made by the different time lengths in music are called rhythm.

Notes can also have a definite pitch (high or low sound). By using notes of different pitches, one after another, we get patterns of notes called melodies or tunes. Playing two or more notes at the same time produces an effect called harmony. A note can have any pitch, but most music uses only a certain number of notes of different pitches. Arranged in order from low to high (or high to low), such notes form scales. So a scale is a set of notes from which the notes of a tune are chosen. The main kind of scale has seven notes with different names. Starting with the lowest they are called C, D, E, F, G, A and B. The next note after B is called C again. It sounds like the first C but is higher in pitch. This kind of scale is called a diatonic scale, and you can play it on the white notes of a piano. You can use the black notes to play diatonic scales beginning on notes other than C, or different kinds of scales.

The other main things in music are its loudness or softness, and its timbre. The loudness and softness of music is called dynamics. Timbre means the particular kind of sound, or tone, made by different instruments; for example a violin, a saxophone and a guitar have very different timbres.

In various times and places people have made many kinds of music. Among tribal people music is

Left: Colin Davis conducts a symphony orchestra.

Below: Elton John, singer of popular music.

used in religion and to celebrate birth, growing up, marrying, dying and anything else that is important in their lives. In modern societies music is also important, but people make and listen to music more for entertainment than for any other purpose, though they also use it for religious worship.

The two main kinds of music that are played today are popular or 'pop' music, and classical or 'serious' music. Music is usually composed (thought up by one person) and written down in detail, so that the musicians know exactly what to play. Much classical music is played by large symphony orchestras, and a piece of music specially written for such an orchestra is called a symphony.

Classical music started about 1,000 years ago in Europe, when ways of writing music down were invented. In many parts of the world music is not written down, but is memorized instead. A piece of music can be played the same way each time, or it can be varied by the performer. This kind of variation is called improvising, and it is important in much pop music and also in jazz and blues – kinds of music which were developed by Negro musicians in the United States.

There has always been popular music, that is, songs and dances that were important in the everyday life of ordinary people in the countryside and cities. Today such traditional music is usually called folk music. Modern pop music is not quite the same. It began in the 1950s with rock 'n' roll, a loud and lively style based on American blues. The more blues-influenced kind of pop music is usually called rock. Both pop and rock are usually performed by groups which have singers, guitarists and a drummer. The voices and instruments are amplified by electronic equipment.

Dance and gymnastics

Dancing is moving our bodies to express our feelings. Together with singing dance was probably the first of the arts. In early and ancient times dancing, singing and playing instruments all went together as part of ritual and religion. This is still true among tribal peoples today.

Dancing was an important part of ancient Greek drama. Indian, Chinese and Japanese dancing all developed as part of drama, which, as in Greece, grew out of religious worship.

Tribal dancing, for instance in Africa, is very important in the lives of the people. All important events, such as births, growing up, weddings and funerals are celebrated by dances, with everybody joining in. Among peasants in Europe what we now call country dancing or folk dancing was performed for the same kinds of reasons.

In modern society there are two main sorts of dancing. One is social dancing, all the different kinds of dancing that are done for fun, such as disco dancing and ballroom dancing. The other sort is stage dancing, which includes ballet and modern dance routines.

Ballroom dancing started with the 17th-century court dances of the nobility, which were mostly 'polished-up' peasant dances. By the 18th century court dances included the minuet, allemande,

courante, gigue and gavotte. The most popular 19th-century ballroom dance was the waltz, which began in Vienna.

Today popular ballroom dances include many Latin American dances, such as the tango, rumba, samba and cha-cha-cha, and dances from the United States such as the foxtrot and the Charleston. Many of these dances started off as Afro-American dances performed by Negroes in Brazil, Cuba, the United States and other countries.

Modern disco dancing goes with pop, rock and soul music. The styles change very quickly, but many of them start off as 'Black' dances, such as the watutsi and the funky chicken.

Classical ballet, like ballroom dancing, grew out of court dancing. It started in France in the 17th century, and developed greatly in Russia during the 19th century. The idea of ballet is to use artistic dancing to tell a story, much as opera uses music. Ballet employs a number of standard body movements and positions. From these, choreographers plan dances in the same kind of way that a composer writes music. Modern dance is similar

Left: Dancers of the Masai tribe in Kenya perform a centuries-old traditional tribal routine.

Below: Ballet is the height of dancing skill in the West. Here, Svetlana Beriosova and Donald MacLeary act out in dance the fairy story of Cinderella.

to ballet, but freer in style. It is often used in stage musicals and variety performances.

Gymnastics is using body movement to exercise and develop the body. It started with the public games of the ancient Greeks. Modern gymnastics began in the late 19th century, in the same period that the Olympic Games were revived. The two main kinds are German gymnastics, which is mainly meant to develop the muscles; and Swedish gymnastics, which develops perfect rhythm in movement.

In competition gymnastics the performers are given points by expert judges. A world championship is held every four years, two years after the

A great gymnast in action: Russia's Olga Korbut in a spectacular leap from the asymmetrical bars.

Olympic Games. There is also a gymnastics section in the Olympics. Men's competitions have six events: horizontal bar, parallel bars, pommel horse, vaulting horse, floor exercises and stationary rings. The women's competition has four events: balancing beam, asymmetrical bars, vaulting horse and floor exercises. For each event the competitors must perform one set exercise and one which they choose themselves.

Trampolining is a form of gymnastics, but it is not included as an Olympics competition.

Photography

Frenchman, Louis Daguerre. His photographs, called daguerreotypes, became widely popular, but because they were still negatives, daguerreotypes were not entirely realistic. This problem was solved the same year by an English scientist, W. H. Fox Talbot. He developed the method of contact printing which transferred the picture on the negative to another plate, the positive, on which the dark and light of the negative were reversed so as to look like the original scene.

In the past hundred years there have been many improvements in the design of cameras and the materials used in them, such as colour film. Photography has become an important art in its own right. It has also had a big influence on the development of modern painting. Artists could not compete with the camera for realism, and this was one reason why many painters turned to abstract art.

Nowadays a huge selection of cameras is available, ranging from cheap, simple ones for snapshots to expensive, complex models for professional use.

All work on the same principle: light from a scene enters the closed box through a lens (called the

Left: In the early days of photography people had to keep still for a very long time; film was slow.

Below: Using black and white film, a camera takes a negative (upper picture) in which all the blacks and whites are reversed. From this negative a print is made in which the tones come out the right way round.

Photography literally means 'light-drawing'. Today photography is the art and craft of producing flat pictures on film by means of a camera. Cameras themselves were invented long before photography. In the late 1400s the artist Leonardo da Vinci used a *camera obscura* (meaning 'dark room') as an aid to drawing. It was simply a small room, light-proof except for a very small hole in one side. An upside-down image of the scene outside was formed on the inside wall opposite to it. Later, an improved *camera obscura* was invented, which used a mirror to turn the image the right way up. All the artist needed to do was to trace the image to have a realistic drawing of the scene outside. In 1600 the astronomer Johann Kepler used lenses to magnify the image.

By the early 19th century there was a big demand for cheap pictures, and it was this which stimulated the discovery of photography. A French scientist, Joseph Niepce, took the first photograph in 1826. He used a *camera obscura* and a photographic plate coated with a silver halide compound. When exposed to light the plate turned dark. Where the light coming from the subject was strongest (that is, lightest) the plate turned darkest. In this way a negative was formed, with the dark and light parts of the original scene reversed.

In 1839 Niepce's method was improved by another

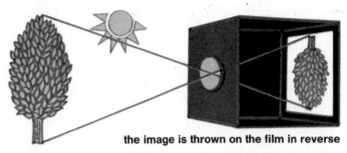

the image is thrown on the film in reverse

aperture) in front, and throws an image on to a film at the back. The film is removed from the camera (in the dark) and is developed, fixed and printed to give a permanent picture. Polaroid cameras provide a finished print (in black-and-white or colour) in less than one minute.

Almost anyone can take a reasonable snapshot, but a great deal of skill is needed to take good, artistic photographs. This is a matter of balancing a number of different things. The size of the aperture, which lets light into the camera, can be made larger or smaller by the diaphragm (a mechanical version of the iris in your eye). It is important that the right amount of light enters the camera, so that the picture is not overexposed (too light) or under-exposed (too dark). When there is plenty of light, as on a bright day, a small aperture is used; a large one is used when there is not much light about.

Another factor is the exposure time: the length of time that the aperture is open. This is controlled by a shutter which can be made to open for varying lengths of time, possibly as little as 1/1000 of a second – and some cameras are faster still.

All cameras except pin-hole cameras have lenses, through which the light passes on to the film. Except in the cheapest cameras the position of the lens can be adjusted to focus the picture sharply.

The camera does not simply copy nature. A good photographer can 'compose' his picture in several ways, for instance by moving the position and angle of the camera, or by special lighting. By being in the right spot at the right time a quick-thinking photographer can capture an event which would be over before an artist had time to draw or paint it.

A colour negative film contains three layers of emulsion (light sensitive material). The yellow layer (top) records the blue light in the subject. The magenta layer (centre) records the image made by green light, while the cyan layer (bottom) records the image made by red light. The printing paper used in colour photography also has three layers, each of which is sensitive to one of the three 'negative' colours, producing the final picture, right, in its true colours.

Radio and television

Many people tend to take radio and television for granted, but the fact that they make it possible to communicate with millions of people at the same time is a comparatively new thing in human history. Television especially has an enormous influence on modern society.

Radio and television were both made possible by the discovery of radio waves by the German scientist Heinrich Hertz in 1887. Radio waves are one form of electromagnetic radiation, which also includes light rays and X-rays. In 1895 a young Italian, Guglielmo Marconi, discovered how to use Hertz's radio waves to send and receive morse messages without the wires used in the electric telegraph. Marconi's invention, known as wireless telegraphy (from which we get the term 'wireless' for radio) was soon used to keep ships in touch with the shore. The invention of radio valves (tubes) in 1904 made it possible to use Marconi's system to transmit actual sounds, and by the 1920s radio broadcasting was established.

The invention of television depended on finding a way to turn moving pictures into a series of electrical signals which could be sent by radio. Many people worked on it, including the Scotsman John Logie Baird, who built his first TV apparatus in 1925. Television broadcasting began in the 1930s, but it was only after World War II that it really became established.

Radio has continued to be popular because it puts across certain subjects just as well as television, if not better. Music is an example. It can be interesting to see music being played, as well as hearing it, but TV does not do all that much for music, and you get better sound reception on a good radio than on most TV sets. For these reasons most broadcast music is on radio. Other radio specialities are talks on a wide range of subjects. Radio drama is interestingly different from either stage or TV drama because it has to achieve its effect through voices and sound effects only. A famous example was a 1938 radio version of **The War of the Worlds** by H. G. Wells. This was so realistic that many people thought that Martians were actually invading Earth.

Radio and television both do news and current affairs programmes very well, but TV has the added advantage of being able to take you to the spot and show you the news as it actually happens. Using

Above: **Maurice Denham and Peggy Ashcroft recording a play for radio in a broadcasting studio.**

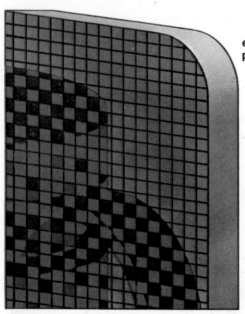

enlarged view of phosphor dot screen

A colour television screen is made up of hundreds of very small phosphor dots. When the set is switched on, the electronic signals picked up by the receiver are distributed by the three electron phosphor dots. This gives an overall picture which appears to the human eye to have many variations in colour.

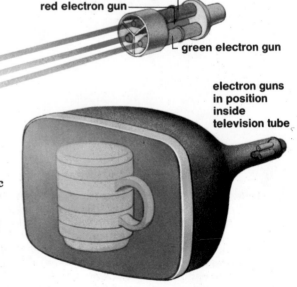

blue electron gun
red electron gun
green electron gun

electron guns in position inside television tube

communications satellites, coverage of historic events such as the Moon landing in 1969 can be watched by viewers all over the world. TV is also very good at plays and documentaries, and programmes showing aspects of natural history.

The many technical 'tricks' now available have made television even more flexible as a form of art than the cinema. People can be made to appear and disappear, backgrounds can be changed during a live broadcast, and two or more pictures can be shown at once. A great many programmes are recorded on film or on magnetic tape, and film and tape can be edited–cut and spliced together–to make quick changes of scene possible. A big variety show, for example, may consist of a dozen or more items, filmed or taped at different times and arranged to produce one fast-moving show. A natural history programme lasting an hour may have been edited down from ten or twenty times as much film, so that the viewer sees only the most interesting and important shots. Instant playback

of recordings enables a producer to give an immediate repeat of a thrilling live event, such as a goal in football or the end of a horse race. This recording can now be done in your own home using a videotape recorder which plugs into your TV. Other additions to the television in our homes which are now widely available are video games. These systems, also using magnetic tape, allow the TV screen to be used as a 'board' for games such as tennis where 'players' are moved by hand controls.

Teletext is the system of displaying printed information and simple diagrams on adapted TV screens. Access to the pages of information is by the use of a hand held keypad.

A television studio during the recording of a show. The small screens suspended from the ceiling are monitors, which allow the technicians and studio audience to see what image the camera is actually projecting. The monitor facing the stage is to show the presenter what the programme looks like. He is using a hand microphone, and there is another microphone at the end of the boom projecting towards the stage

The cinema

After the invention of photography in the early 1800s, many scientists tried to find ways of making photographs appear to move. They knew of a strange thing about the human eye, called *persistence of vision*. This means that any image remains imprinted on the brain for a split second after it has disappeared. For example, if you rotate a lighted sparkler quickly in the dark you will see a circle of light. Inventors realised that if they could show a series of still pictures quickly, those pictures would form a moving image.

To make moving pictures a camera was wanted to take pictures in rapid succession. To make this possible flexible film was needed. In 1889, the American George Eastman made film of celluloid in long strips. Three years later an inventor, William Dickson, made a camera that took 46 pictures a second. When strips of exposed film in 15-metre (50-foot) loops were projected at the same speed, at which they had been shot, the pictures appeared to move. A viewing cabinet, a kinetoscope, was invented by Thomas Edison, another American.

The first public film show took place in France in 1895. By the early 1900s short, silent films were being made all over the world. The most successful

Above: Minnie Mouse, Mickey's companion, was one of Walt Disney's popular cartoon characters.

Left: At one time Westerns were fast-moving adventure stories, all about rugged heroes. Modern Western films still have tough guys and plenty of action, but they also try to recreate the atmosphere of the real 'wild frontier', as in this dramatic shot from Andrew V. McLagen's 'Firecreek'.

films told stories, and longer films made it possible to tell more complicated stories. In 1915 an American film director, D. W. Griffith, made a three-hour film **The Birth of a Nation**, followed, in 1916, by another called **Intolerance**. These films were skilfully made and exciting to watch. They influenced film-makers everywhere.

The success of films led to the growth of huge companies, or studios. The studios contained offices and vast areas of sets, such as streets, palaces and so on, where scenes were filmed. Sometimes film-makers shot scenes in real locations. But location filming could be difficult. For example, no film could be shot on a cloudy day. Popular studio actors and actresses became film stars. Some early stars included Charles Chaplin, Douglas Fairbanks Senior and Mary Pickford. Silent films were very popular and could be shown anywhere. There was no language problem.

In 1927 a film called **The Jazz Singer** was made. It had a musical soundtrack and contained a few words spoken by its star, Al Jolson. The film caused such excitement that all studios switched to making sound films.

The heyday of sound films was the 1930s to the 1950s. Hollywood, in the United States, became the world's leading film centre. Film-makers and performers from many countries went to Hollywood

Shooting a scene in the British film 'Chitty Chitty Bang Bang'. Besides all the actors, the gigantic 'A' stage at Pinewood Studios holds a host of other people operating cameras, microphones and lights, with the director and his immediate assistants.

to make their fortunes. Animated cartoon films, especially those of Walt Disney, were popular, alongside the all-important story films. From the late 1930s more and more films were made in colour.

During the 1940s foreign-language films became available to large audiences. Some films were *dubbed* – that is, a soundtrack in another language was substituted for the original. Other films were *sub-titled*, with printed words on the bottom of the picture translating the dialogue. As a result film-makers such as Vittorio De Sica (Italy), Akira Kurosawa (Japan) and Ingmar Bergman (Sweden), became internationally popular.

The arrival of television in the 1950s led to a decline in cinema audiences. The studios tried to win back their audiences with more spectacular films and wide screens, such as CinemaScope and Cinerama. But the studios still declined. Many went out of business, and others made films for TV. Fine films are still being made, and although it is no longer universally popular, the cinema is now regarded as a major art form, alongside the theatre or ballet.

FINGERTIP FACTS ON THE ARTS

THE PRIMARY COLOURS

In painting, the primary colours are red, blue and yellow, and they are called primary colours because all other shades can be made by mixing two or more together. Thus red and yellow make orange, and blue and yellow make green. Black and white are not counted as colours.

In light, and therefore in television, the primary colours are red, blue and green. Red and green light together make yellow.

Abstract art Painting or sculpture which relies on shapes and does not look like a real object.

Acrylic paint A kind of emulsion paint which has some of the properties of water-colours and also some of those of oil-colours.

Action painting Splashing paint on to canvas in the hope that a work of art will result.

Armature An internal metal frame used to support a clay sculpture.

Collage A picture made by sticking bits of cloth, paper and other materials on to a background.

Cubism A form of abstract art which shows several views of an object one on top of another.

Fresco Painting on wet plaster.

Gouache An opaque water-colour paint, also called poster paint.

Impressionism A style of painting in which the artist tries to give an impression of a scene rather than showing it in detail.

Lay figure An often large jointed wooden figure of a person which can be used as a guide for drawing or painting.

Lino-cut A print made from a piece of linoleum, in which part has been cut away to leave the design, which is then inked for printing.

Mobile A sculpture in which shapes cut in card or metal hang from threads and rods. A touch or a puff of wind makes it move and change shape.

Montage Sticking one layer over another – a technique used in collage.

Mural A painting on a wall.

Oil-colours Paints which are mixed with linseed oil. They dry hard, and one layer can go over another, making corrections easy.

Op Art A style of painting which creates optical illusions.

Pastel Sticks of colour with which the artist can draw. Pastel smudges easily.

Pop Art Pictures made in the style of strip cartoons, advertisements and photographs.

Relief A sculpture in which the figures are attached to the background.

Water-colours Paints which are mixed with water to give a transparent wash.

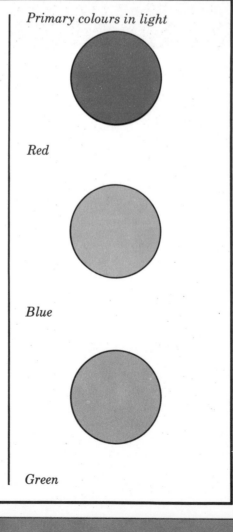

Primary colours in painting

Red

Blue

Yellow

Primary colours in light

Red

Blue

Green

TERMS USED IN MUSIC

Cantata A work for solo singers, possibly with chorus and orchestra, often on a religious theme.

Concerto A work for a soloist and an orchestra.

Counterpoint Two or more tunes played simultaneously.

Fugue (which literally means 'flight') is a special kind of counterpoint in which each part in turn begins with the same melody until all are playing or singing.

Harmony Two or more notes sounded together to form a chord.

Opus means 'work', and is used to list a composer's published pieces. 'Op. 32' means the musician's 32nd published composition.

Overture is a piece of music that comes before something else, usually an opera.

Rondo A kind of music in which the same theme comes round again and again, so you might have Tune A, Tune B, Tune A, Tune C, Tune A, and so on.

Sonata A composition for one or two instruments, in several movements (sections) of contrasting speeds and styles.

Symphony A sonata-like piece for full orchestra.

TWENTY GREAT ARTISTS

Gianlorenzo Bernini (1598–1680) was an Italian sculptor whose work influenced European sculpture for 100 years.

Georges Braque (1882–1963), a French painter, was one of the founders of Cubism.

Alexander Calder (1898–1976), an American sculptor, invented mobiles and also made non-moving sculptures in bent wire.

John Constable (1776–1837) was an English landscape painter who greatly influenced French artists.

Donatello (1386–1466) was an Italian sculptor whose real name was Donato di Bardi. He created a realistic, dramatic style of sculpture.

Albrecht Dürer (1471–1528) was the greatest German painter of his age. A noted engraver, he invented the art of etching (chemical engraving).

Paul Gauguin (1848–1903), a French artist, spent part of his life in Tahiti. He used brilliant colours to express ideas as well as portray scenes.

Giotto di Bondone (1266–1337), an Italian painter, sculptor and architect, revolutionized art by making natural-looking paintings in contrast to the stylized art of the Middle Ages.

Leonardo da Vinci (1452–1519) was the greatest all-round genius of the Italian Renaissance, being architect, engineer, musician, botanist, anatomist, painter, sculptor and astronomer. He left comparatively few finished works.

Michelangelo Buonarroti (1475–1564) was the greatest artist of the Italian Renaissance, excelling as painter, sculptor, architect and poet. His masterpieces are the statue of *David* and the ceiling of the Sistine Chapel, Rome.

Henry Moore (born 1898) is one of the greatest 20th century English sculptors. He is noted for sculptures with a hole in them.

Phidias, who lived in the 400s BC, was the greatest of the ancient Greek sculptors.

Pablo Picasso (1881–1973), a Spanish painter, sculptor and potter, was the most influential artist of the 20th century, and one of the founders of Cubism.

Raphael (1483–1520) was an Italian painter whose full name was Raffaello Santi. He was one of the finest artists of the Renaissance.

Rembrandt van Rijn (1606–1669) was the greatest Dutch artist and a superb portrait painter.

Pierre Renoir (1841–1919) was one of the leading French Impressionist artists.

Auguste Rodin (1840–1917) was the greatest sculptor of the late 19th century.

Titian (1477–1576), an Italian painter whose real name was Tiziano Vecelli, was renowned for his care in finishing his work and for his liking for a shade of red now called after him.

Joseph Turner (1775–1851) was one of the greatest English watercolour artists, renowned for his dramatic sunsets.

Diego Velázquez (1599–1660) was the greatest Spanish painter, famed for his portraits.

IMPORTANT DATES IN RADIO AND TELEVISION

1878 Sir William Crookes (UK) invented the first kind of cathode-ray tube.

1887 Heinrich Hertz (Germany) transmitted a radio wave across a room.

1895 Guglielmo Marconi (Italy) transmitted radio signals out of doors.

1900 R. A. Fessenden (US) made the first voice broadcast.

1901 Marconi sent the first radio signal across the Atlantic Ocean.

1904 John Ambrose Fleming (UK) invented the thermionic valve.

1920 First regular radio broadcasts began in the United States.

1925 John Logie Baird (UK) and Charles Francis Jenkins (US) invented the first TV sets.

1928 First regular TV broadcasts began in the United States.

1929 Baird produced the first colour TV pictures.

1953 Tape recording of television pictures began.

1956 First regular colour TV service began in the United States.

1964 Television pictures were sent from the Moon.

IMPORTANT DATES IN THE CINEMA

1832 Joseph Plateau (Belgium) invented the phenakistoscope, which made pictures appear to move.

1872 Eadweard Muybridge (UK) made the first photographs of a running horse.

1889 George Eastman (US) invented flexible film.

1893 Thomas Edison (US) invented a cine camera and a kinetoscope, which showed 50 feet (15 metres) of film at a time.

1895 Several people invented projectors.

1896 Georges Méliès (France) began making trick films.

1903 *The Great Train Robbery* (the first Western) was made in the United States.

1906 G. A. Smith (UK) invented the first practical method of filming in colour.

1910 The first newsreels were shown regularly.

1917 The first cartoon films were shown.

1927 *The Jazz Singer*, the first sound film, was shown.

1937 Walt Disney (US) made the first full-length cartoon film, *Snow White and the Seven Dwarfs*.

1952 The first wide-screen process, Cinerama, was produced.

Science and technology

The world around us is fascinating. For thousands of years people have tried to find out how things work. Thanks to the efforts of the great scientists of the past we now have a vast store of knowledge. We know what matter is made of, how electricity works, and how the human body keeps going. The knowledge of these and many other things is used in our everyday life. We use it to build the machines, ships, aeroplanes and houses that we need in our modern world. At the same time we use our knowledge to explore still further into the nature of matter, and extend our explorations out from Earth into space.

The particles of matter

A block of iron is solid and heavy. But what is it made of? With a hacksaw you can cut it into two pieces. You can then cut one of these pieces into two more, and so on as the pieces get smaller and smaller. If your saw was small enough you could cut pieces too tiny to see without a microscope. In theory, you might think that you could go on halving the pieces of iron forever; but you could not. Eventually you would find a particle of iron that you could not cut into two. The original block of iron is made up of millions of these particles, too small to see even with the most powerful microscope. They are called atoms.

A single atom is also composed of smaller particles. There is a central group called the nucleus, which consists of particles called protons and neutrons. The outer part of the atom is made up of a cloud of particles called electrons. Enormous forces hold all these particles together. Scientists have found ways of splitting atoms, but this process releases vast amounts of energy.

Electrons and protons have electrical charges.

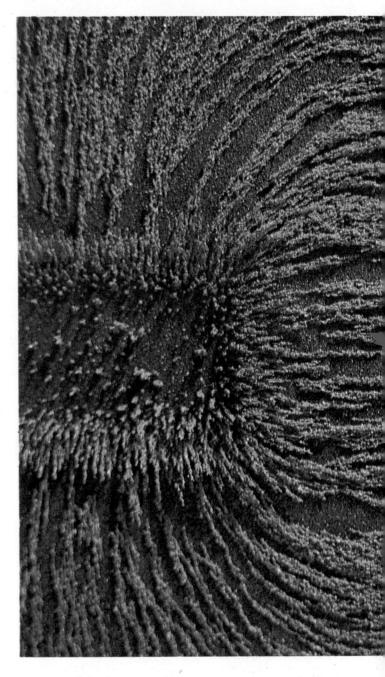

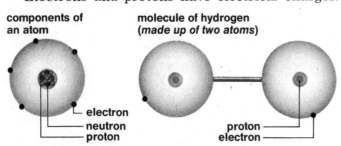

components of an atom

molecule of hydrogen
(*made up of two atoms*)

electron
neutron
proton

proton
electron

Above: These simple diagrams show the structure of an atom – of the element boron, which contains five electrons, five protons and five neutrons – and of a molecule of hydrogen, two atoms bonded together.

Below: How electrons flow through a wire.

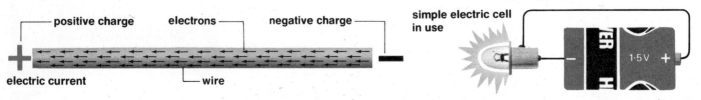

positive charge   electrons   negative charge   simple electric cell in use

electric current   wire   1·5V

Electrons are negatively charged and protons are positively charged. In a stable atom the number of electrons is the same as the number of protons, and so the charges are balanced. Different elements have different numbers of these particles in their atoms. For example, iron has 26 electrons and 26 protons. Hydrogen, the simplest element, has one electron and one proton in each atom. The number of neutrons in the nucleus varies.

Many elements, such as iron and sulphur, are made up of single atoms, but some elements cannot exist in this form. For example, hydrogen consists of two atoms joined together. These two atoms form a molecule. Most of the materials we use are made of molecules, some containing a great many atoms. For example, the paper of this book consists of several kinds of molecules, and these molecules contain atoms of more than one element. Most of the molecules in this paper are built up from atoms of carbon, hydrogen and oxygen.

Electrons can be made to leave atoms. If you rub a balloon with a cloth you cause electrons to pass from the cloth to the balloon. As a result the balloon has too many electrons and is negatively charged. The cloth now has too few electrons, and so the protons in the cloth give it a positive charge. This kind of electricity is static—that is, it does not move—and is therefore called static electricity. But electrons can be made to move in a wire. If there is a positive charge at one end of the wire and a negative charge at the other end, electrons in the wire are attracted towards the positive end. This movement of electrons give us an electric current.

Magnetism is a property of certain elements, such as iron and nickel. In a bar of iron there are groups of atoms called magnetic domains. These can be made to line up together so that a magnetic north pole forms at one end and a south pole forms at the other. The bar thus becomes magnetized. Its south pole always tries to point towards the magnetic North Pole of the Earth.

Above: An ordinary horseshoe magnet produces lines of 'pull' known as its magnetic field. This picture of magnetized iron filings shows a magnetic field.

Right: If you rub an inflated balloon briskly it becomes charged with static electricity, and will cling to the wall or other objects for a few minutes.

Waves and energy

The Sun's energy comes to us in the form of light and heat. These are both kinds of energy that move as waves. If you drop a stone into a calm pond you create waves. Similarly, if you jerk the end of a rope a wave passes down the rope. Light and heat move in the same way as the wave that passes down the rope. They do so because of electrical and magnetic forces. Hence, light and heat are known as electromagnetic waves.

Natural light consists of electromagnetic waves which we can see as different colours. We call the range of colours we can see the visible spectrum, with red having the longest wavelength and violet the shortest. The wavelength is the distance from one wave crest to the next. Although these waves are regular, because natural light is made up of a number of different wavelengths it is easily distorted and is known as *in-coherent* light.

Coherent light can be produced by lasers which were discovered in 1960. This kind of light, although it is also made up of waves, is much more stable because the waves move in regular patterns. Lasers can be used over vast distances, particularly for telephone messages. They are also used to produce holograms which are three dimensional photographs.

However, although natural light can be easily deflected this property can be very useful. Most objects, such as the pages of this book, distort light by reflecting it in all directions. A silvered mirror does not distort the light rays, and for that reason we can see images in a mirror.

Light can also be bent by transparent objects

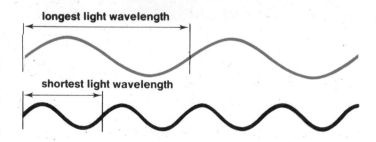

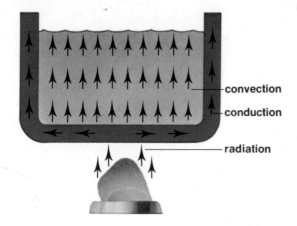

convection
conduction

radiation

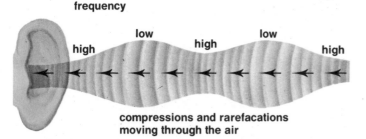

frequency

low   low

high   high   high

compressions and rarefacations
moving through the air

Left: The upper part of the diagram shows, with the aid of a pan of water over a flame, the three ways heat travels: from the flame through the air as radiation; through the metal of the pan as conduction; and through the water in the pan as convection. The lower part of the diagram shows how sound waves travel through the air, compressing the air slightly for high notes and becoming less compressed for low ones.

Although an object may seem completely transparent, it is not as clear as air, and light moves at different speeds through the object and through air. The glass of water on the left makes the spoon seem bent. It is only slightly distorted by glass (right).

such as water and glass. Glass lenses cause light to be bent in such a way that we can see magnified images of things we want to study more closely. When white light is bent by a prism it is split into a wide band of colours. Thus we can see that white light actually consists of all the colours of the spectrum. Rainbows are formed in the same way: the raindrops act as tiny prisms that split the Sun's light into its colours.

Heat comes to us from the Sun in the form of infra-red rays, which are electromagnetic waves beyond the red end of the spectrum. We feel heat because of the effect that these waves have on atoms. In any object the atoms are always moving. They do not move far, but they are always bumping their neighbours. When heat rays reach an object, extra energy is given to the atoms and they move faster, and the object itself gives off heat.

Heat moves in three ways. Radiation is the movement of heat by infra-red rays. Conduction occurs when heat travels through a solid object, and energy is passed from atom to atom down the object. Convection occurs in fluids. The hotter atoms or molecules rise above the cooler ones and cause currents. You can see convection currents if you watch a saucepan of water boiling.

Sound is also a form of energy that travels as waves, but it is produced by vibrations, and the waves are different from those of light and heat. Sound travels through the air at about 340 metres (1120 feet) per second. The 'crests' of the waves are actually areas where the molecules of air are compressed together, and are called compressions. A

Above left: When white light is passed through a prism – a wedge of glass – it forms a spectrum of all the colours we can see, from red to violet. The diagram at left shows the relative lengths of the wavelengths of red (longest) and violet (shortest).

single sound wave can be made by beating a drum sharply once. Either side of the compression are areas where the molecules of air are further apart – called rarefactions. A musical note produced by a vibrating string consists of many compressions and rarefactions moving through the air. The pitch of the note depends on the number of compressions that reach your ear in a given time. This is called the frequency. If the compressions are close together – that is, the note has a short wavelength – the frequency of the note is high.

Heat, light and sound can all be transformed into electrical energy. This is often a more convenient form of energy to store and transfer from place to place. Electrical energy is easy to handle today because we now have sophisticated electronic equipment, such as radios, televisions and computers. The science of electronics deals with the movement of electrons (see pages 122–123) through transistors, vacuum tubes, and similar devices.

Molecules and matter

The smallest form of matter is an atom, but matter can exist as combinations of atoms called molecules. Hydrogen gas contains molecules composed of two atoms. Oxygen also has two atoms in each molecule. A molecule of water consists of two atoms of hydrogen and one atom of oxygen.

Why do atoms need to join together? And how do they do it? To answer these questions we must once again look at the structure of an atom, and particularly at the electrons. The study of this form of science is called chemistry.

A hydrogen atom (symbol: H) has one electron, but it would be more stable if it had two. Therefore two hydrogen atoms share their electrons between them. In this way the bond of the hydrogen molecule (H_2) is formed. An oxygen atom (symbol: O) has 8 electrons, arranged in two layers or shells. The inner shell has two electrons and is filled. The outer shell has 6 electrons, but it would be more stable if it had 8. So each oxygen atom shares two of its electrons with another oxygen atom. As a result, both oxygen atoms have 8 electrons in their outer shells, and the oxygen molecule (O_2) is formed.

Hydrogen and oxygen both have molecules containing a single kind of atom. They are therefore called *elements*. *Compounds* contain atoms of more than one kind, but their molecules are often formed in the same way. In a molecule of water (H_2O) the oxygen atom shares one electron with each hydrogen atom, and the hydrogen atoms both share their single electrons with the oxygen atom.

Some molecules are formed in a slightly different way. The salt that you eat on your food is a chemical called sodium chloride. The symbol for sodium is Na; the symbol for chlorine is Cl; and sodium chloride is written as NaCl. The sodium atom gives the chlorine atom one electron. As a result,

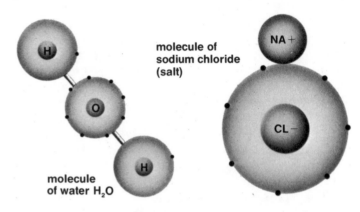

molecule of
sodium chloride
(salt)

molecule
of water H_2O

Above: Most of the substances we know are made up of molecules containing more than one element. Water (left) consists of two atoms of hydrogen combined with one of oxygen; the salt you put on your egg has one atom of chlorine and one of sodium (the symbol for sodium, Na, comes from its old name natrium).

Left: A magnified picture of crystals of salt.

the sodium atom ends up with a small positive charge (Na+) and the chlorine atom has a small negative charge (Cl–). These two unlike charges attract each other, and in this way salt crystals are formed from many charged sodium and chlorine atoms. When the salt is mixed with water the charged atoms separate. The salt thus dissolves and the charged atoms in the solution are called *ions*.

Chemical changes involve molecules being altered in some way. For example, if you put a piece of zinc (Zn) into sulphuric acid (H_2SO_4), it fizzes rapidly. The fizzing is caused by hydrogen (H_2) being formed. At the same time zinc sulphate ($ZnSO_4$) is made.

Elements and compounds may be solids, liquids, or gases, and it is often possible to change from one of these states to another. The difference between them is in the way in which their atoms or molecules are arranged. The atoms of a solid piece of metal are tightly bound together by great forces, but if the

metal is heated beyond a certain temperature the increased energy of the atoms partly overcomes these forces. Clusters of atoms are then free to move about among each other, and the metal becomes liquid, but it still has a definite size.

Different substances are solids, liquids or gases at different temperatures. Most metals must be heated to high temperatures before they melt and become liquid, but water is a liquid at normal temperatures. If a pan of water is boiled molecules leave the surface and become gas, or vapour. In this state the energy of the molecules has completely

This picture of the continuous casting of steel shows how the metal is molten when it is very hot, and becomes a solid bar as soon as it cools down.

overcome the binding forces, and they can move about freely, expanding indefinitely.

If water is cooled to below 0° centigrade the molecules have so little energy that the binding forces win, and ice, a solid, is formed. Hydrogen and oxygen are gases at normal temperatures, but if they are cooled to very low temperatures they can be turned into liquids.

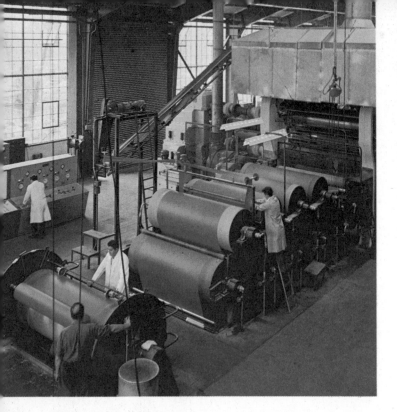

Chemistry in everyday life

Until a hundred years ago people wore clothes made only from natural materials; wool and leather from animals; cotton and linen from plants. In the past 100 years there have been tremendous advances in chemistry, and today we can make any item of clothing from chemicals.

There is a vast range of chemicals that we now take for granted. For example, it is sometimes difficult to understand how our ancestors managed without washing powders, disinfectants and safety matches. These and many other chemically-produced household items make our life much easier today.

We use chemical fertilizers to make the land grow better plants for food, and we wage war with chemical pesticides on the insects and other pests that attack our crops. Many people believe that the use of these fertilizers and pesticides is wrong, but it is certain that without them we could not feed everybody. The world's population has more

Above: Plastic sheeting being produced in a calendering mill. In calendering, resin is squeezed between a series of rollers; it forms a thin sheet which is pulled off and wound on to a drum.

than doubled in the past 100 years, and the increase is partly due to our present knowledge of drugs (medicines), chemicals that help to keep people alive and cure their illnesses.

Chemicals are also used in many industrial processes. Metals are extracted from their ores by chemical treatment. Some foods are prepared with chemical preservatives, colourings and flavours. Fabrics are treated with chemicals to make them waterproof or resistant to fire.

The chemicals that have done most to revolutionize our way of life are the plastics. They are found in almost every part of the home. Clothes, curtains, carpets, floor tiles, non-stick pans and food containers are among the many plastics items that we use today. The first plastics, such as Bakelite, were only substitutes for other materials, but today plastics are used where no other material will do. For example, plastics tubes are used to replace arteries in heart surgery. Other materials would react with the chemicals of the body.

The molecules of plastics contain long chains of carbon atoms, and it is these molecules that give plastics their special properties. There are two kinds of man-made plastics. Thermosetting (heat-setting) plastics are hard and unbendable. Their long chains of atoms are linked to each other in a network, and as a result the molecules cannot slide over each other. These plastics, such as Bakelite and Melamine, are resistant to heat, and so are particularly useful for use as table mats and kitchen work tops. Polyurethanes are used in the manufacture of paints and varnishes.

Thermosoftening plastics (also known as thermoplastics) are much softer, and they melt when heated. Their long chains of carbon atoms slide over each other, and so these plastics can be bent and stretched, and they are easy to shape. The most common method of shaping is by pressing plastics into moulds. Polythene (polyethylene) is often moulded into buckets, bowls and children's toys. Nylon and polyesters are drawn out into long fibres, which can be woven into fabrics. Polyesters are also used together with fibreglass to make boat hulls and car bodies. PVC (polyvinyl chloride) is made into pipes, and is added to fabrics to make them waterproof. PTFE (polytetrafluoroethylene) is used as a coating in non-stick pans. Perspex is used as a lightweight substitute for glass.

Many of our plastics and other chemicals come from oil. Crude oil is a mixture of many simple chemicals. These are separated at an oil refinery, and one of the products we get directly from the refinery is petrol. Other chemicals from oil are used by various industries to give us products such as plastics, drugs, explosives, dyes and animal foods.

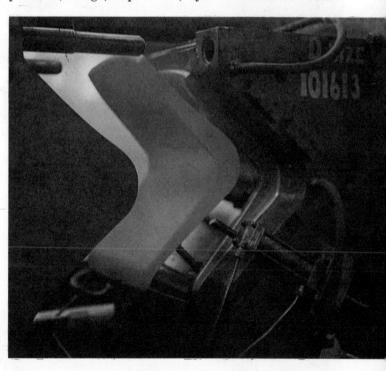

Above: Opening a mould to remove a plastic chair seat. The plastic, polypropylene, is injected into the mould when hot and sets as it cools.

Left: A giant oil refinery in Peru, seen at night. A refinery turns crude oil into a number of useful products, including petrol (gasoline), fuel oil as used in central heating, kerosene (paraffin), lubricants for machinery, and asphalt for roads.

Life

Cats, beetles, trees and seaweeds are all living things. Rocks and metals are non-living. The difference may seem obvious. But what really makes a living thing different? By studying living things we can say that there are seven features that clearly distinguish them from non-living things.

All living things feed. Animals take in all kinds of foods and use them to make new chemicals. Plants take some of their food from the soil. The rest they make themselves, using water and carbon dioxide, one of the gases of the air. This process is called photosynthesis.

All living things get rid of their waste products. The name of this process is excretion.

All living things grow. Both plants and animals use the chemicals in their food to make new body material for growth.

All living things breathe. When we breathe we take in oxygen from the air and get rid of carbon dioxide. Oxygen gets into our blood, and our bodies use it to 'burn' food chemicals to give us energy. All organisms except some bacteria take in oxygen for this purpose. The process of using oxygen to make energy is called respiration.

All living things move, and movement uses some of the energy created during respiration. Most animals can move from one place to another, and even those that remain still have movements inside their bodies. Most plants remain in one place, but they do have some movements. They can bend towards light, and plant stems always grow upwards and roots always grow downwards.

All living things are sensitive. Both plants and animals react to certain stimuli – those things that arouse a response. These stimuli include touch, pain, gravity, light, moisture, heat, cold and chemicals.

Finally, all living things reproduce. By various methods animals and plants produce new individuals. This characteristic of living things is very important. It is essential for life to continue, as nearly all individuals eventually die.

The bodies of animals and plants are built up from tiny enclosed boxes called cells. Some organisms consist of only one cell, and these can only be seen by using a microscope. Large animals and plants are composed of millions of cells linked

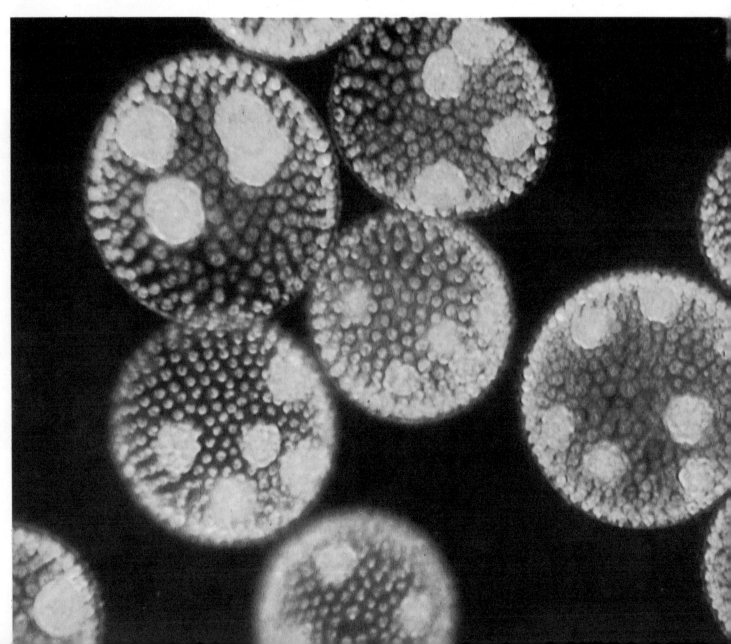

together. A single animal cell is surrounded by a thin membrane. A plant cell has a more solid wall made of a substance called cellulose, which surrounds the cell membrane. Inside the cells of both plants and animals there is a watery liquid called cytoplasm, and a structure called the nucleus.

The nucleus of a cell contains chemicals that hold information, and it acts as the headquarters or controller of the cell. From it information and commands are passed to the rest of the cell. According to these commands, other structures in the cytoplasm perform various functions. Some help to make energy by the process of respiration. Others make chemicals for growth. One important group of growth chemicals consists of the proteins, which have large, complicated molecules and are built up from simpler chemicals called amino-acids.

Animals and plants grow by increasing the numbers of their cells. This happens when cells divide into two. The most important part of the cell

Right: How a cell divides to form two new ones.
Below: The simple, single-celled alga *Volvox* forms colonies with several thousand cells inside a jelly-like casing. *Volvox* is one of many algae found in water which help to turn it green in colour.

is the nucleus, and this divides first. In a cell that is about to divide the chemicals that contain the information can be seen as thread-like structures, chromosomes. Each chromosome divides into two new identical ones, and these are pulled to different ends of the cell. The two groups of chromosomes form two new nuclei, and a new cell wall is formed in between them. In this way two new cells are formed, and they are identical in every way to the original cell which divided.

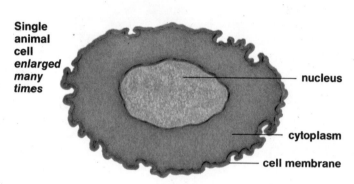

Single animal cell *enlarged many times*

nucleus

cytoplasm

cell membrane

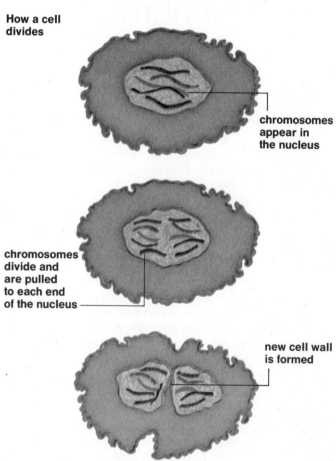

How a cell divides

chromosomes appear in the nucleus

chromosomes divide and are pulled to each end of the nucleus

new cell wall is formed

two identical new cells are formed

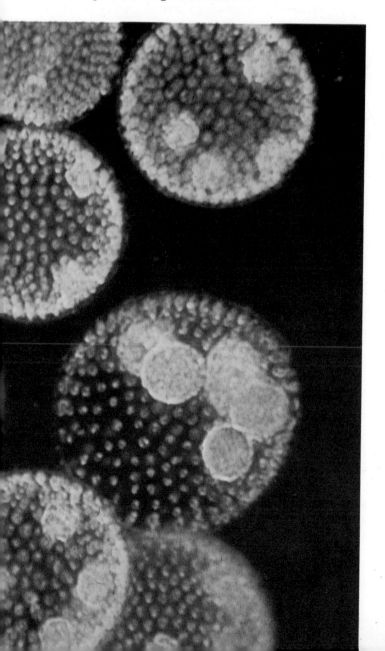

Left: The human body is capable of remarkable feats, as this picture of a gymnast turning a somersault shows, but none of them is half as remarkable as the feats carried out by the organs inside our bodies every day.

Right: This greatly simplified diagram shows the main organs of the human body, together with some of the bones and muscles.

The human body

Our bodies are wonderful machines, but they are also very complicated. They enable us to perform the functions that keep us alive, such as feeding, breathing and excretion, and they allow us to perform acts that make our lives enjoyable, such as walking, reading, listening to music, thinking and creating things with our hands.

The most important part of the body is the brain. This controls all the other parts of the body. Particular centres in the brain control such things as sight, hearing and the movements of our legs and arms. The brain also receives information from all parts of the body. Sensations such as touch, pain, cold, heat and the position of the body are all passed to the brain. Information and instructions are sent round the body by nerves, which are linked to the brain by the spinal cord which runs up the back of the body and through the neck.

We move by using our muscles, structures that can contract. They are attached to the bones of the body, and opposing muscles are used to stretch and bend our arms and legs. The bones of the body form the skeleton; the body contains over 200 bones.

We breathe by taking oxygen into our lungs. Stretched across the bottom of the rib cage is a membrane called the diaphragm. When the muscles of the diaphragm contract it is pulled downwards and air is drawn into the lungs through the nose and windpipe. Oxygen from the air enters the blood; carbon dioxide is expelled from the lungs when we breathe out

The blood system is used to pass oxygen and chemicals to all the parts of the body. Oxygen-rich blood from the lungs flows to the heart. The heart is simply a pump which keeps the blood flowing round the body. From the heart blood is pumped into tubes called arteries. Blood leaves the heart at high pressure, and so the arteries have thick walls. When the blood reaches its destination in the body it gives up its oxygen and removes carbon dioxide from the cells. It then flows back to the heart through thin-walled tubes, the veins. From there it is pumped once again to the lungs, where the carbon dioxide is removed.

In the trunk of the body there are several organs used for taking in food and processing the chemicals it contains. Food taken in through the mouth passes down the gullet and into the stomach. The body deals with food by the process of digestion. It produces enzymes, chemicals which help to break down the large molecules of the chemicals in food into smaller molecules. Digestion begins in the mouth, where enzymes in the saliva act on the food, and continues in the stomach and the small intestine. The chemicals that the body needs are absorbed through the wall of the small intestine. The waste matter passes on into the large intestine, and is finally excreted.

There are also several other essential organs, such as the reproductive organs (see pages 134–135), the liver and the kidneys. The liver is one of the main chemical factories of the body. It carries out several vital functions concerned with digestion, removing waste materials from the blood, and storing reserves of chemicals. The two kidneys are concerned with removing certain waste materials from the body. These materials are then passed on to the bladder, and they are excreted in urine.

The liver is a gland, and there are several other glands around the body. Some glands produce enzymes for digestion; others produce hormones, chemicals that act as messengers. Hormones control various functions of the body. For example, adrenalin, a hormone produced by the adrenal glands, regulates the speed at which the heart beats.

THE BODY

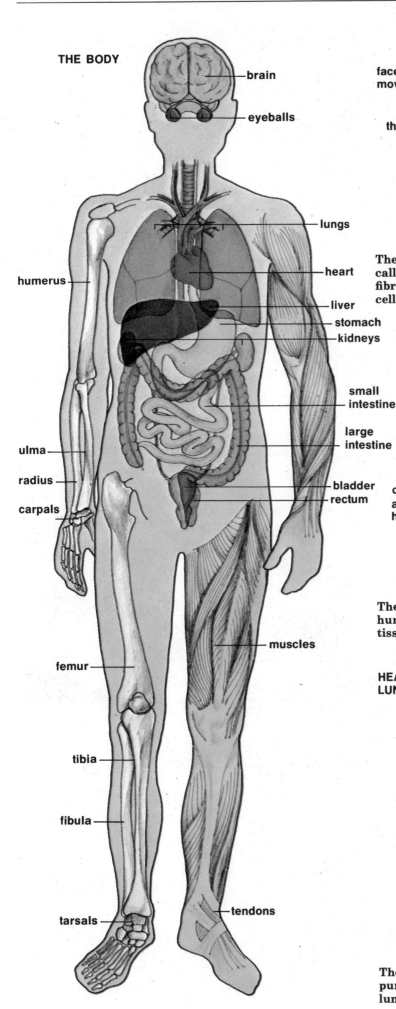

brain

eyeballs

lungs

heart

liver

stomach

kidneys

small intestine

large intestine

bladder

rectum

muscles

humerus

ulma

radius

carpals

femur

tibia

fibula

tarsals

tendons

THE BRAIN

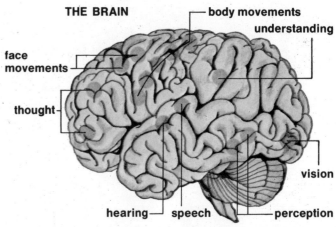

body movements

understanding

face movements

thought

hearing

speech

vision

perception

The human brain consists of many millions of grey cells called neurons. The neurons are connected by fine fibres: dendrites carry incoming messages from other cells of the body, and axons outgoing messages.

THE EYE

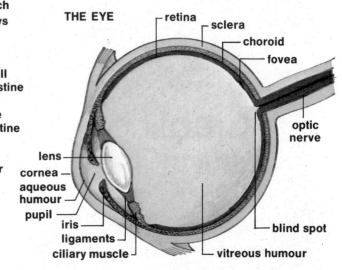

retina

sclera

choroid

fovea

optic nerve

lens

cornea

aqueous humour

pupil

iris

ligaments

ciliary muscle

blind spot

vitreous humour

The eye is filled with jelly-like substance, the vitreous humour, behind the lens. The scelera is the outer tissue, and the choroid carries blood vessels.

HEART AND LUNGS

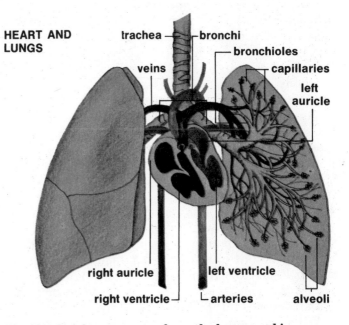

trachea

bronchi

bronchioles

capillaries

left auricle

veins

right auricle

left ventricle

right ventricle

arteries

alveoli

The blood picks up oxygen from the lungs, and is pumped around the body by the heart. It returns to the lungs with carbon dioxide waste, to pick up more oxygen.

Creating a family

All animals produce young, and many care for them for some time after they are born. Human beings in particular care for their children for a number of years. The best way of doing this is within a family unit, in which all the members of the family have great affection for each other.

Human beings, like many other animals, are divided into two sexes, male and female, for the purpose of producing children. The main physical difference between a man and a woman is in the reproductive organs. A man has a penis and two testicles in which he produces sex cells called sperms. A woman's reproductive organs are inside her body. They consist of a vagina, womb, and two ovaries in which she produces sex cells called eggs.

The woman produces one egg cell each month. This passes down a tube towards the womb. At this stage a sperm from the man may enter the egg cell, a process called fertilization. The fertilized egg then begins to divide and continues down the tube into the womb. There it becomes attached to the wall of the womb, and starts to grow into a child. From the time that the egg is fertilized until the baby is born is about nine months. During this time the baby is continually growing inside the mother's womb. It gets food from its mother through an organ called the placenta. In this organ food chemicals pass from the mother's blood into the baby's blood.

When the baby is born it has all its organs, but they are much smaller than those of an adult. They all continue to grow for the next 16 to 20

Top: A baby at three weeks old is helpless, and needs the care of its parents. It cannot fend for itself for several years, until it is almost fully grown.

Above: Many animals care for their young until they can look after themselves.

years. During the first few months the baby cannot eat solid food, and so it is given milk from its mother's breasts. Sometimes this is not possible, in which case the baby is fed with milk from a bottle.

For about a year the young baby is totally helpless. During this time the parents, and particularly the mother, have to look after all its needs. The most important of these are food and cleanliness. Gradually the child learns to feed itself, walk and use the lavatory. All the time the child is learning more about the world around it, and this process

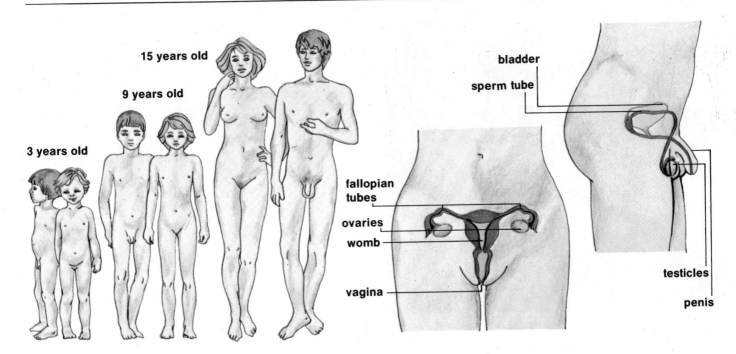

Girls and boys grow at different rates. At three years a girl and a boy are much the same size, but by the time they are nine the girl may be taller. A few years later the boy is taller than the girl.

The reproductive organs of a woman – ovaries, womb and vagina – are all internal, as shown in the diagram on the left. The male reproductive organs are partly inside the body, and partly external.

continues for many years at school and at home. The family is very important during these years. It provides happiness and security, and in these conditions it is easier to learn.

Parents continue to care for their children until they are about 18 years old (younger in some communities). By this time the children have learned, through teaching and experience, enough to be able to leave home and cope with adult life. However, even after the children have left home the family ties remain.

When a baby is born, it is of course either a boy or a girl. It has been a boy or a girl ever since fertilization took place. The father produces millions of sperms, half of which contain a special chromosome for a boy. If one of these sperms fertilizes the egg, the child is a boy, but if a sperm without one of the special chromosomes fertilizes the egg, the child is a girl.

At birth boys and girls have different reproductive organs, although they do not function until several years later. Apart from this, young boys and girls are very similar until a stage called puberty is reached. In girls this occurs at about the age of 11 or 12. Their hips grow wider and they begin to develop breasts. Hair begins to grow under the armpits and between the legs. At the same time they begin to have periods. These are normal events that occur in all women. Some bleeding usually occurs for a few days each month, when an unfertilized egg cell leaves the body.

In boys puberty begins later, between the ages of 13 and 14. Boys' shoulders become broader and their voices become deeper. Hair begins to grow on the face and chest, in the armpits, and around the base of the penis.

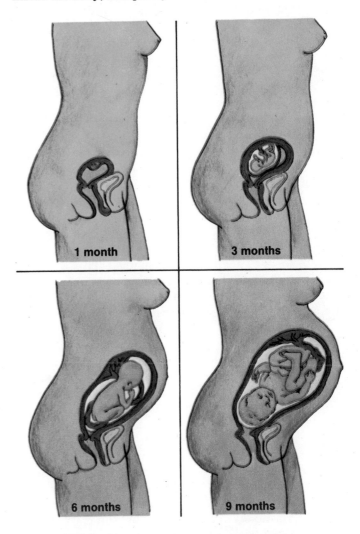

Four stages in the development of a baby in its mother's womb. Top left, at one month, it is very small indeed. Top right; at three months and bottom left, six months; bottom right, ready to be born.

Mathematics in action

Have you ever wondered what would happen if there were numbers and no mathematics? This is not a ridiculous idea–even recently there were some tribes whose languages had words only for numbers up to three, any number over three being referred to by the word for 'many'.

Obviously, without numbers or mathematics we would not be able to count or measure anything. But in our modern, scientific world mathematics is involved in so many aspects of life that it is impossible to list them all. However, here are a few examples of how the mathematics we learn in school and college are applied.

One application is in map-making. Few people who use maps wonder how they are constructed. Because maps are used for many purposes, they need to be very accurately measured. This is where that branch of mathematics known as trigonometry comes in. It deals with the measurements of triangles and how to use them.

For example, if a surveyor wants to know how far away from him a marker on a nearby hill is, he can do so without measuring the distance directly. From where he is standing, he measures the marker's bearing–that is, how many degrees off it is from being exactly north of him. Then he moves a fixed distance, such as 100 metres, in a suitable direction, to one side or the other, and measures the marker's bearing from his new position. This gives him two angles and one line of a triangle. From these figures, the surveyor can, using mathematical tables and various mathematical methods, work out how far the marker was from his original position. There are many other possible methods of working out the same problem.

An interesting mathematical problem occurs in making maps of large areas. The difficulty is that,

while most maps are flat, the Earth's surface is round. As a result, it is impossible to make a perfectly accurate flat map of really big sections of the Earth. Either distances or angles between places must be distorted at the edges of the map. There are various ways of distorting the Earth's surface to make a map, which are called 'projections'. Perhaps the best known is Mercator's projection, named after a Flemish geographer who lived 400 years ago. The continent maps in this book are drawn using this projection.

Mathematics of some kind is involved in nearly all science, technology and engineering. For instance, an engineer designing a suspension bridge needs to know exactly what way the bridge will be under stress, in order to know at what points the structure must be strongest. He uses the mathematics of forces and the way in which they react with each other. He must also study the way in which various materials such as steel behave under stress, a subject which involves many mathematical calculations.

Perhaps the best-known field in which mathematics is involved is space travel. The mathematical problems involved in getting a spacecraft, whether manned or not, to the Moon or another planet are so great that scientists have to use a computer to control the flight. The reason is that, since the position of the spacecraft is changing all the time, by the time a human brain had worked out a particular problem the answers would be too late to be of any use.

Not the least of our problems is that when we send a spacecraft from the Earth to, say, Mars, we must not aim it at Mars's position at the time we fire the rockets. If we do, by the time the spacecraft gets to that point Mars will no longer be there. We need to calculate Mars's path through the sky, and then plot a course so that Mars and the spacecraft both reach the appropriate point at the same time. All this goes some way to explain why man's venture into space represents one of the most challenging practical achievements of mathematics.

Top: A shopper adds her purchases with a calculator.

Below: Mathematics helped to put Skylab into orbit.

A surveyor measures angles with a theodolite–as shown below–to prepare a plan of a building site.

angles of elevation

How far is the house from the top of the hill?

?

20°

10°

40m

horizontal plane

Ideas in action

The modern world depends a great deal on technology. Cars, aeroplanes, radios and telephones are all essential parts of our lives, and we would find it hard to do without them. All these things and many others are the result of the ingenious ideas of clever men, whom we call inventors.

Inventions have been going on since the dawn of history. Stone Age men invented tools for hunting and carving. Much later people discovered how to melt metals and fashion them into more efficient tools and weapons.

Perhaps the most important invention of ancient civilizations was the wheel, about 5,000 years ago. It was probably not invented by one person, but by a number of people who separately discovered an easier way of moving things around. The first wheel was probably a tree trunk that could be rolled along the ground. Such inventions took thousands of years of slow progress, until today we have wheels of all types and sizes, used for many different purposes.

A great period of invention in Europe began in the Middle Ages, and by the time they ended in the 1500s men had invented machinery for mining coal and metals, and furnaces for making cast iron. Gunpowder had already been invented by then, and so large cast-iron cannons were made for use in war.

Since the 1500s there have been many thousands of inventions. People's knowledge and understanding of mechanical things grew, and this led to better and better ideas. The Italian artist Leonardo da Vinci is best known today for his achievements in sculpture and painting, but he also designed a helicopter, a machine for digging canals, and many other devices. However, neither he nor anyone else could put these ideas into practice at the time.

As technology grew, more inventions became possible. In 1698 an English engineer, Thomas Savery, discovered how to use the energy in steam to make a steam pump, and in 1712 Thomas Newcomen invented the first steam engine. Newcomen's engine was very inefficient, and modern steam engines are all based on James Watt's version, produced in 1765.

For the next hundred years all engines were powered by steam, but in 1876 a practical internal combustion engine was invented by a German, Nikolas Otto. This was quickly followed by two more German inventions–the petrol engine by Karl Benz and Gottleib Daimler in 1885, and the diesel engine by Rudolf Diesel in 1893. These engines could be made small and light, and it was this feature that made it possible for man to achieve a very long-standing ambition–to fly. The first engine-powered flight took place on 17 December, 1903, when two American engineers, Wilbur and Orville Wright, flew their aeroplane a little way.

The first aeroplanes were slow, but inventors made many modifications so that men could fly faster and faster. In 1937 a Briton, Sir Frank Whittle, invented the jet engine, and soon aeroplanes were flying faster than the speed of sound.

Another series of inventions that changed the

This steam-driven patent excavator was an American invention of the 1860s, and the ancestor of the sophisticated earth-moving machinery of the present day. It was capable of digging out cuttings and building up embankments for the railways that were then being constructed.

Above: Many modern inventions are centred on electronics, as in this microprocessor board from a computer.

Left: A giant radio telescope in West Germany. Devices of this kind are used to 'listen-in' to radio signals coming from outer space. With their aid astronomers are able to learn about stars and other objects that are too far away to see with ordinary telescopes.

way people lived was concerned with electricity. Great scientists of the 1700s and 1800s such as Alessandro Volta and Michael Faraday discovered how to make and use electricity. With this knowledge Alexander Graham Bell (Scottish-American) invented the telephone (1876); Thomas Alva Edison (American) invented the phonograph, ancestor of today's record-player (1877), and electric light (1879); Guglielmo Marconi (Italian) invented radio (1895); and John Logie Baird (British) invented television (1925).

Modern technology is very complicated, As a result, inventions today are often due to the efforts of teams of people rather than individuals. For example, the transistor was invented in 1948 by three Americans–William Shockley, John Bardeen and W. H. Brattain. However, there are still opportunities for individual inventions, such as the hovercraft, devised by the Englishman Sir Christopher Cockerill in the 1950s.

Below: The Great Wall of China runs for more than 2,700 kilometres (1,700 miles) through northern China. It was completed about 2,100 years ago after many years' work by 300,000 men as a defence against the barbarians who threatened China from the north. A roadway runs along the top, and there are watch towers at frequent intervals. The wall has been restored and extended several times in its long history.

The feats of Man

About 10,000 years ago men gave up their wandering life to become farmers. They built houses, and slowly villages and towns grew. From these small beginnings arose the great civilizations. Some men remained farmers and supplied everyone with food; others were able to do different kinds of work, and some of them concentrated on building.

As towns and cities grew they had to be protected from invaders, and so some of the earliest engineering feats were fortifications. Maiden Castle, the Iron Age fort in southern England, consists of four massive rings of earthworks that once surrounded the buildings of the town. Later fortifications include Hadrian's Wall, which lies on the border between England and Scotland. It was built as a defence against the Scots in AD 122–6. The Great Wall of China was built in 246–210 BC and is 2,700 kilometres (1,700 miles) long. The Incas, who ruled part of South America in the 1400s, built town walls from massive stones, which are still standing.

The people of early civilizations paid much attention to their gods. Many enormous buildings were constructed to honour and pacify these gods. The ruins of many Greek and Roman temples can still be seen. The Maya Indians, who ruled a large part of what is now Mexico, Guatemala and Belize, built gigantic pyramid-shaped temples. The Aztecs, who also lived in Mexico, constructed elaborate places of worship.

Three thousand years earlier the Egyptians built

their pyramids, which are among the most spectacular monuments left to us by any of the ancient peoples. They were built as tombs for the pharaohs (kings), who were believed to become immortal gods when they died. The building of the pyramids must have taken many years, and thousands of men were employed. They had only the simplest of mechanical devices, such as levers, rollers and slopes, to help them in this great feat of engineering, and the work must have been very hard.

Engineering today is not primarily concerned with religion, although many fine cathedrals and temples have been built during the past thousand years. Modern engineering feats are the result of technology. For example, when the steam engine was invented, railways soon followed. The easiest route for a railway is as straight and level as possible, and this means that bridges have to be built to cross rivers, and tunnels must be bored through hills and mountains.

One of the greatest railway engineers was Isambard Kingdom Brunel, who built England's Great Western Railway. His brick bridge across the River Thames at Maidenhead is still used by trains, although Brunel's critics said that its design would never carry the weight of a train. Other bridges of the world include many landmarks such as Sydney

Some of the biggest modern engineering works are dams to hold back rivers and supply water and electrical power. Here you see the Bratsk Dam under construction in Siberia, in the Soviet Union.

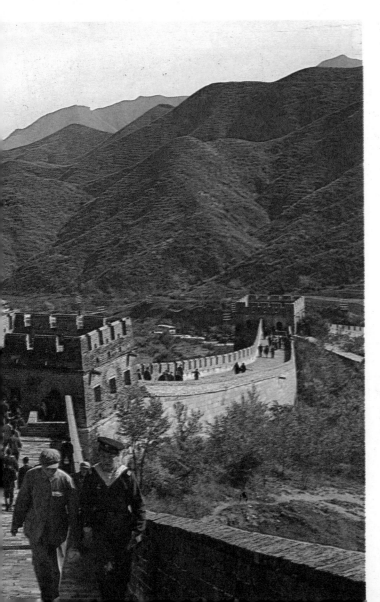

Harbour Bridge in Australia, the Verrazano-Narrows suspension bridge that soars 2,040 metres (6,690 feet) across the entrance to New York Harbour, and the Royal Gorge Bridge over the Arkansas River in Colorado, which is a dizzy 320 metres (1,050 feet) above the river's surface.

Other engineering feats of the modern world include tunnels, canals and skyscrapers. Tunnels have made mountain ranges such as the Alps no longer the almost impassable barriers that they used to be. Skyscrapers, the lofty buildings which dominate the skyline of so many cities, have become possible through the development of steel frames for constructing buildings. Steel used with concrete produces structures of enormous strength. Strength of this kind is needed for dams, which have to hold back incredible weights of water. The world's largest concrete dam is the Grand Coulee Dam, on the Columbia River in Washington, which is 1,270 metres (4,170 feet) wide.

Energy and
power

Energy is a popular word today. Manufacturers of breakfast cereals inform us that their foods are 'full of energy' – and yet we are told that the world is in an 'energy crisis'. You might think that the word energy means several things, but it actually has only one meaning. It is simply the capacity to do some work. For example, the muscles of your arm are able to lift things. They therefore contain energy, which is used when the muscles work.

There are several forms of energy, but all the energy in the world comes from two sources only – the Sun and minerals. The Sun's energy reaches us as light and heat; minerals give us energy in chemical form.

One of the main laws of energy is that it cannot be destroyed. However, it can be converted from one form into another. For example, the Sun's heat causes water vapour to rise from the sea and form clouds. These contain water that is capable of falling, and we call this capability potential energy. As the water falls to the ground and runs down the hills the potential energy is converted into moving energy, or kinetic energy. This form of energy in falling or running water can be converted into electrical energy in a hydro-electric plant.

Plants use the Sun's light to make chemicals, which are used to provide chemical energy for both plants and animals. Long ago the bodies of many plants and animals were turned into coal and oil, which we now use as fuels to provide us with heat and light when they are burned. At power stations some of this heat is converted into electrical energy.

Petrol and diesel fuel, two of the chemicals contained in oil, are used to power our trucks, cars and trains. Here, chemical energy is turned into heat energy, which is used to provide mechanical energy to propel the vehicle.

The chemical energy contained in minerals can also be converted into other forms of energy. For example, chemical energy stored in a car battery is used to provide an electric current. Some minerals produce a very different kind of energy, called nuclear energy. The atoms of such minerals as uranium and plutonium are unstable – that is, they do not keep their form, but break down. In doing so they give off energy and particles. The particles strike other atoms and cause them to break down as well. Soon, more and more atoms are breaking down, and this process is called a chain reaction. If there is enough of the mineral present, vast amounts of energy are released, and this leads to a nuclear explosion. However, the speed of a chain reaction can be controlled in a nuclear reactor, so that the energy is released comparatively slowly – as heat and not as an explosion. The heat can be converted into electrical energy in a power station.

Nuclear energy is dangerous, and the world's coal and oil cannot last for ever, so people are looking at alternative sources of energy. The Sun's energy can be used more directly: for example photoelectric cells convert light into electricity, and the Sun's heat can be trapped by water flowing through large solar panels. The Earth is also hot inside, and some power stations in New Zealand, Iceland and the United States use heat obtained from steam and hot water that gush out from the ground. Wind can also be used to provide power; windmills which used to drive corn-grinding machinery, today turn electrical generators to provide electricity. The waves and tides of the sea contain a great deal of energy. Many experiments are being done to try to harness wave power, and the Rance river project in France converts the rise and fall of the tide into electricity.

The greatest source of power available to Man: a thermo-nuclear test explosion in the Pacific Ocean unleashes the energy locked inside the atom.

The Rance river barrage in Brittany, France, uses the rise and fall of the tide to drive turbo-generators. The generators work whichever way the tide is flowing.

FINGERTIP FACTS ON SCIENCE

NEWTON'S LAWS

The English scientist Sir Isaac Newton (1642–1727) discovered three important laws of motion which are named after him.

Newton's First Law says that unless some outside force acts on them, a stationary body will stay still, and a moving body will travel in a straight line.

Newton's Second Law says that a change of momentum produced by a force is in proportion to the strength of the force and the time for which it acts.

Newton's Third Law says that to every action there is an equal and opposite reaction.

The first law governs such things as satellites. For example, the Moon would go through space in a straight line if it were not pulled into orbit around the Earth by the Earth's gravity.

The second law affects the way in which a force acts on an object—such as the force of an explosion in a gun on a bullet.

The third law shows that if one object pushes against another, it meets an equal resistance—so if you push yourself away from a wall, the wall is supplying a resistance equal to the strength with which you push. If the resistance were less you would push the wall over!

THIRTY GREAT INVENTIONS

Name	Inventor	Date
Aeroplane	Wilbur and Orville Wright (US)	1903
Balloon	Jacques and Joseph Montgolfier (Fr)	1783
Barbed wire	Joseph Glidden (US)	1873
Bicycle	Pierre and Ernest Michaux (Fr)	1861
Canned food	Nicolas Appert (Fr)	1810
Electric light	Thomas Edison (US)	1879
Fountain pen	Lewis Waterman (US)	1884
Helicopter	Paul Cornu (Fr)	1907
Hovercraft	Christopher Cockerell (UK)	1955
Lawn mower	Amariah Hills (US)	1868
Lightning conductor	Benjamin Franklin (US)	1752
Margarine	Hippolyte Mourries (Fr)	1870
Microscope	Zacharias Janssen (Neth)	1590
Motor car	Karl Benz (Ger)	1885
Pneumatic tyre	Robert Thomson (UK)	1845
Printing from type	Johannes Gutenberg (Ger)	1440
Radio	Guglielmo Marconi (It)	1895
Record-player	Thomas Edison (US)	1877
Refrigerator	Jacob Perkins (US)	1834
Safety pin	Walter Hunt (US)	1846
Safety match	Gustave Pasch (Swe)	1844
Sewing machine	Thomas Saint (UK)	1790
Steam engine	Hero of Alexandria	100
Telescope	Hans Lippershey (Neth)	1608
Telephone	Alexander Bell (UK)	1876
Thermometer	Galileo Galilei (It)	1593
Vacuum flask	James Dewar (UK)	1885
Washing machine	Joel Houghton (US)	1850
Wheel	Unknown	About 3000 BC
X-Rays	Wilhelm Roentgen (Ger)	1895

THE CHEMICAL ELEMENTS

There are 92 elements which occur naturally in the Earth's crust, and in addition scientists have made another 15 artificially.

Each element has a symbol (a one-letter or two-letter abbreviation of its name or a Latin form of its name) which is used in writing down chemical formulae. It also has an atomic number, which is equal to both the number of protons in the nucleus and the number of electrons orbiting the nucleus.

The total mass (sometimes called weight) of all the particles within an atom is called its atomic mass or weight.

Isotopes are atoms of the same element that have differing atomic mass. This is caused because they have different numbers of particles called neutrons in the nucleus.

The artificial elements are sometimes called transuranium elements, because they have higher numbers than uranium, the natural element with the largest number of protons and electrons.

ARCHIMEDES' PROBLEM

The Greek mathematician Archimedes, who lived in the 200s BC, had a problem. The King of Syracuse had asked him to find out if his crown were made of pure gold. Archimedes puzzled over this for a long time. Then one day as he lowered himself into the bath he noticed that water spilled over the side (he liked a very full bath).

Suddenly he realized that if he took a lump of pure gold that weighed the same as the crown and put it in water, and measured the amount spilled, and then did the same with the crown, he could tell the answer to the problem at once. Because if the crown were indeed made of gold mixed with a lighter metal, it would be bulkier than a lump of pure gold and more water would spill.

According to tradition, Archimedes was so excited that he leaped out of the bath and ran into the street without his clothes, crying 'Eureka!' (I have found it). Ever since, scientists have made use of Archimedes' principle, which is that if you immerse an object in liquid, the apparent loss of weight of that object equals the amount of water it displaces.

TABLE OF THE ELEMENTS

Name	Symbol	No
Actinium	Ac	89
Aluminium	Al	13
Americium	Am	95
Antimony	Sb	51
Argon	Ar	18
Arsenic	As	33
Astatine	At	85
Barium	Ba	56
Berkelium	Bk	97
Beryllium	Be	4
Bismuth	Bi	83
Boron	B	5
Bromine	Br	35
Cadmium	Cd	48
Caesium	Cs	55
Calcium	Ca	20
Californium	Cf	98
Carbon	C	6
Cerium	Ce	58
Chlorine	Cl	17
Chromium	Cr	24
Cobalt	Co	27
Copper	Cu	29
Curium	Cm	96
Dysprosium	Dy	66
Einsteinium	Es	99
Erbium	Er	68
Europium	Eu	63
Fermium	Fm	100
Fluorine	F	9
Francium	Fr	87
Gadolinium	Gd	64
Gallium	Ga	31
Germanium	Ge	32
Gold	Au	79
Hafnium	Hf	72
Helium	He	2
Holmium	Ho	67
Hydrogen	H	1
Indium	In	49
Iodine	I	53
Iridium	Ir	77
Iron	Fe	26
Krypton	Kr	36
Lanthanum	La	57
Lawrencium	Lr	103
Lead	Pb	82
Lithium	Li	3
Lutetium	Lu	71
Magnesium	Mg	12
Manganese	Mn	25
Mendelevium	Md	101
Mercury	Hg	80
Molybdenum	Mo	42
Neodymium	Nd	60
Neon	Ne	10
Neptunium	Np	93
Nickel	Ni	28
Niobium	Nb	41
Nitrogen	N	7
Nobelium	No	102
Osmium	Os	76
Oxygen	O	8
Palladium	Pd	46
Phosphorus	P	15
Platinum	Pt	78
Plutonium	Pu	94
Polonium	Po	84
Potassium	K	19
Praesodymium	Pr	59
Promethium	Pm	61
Protactinium	Pa	91
Radium	Ra	88
Radon	Rn	86
Rhenium	Re	75
Rhodium	Rh	45
Rubidium	Rb	37
Ruthenium	Ru	44
Samarium	Sm	62
Scandium	Sc	21
Selenium	Se	34
Silicon	Si	14
Silver	Ag	47
Sodium	Na	11
Strontium	Sr	38
Sulphur	S	16
Tantalum	Ta	73
Technetium	Tc	43
Tellurium	Te	52
Terbium	Tb	65
Thallium	Tl	81
Thorium	Th	90
Thulium	Tm	69
Tin	Sn	50
Titanium	Ti	22
Tungsten (Wolfram)	W	74
Uranium	U	92
Vanadium	V	23
Xenon	Xe	54
Ytterbium	Yb	70
Yttrium	Y	39
Zinc	Zn	30
Zirconium	Zr	40

Elements 104, 105, 106 and 107 have been discovered by Russian and American scientists, but names have not yet been agreed for them. The Americans call elements 104 and 105 rutherfordium and hahnium, but the Russians call them kurchatovium and niels borium.

Transport and communications

Until about 200 years ago very few people ever went far from their homes. People living in the country would perhaps visit the nearest big town once or twice a year–and some did not even do that. There were no telephones, no telegraph wires, no radio or television. There were very few newspapers, and many people could not read. News travelled slowly and was often carried by word of mouth by travellers who journeyed from one place to another on horseback, in horse-drawn carriages, and on foot. There were no motor-cars or railways or aeroplanes, and travel was very slow indeed.

Today all that has changed. People spend a great deal of time travelling. You can fly from one side of the Earth to the other in a day, and hear news of an event a few minutes after it has happened–and with television you can even watch things going on in far countries just as if you were there. In these pages we look at some of the ways in which people travel and communicate with one another.

Travelling by road

Almost every place on Earth is linked to other places by roads, and for this reason road transport is the most important way of getting about. You can get to almost anywhere by road unless you have to cross the sea, and even if you make most of your journey by plane or train or ship, you have to use roads to reach these other means of travel.

The simplest form of road is a dirt road, which is just a clear track with perhaps a layer of stones on top to keep it as dry as possible. Many roads in the developing countries or in the wilder parts of developed countries are like this. For example, many roads in Turkey, Iran and Afghanistan are surfaced with loose gravel – very dusty in summer and muddy in wet weather. A modern road is made by tamping the soil with rollers until it is hard, covering it with a thick layer of small stones, and covering the stones with an even thicker layer of concrete. The surface may be just the concrete or a layer of asphalt or stones and tar, which keeps the water out and prevents damage.

Engineers try to make main roads as straight and flat as possible. To do this they must cut their way through low hills, build up embankments on low ground, and build bridges to cross rivers, railways or deep valleys. In mountainous areas some roads

Modern multi-lane highways carry fast traffic clear of built-up areas. They connect with local roads by elaborate, clover-leaf junctions. This junction is in Kuala Lumpur, the capital of Malaysia.

go through tunnels to avoid very high passes. All countries are constantly working to improve their roads because the number of cars and trucks using them is increasing all the time. In some countries, such as the United States, there are two cars for every five people, but developing countries have comparatively few cars. An increasing amount of long-distance freight travels by road because it can go from door to door without being loaded from one form of transport on to another. In the past 20 years there has been an increasing use of containers, large boxes built like the body of a big truck. A container can be filled at a factory, travel to a port on a truck, be loaded on to a ship and carried half across the world, and then finish its journey on another truck.

One of the big problems of today is that many roads, especially in developed countries, are carrying much more traffic than they were built for. To make roads wider or build new ones in such places means taking land already used for something else, and may mean pulling down buildings.

Public transport by road, in buses, is used mostly for short journeys, such as people make every day. However, there are a number of long-distance bus services. For example, the Greyhound Bus service links most of the major cities of the United States, while specially air-conditioned buses run on desert routes, such as the service between Beirut, Lebanon, and Baghdad, Iraq.

Travelling by rail

Above: Pioneer days – the locomotive 'Derwent' on the Stockton and Darlington Railway in 1845.

Above right: The heyday of steam – a locomotive on a Melbourne-bound train in Victoria, Australia.

The coming of the railways brought the biggest-ever change in people's ways of travel. For thousands of years, until the early 1800s, the fastest ways in which people could go from one place to another overland were on horseback or in carriages drawn by horses.

The first passenger-carrying railway was opened in England in 1830. It was possible because engineers had adapted steam engines to run on rails. People had been pushing and pulling trucks along rails ever since the 1500s, because they ran more easily than on the ground and heavy loads could be moved

that way. The trucks were moved either by people or by horses. Steam engines were used for hauling goods trucks as early as 1812. By the 1870s most of the major countries of the world had a network of railway lines, and more were being built every year.

Steam engines burned coal or, in some parts of the world such as the wilder parts of North America, wood. They were dirty, and they needed regular supplies of fuel and water, while to 'raise steam' – start up an engine from cold – takes several hours. Engineers quickly began looking for other forms of power, and the first electric locomotive was built

Main-line railways run between large cities, carrying passengers and freight at high speed. The trains on them make few stops. Suburban trains provide a frequent service over short distances, carrying passengers to and from towns. Most of their passengers are commuters – people who travel to work and back. Suburban trains make frequent stops, and many of them are powered by electricity. Because of shortage of space many large cities have underground railways, burrowing deep beneath the ground, to carry commuters. They are always electrically powered to avoid having smoke or fumes in the tunnels.

In mountainous countries, such as Switzerland, there are funicular railways, in which the cars are hauled up steep slopes by cables, and rack railways. A rack railway has a centre toothed rail, and a cog in the engine meshes with it. In this way the engine can get a grip on the rail however steep it is.

The track is a vital part of a railway, and it must be kept in first-class condition for safety. The bed of a railway is made of stone chips (ballast) which form a firm but flexible base. On the ballast are laid sleepers, crosspieces made of wood, steel or concrete. The rails are fixed on the sleepers by means of metal frames called chairs. For smooth running rails are often welded together into lengths of a kilometre or more.

One of the most modern trains is the lightweight electric advanced passenger train (APT). Placed in service in 1980, they reach speeds of 150 miles (240 km) per hour.

Finally, to guide the drivers there is an elaborate system of signals – which are controlled from signal boxes.

and ran in 1879. Electric trains are clean and fast and have no starting problems, but they need overhead wires or a third rail at ground level to carry the current, and for this reason they are not suitable for very long distances or for country where there is a great deal of snow. In 1912 railways began using diesel locomotives, powered by internal combustion engines like those which drive giant trucks. Because electric motors make for smoother running than diesel engines, most diesel locomotives are really travelling power-stations – the diesel engine drives a generator which provides power for electric motors that drive the wheels. By the 1970s most of the world's railways had stopped using steam and relied on diesel and electric locomotives.

There are various kinds of railways, according to where they run and the kind of traffic they carry.

A powerful modern diesel locomotive on the Santa Fe railroad in the United States hauling 'The Grand Canyon' passenger train up a steep pass in New Mexico.

Travelling by water

The best way to carry bulky objects over long distances is by sea. There is plenty of room at sea, so ships can be made very large indeed–today's giant tankers are more than 350 metres (1,150 feet) long and can carry almost 400,000 tonnes of oil.

There are many kinds of ships in use. Passenger ships carry only passengers, often in great comfort. However, for long distance travel more and more people prefer to fly, so the number of large passenger ships is decreasing. On the other hand there is an increasing use of ferries, ships which carry people and freight over narrow stretches of sea such as the English Channel.

Merchant ships, which are sometimes called freighters, are the most important ships today. They are built in all sizes, from small coasters which hug the shore to the giant tankers which are the heavyweights of the sea. Some ships carry mixed cargoes of all kinds, but most freighters are built specially to carry one particular kind of cargo. Tankers are made to carry other liquids besides petroleum, and some carry natural gas in special tanks. Ships with refrigerated holds carry cargoes of meat, butter and cheese, and fruit also travels in ships where the cargo can be kept cool.

Modern ships are masterpieces of technology, and they need only small crews to man them–even a giant tanker can be handled by as few as 40 men. Many seamen today are specialists and technicians,

Above: These frail-looking Chinese junks off Hong Kong are wooden ships of a type that has been in use for hundreds of years. They are much tougher than they look and often brave the open seas.

a far cry from the 'old salt' of tradition. The ships with really big crews are the few remaining ocean liners, such as Britain's *Queen Elizabeth* 2, which needs several hundred people to look after the passengers; but then such a ship is really a floating hotel and carries a hotel's staff.

Sea transport would be impossible without harbours where the ships can load and unload and take on fresh fuel. Most ports have huge cranes which can lift cargo in and out of the hold of a ship, but ships also have their own derricks (cranes) attached to the masts. Many ships have other facilities, such as pumps and conveyor belts, for loading and unloading specialized cargoes. Loading and unloading is handled by dockside workers. If a ship is too large to tie up close to the dock its cargo is off-loaded into small boats, called lighters, which ferry the freight to the shore.

Nobody can tell which country really has the biggest fleet of merchant ships because many ships are registered with a country that does not own them. This is because there are two countries, Liberia and Panama, which charge much lower fees and taxes to shipowners, and also are less strict about rules covering safety at sea and the wages of the crews. A ship registered with another country in this way is said to be 'sailing under a flag of convenience'. As a result, Liberia has the largest apparent merchant fleet, followed by Japan, Britain, Norway, and Greece. However, the United States, a country which seems to have less than one third as many ships as Liberia, probably has many times more.

All the countries of the world co-operate to make life at sea safe. Those with dangerous coasts build lighthouses to warn ships when they come too close, or moor lightships near treacherous sandbanks for the same purpose. Weather forecasters supply constant news about storms and bad weather generally, and they are helped by weather ships, floating weather stations in mid-ocean. Most governments also agree on safety regulations. A branch of the United Nations co-ordinates their efforts to enforce these rules.

The open sea is not the only place where people and goods can travel by water. Countries with navigable rivers use them a great deal, particularly for bulk cargoes, and in North America and continental Europe many rivers have been linked by canals to make an inland waterway network. Important cargo-carrying rivers include the Rhine and the Danube in Europe, the Volga and the Don in the Soviet Union, and the Mississippi-Missouri river system in North America. The St. Lawrence Seaway is a canal system which links the St. Lawrence River with the Great Lakes, so that large ships can sail to ports such as Chicago in the heart of North America.

Left: A bus being loaded on to a ship at Miami harbour in Florida. Sea transport is still the cheapest and best way of transporting bulky cargoes of this sort over very long distances.

A modern giant of the seas, the 195,900 tonne Shell tanker 'Marinula'. Most of the space in ships of this kind is taken up with tanks to carry petroleum, and they require very small crews to navigate them.

Travelling by air

The story of air travel began within the lifetime of many people still living. The first true aeroplane to fly was *Flyer 1*, piloted by American engineer Orville Wright at Kitty Hawk, North Carolina, on 17 December, 1903. Within 16 years an aeroplane flew across the Atlantic Ocean – and aviation has gone on developing as rapidly ever since.

Today there are about 10,000 passenger aircraft in service, ranging from small, twin-engined planes operating local services in such places as the out-

back of Australia to the jumbo-jets which can carry 400 passengers at a time, and the supersonic Concorde which flies daily across the Atlantic Ocean in $3\frac{1}{2}$ hours. A great deal of mail travels by air, but only a small amount of freight does so because of the high cost. Perishable goods such as fruit and flowers are often sent by air, and it is often the best way of transporting animals over long distances. Bulky cargoes or large supplies of things such as oil and wheat are still mostly sent by land

Left: A modern version of the oldest method of flying – a hot-air balloon. Balloons are still used for pleasure flights, but they cannot be steered.

Above: Today's 'Jumbo Jet', the Boeing 747, which can carry up to 362 passengers. Aircraft of this kind went into service in February 1969.

and sea. Early aeroplanes, like some small aircraft today, flew slowly and fairly near the ground. Pilots could sit in open cockpits and breathe comfortably, though they were often cold. Modern planes fly at 9,000 metres (30,000 feet) and more above the ground. At such heights the air is too thin for a person to breathe, so the cabins of such aircraft are pressurized – that is, the air inside them is at a much higher pressure than the air outside.

Men have been trying to fly for thousands of years, but man-powered flight has become possible only in the past 5 years or so, using what is in effect a pair of wings powered by a bicycle-like mechanism. Even so, man-powered machines can fly only slowly and over short distances. The reason is that an athletic man can produce only just enough power to lift his weight, while a bird has a very light body in relation to the power of its wings.

To understand how an aeroplane flies, try holding a large piece of stiff card in a strong wind. You will find, if you keep the card nearly parallel to the ground, that the wind tries to lift it up. When an aeroplane flies, its propeller, or its jet engine, pushes it forward against the air – which is the same in effect as the wind pushing against it – while the wing acts like the piece of cardboard.

The shape of an aircraft's wing is important. Generally a wing is nearly flat underneath, and on top is thick at the front and thin at the back. When air flows over a wing it has to move faster over the top than over the bottom, because the distance 'over the hump' is longer (it is rather as if one lot of air has to go along one side of a triangle, while the rest has to go along two sides). Because the upper air is moving faster, its pressure is less, while the pressure below stays the same. The wing lifts into the area of low pressure and carries the rest of the aircraft up with it.

Engineers have experimented with making aircraft that float in the air – balloons and airships. A balloon is a large bag filled with a gas that is lighter than air, such as helium or hydrogen, but it cannot be steered or guided and is therefore of no use for travelling from one place to another. An airship is a cigar-shaped balloon under which is hung a car carrying an engine and a propeller. Airships are not very fast, and they are more liable to damage than aeroplanes, so they are not used much now, although they can carry heavy loads.

Like ships, aeroplanes need ports from which to go to and fro. An airport needs a great deal of space to allow a plane to run a long way along the ground when landing and taking off. It must have buildings where the passengers can wait and meet their friends, and where customs officers can inspect baggage in case people are smuggling in goods from another country without paying duties (taxes). Above all it must have a control tower, where traffic controllers can regulate flights and keep them safely apart – just as signalmen control trains.

The helicopter, which can land and take off vertically and hover, is a valuable rescue aircraft.

The postal services

A great deal of mail is now sorted by machines like these, which automatically put the letters the right way up, check they have the right stamps on, and 'read' codes which show their destination.

When Abdul drops a letter into a mail-box in Marrakesh, to be delivered a few days later to his pen-friend George half across the world in Vancouver, he is using one of the most important means of communication–the postal services. Yet the great system of mail delivery we have today is less than 150 years old. In the Middle Ages it was very difficult to send a letter from one country to another unless you employed someone to carry it, or knew somebody who was travelling and would take a letter for you. It was nearly as difficult to send a letter inside a country, and also very expensive. Generally the person receiving the letter had to pay for it, and the further it travelled the more he paid.

The modern system of handling mail was invented by a former schoolmaster, Rowland Hill, in England. Hill said that there should be one rate of postage for letters, and that the postage should be paid by the sender by means of adhesive labels–and that was how the postage stamp came into being in 1840. A postage stamp is really a receipt to show that you have paid the post office the fee to carry your letter for you.

If we follow Abdul's letter to Vancouver we can see how it is handled. Abdul has, of course, put a stamp on it. A postman collects the letter from the mail box, together with all the others that have been posted there, and takes them to the local sorting office. The sorting office may be in the same town or in one close by. At the sorting office workers

To help sorting machines work, the post-codes you write on your letters are typed on to the envelope as a series of light-sensitive dots by the operator shown in the lower picture. Once he has done that the machines automatically sort the letters, even down to the part of the road they are going to.

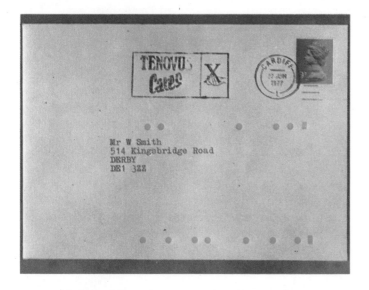

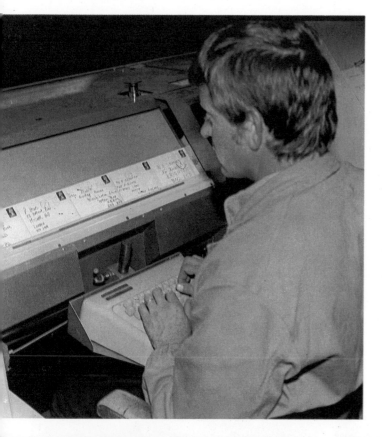

stack the letters so that they are all face up, with the stamps in the same place, and feed them through a machine which cancels them. The cancellation shows the date and place of posting, and also marks the stamp so that it cannot be reused.

Once cancelled, the letters are sorted according to the destination. The first sorting puts the letters into piles for major regions and important cities. Local letters go into a separate section, where in due course they are re-sorted along with letters from other places to Marrakesh. Letters for other countries, such as Abdul's letter to George, go into a special overseas section.

In many countries a great deal of this sorting is carried out by machines, which put the letters the right way up and cancel them. In some countries, such as Britain, the stamps carry invisible lines of phosphor which can be detected by light-sensitive devices. These devices can check that the correct postage has been paid and sort the mail into first and second class letters.

Abdul's letter, together with any others for foreign destinations, is taken to an overseas sorting office, where it is put into a bag containing other letters for Canada. It may travel by van, or part of the way by train. From the overseas sorting office Abdul's letter travels either to an airport, if it is airmail, or to a port if it is surface mail. Surface mail may have to wait some time for a suitable ship. The letter may go direct from Morocco to Canada, or more likely it will be flown to some place such as Paris or London which has direct flights to both Canada and Morocco.

Once the letter reaches Canada it is sorted again and put aboard a train or a plane for Vancouver. In Vancouver it is sorted with all the local mail, and made up into a bundle to take direct to George's house. The postman who delivers in George's road probably sorts the letters himself before he takes them out, because he knows his road well. If George's home is in town the postman will deliver the letters on foot. If it is in a country area where the houses are further apart the postman probably uses a van. In some parts of the world the mail is delivered by boat or on horseback, or even on a sledge if the land is covered with a blanket of snow.

How Abdul's letter reaches George. This strip traces the progress of the letter from the moment Abdul drops it in the mail-box in Marrakesh to the time George receives it in faraway Vancouver.

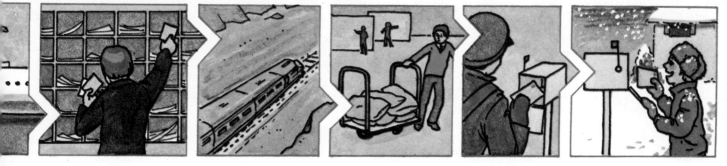

Communicating by wire

A popular, good-humoured American artist was sailing home across the Atlantic in 1832 from a visit to Europe when he fell into conversation with a doctor about the electromagnet, then newly invented. As a result, he started thinking about how he might use electromagnets to send messages by wire – and a few years later the electric telegraph was born.

The painter was Samuel Morse, and he not only invented the telegraph, which he had working by 1835, but also the Morse Code, used ever since for sending messages. Morse was not the only man to invent a telegraph system, and many people helped to make the system in use today.

The telegraph works by making and breaking an electrical circut to send a series of electrical impulses over a wire. You can get the same effect by switching a flashlight or an electric light on and off. For many years all telegraph messages were sent by hand, using a spring-loaded key to tap out the signals. Now nearly all messages are sent by machine. The message is tapped out on a keyboard like that of a typewriter, which either sends the impulses directly over the wire or punches holes in a paper tape. The tape can then be fed through another part of the machine to send the message. The tape method is better because it can send the message faster than an operator can tap it out, so it occupies less time on the wire.

Pictures can also be sent by wire. The black and white of the original are translated into electrical signals of various strengths at the sending end. The receiver decodes the signals and builds up the picture, either by some form of ink on paper or by tiny dots of light on photographic paper.

The telephone grew out of the telegraph. It was invented by a Scottish-born teacher of deaf children, Alexander Graham Bell, in Boston, Mass., in 1876. The basic principle is the same as that of the telegraph: the sounds of the voice are converted by a microphone into electrical signals which travel over a wire and are turned back into sound by a similar device the other end. Sound in radio and television is dealt with in the same way, with a microphone at one end and a loudspeaker – which works like the earpiece of a telephone but on a bigger scale – at the other.

The basic difference between the telephone and

Below: The switchboard in a busy telephone exchange in the early days of the telephone. The operators had to plug in the calls using long wires.

Below right: A modern switchboard has no long trailing wires. Operators press buttons to connect callers.

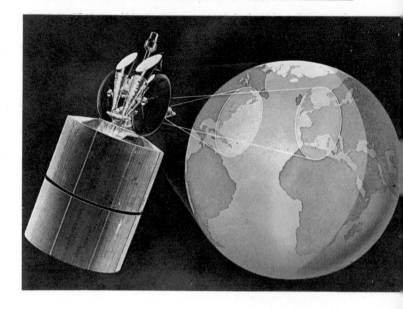

Below: A communication satellite orbits the Earth at the same speed as the Earth's rotation, so it 'hovers' in the same spot in the sky. Signals can be bounced off it and back to Earth, when they could not be sent direct because of the world's curve.

radio is that with radio the signals are carried on radio waves through space, instead of as electrical signals along a wire. Each system is used today to help the other. For example, although there are cables running under the oceans to carry telephone and telegraph signals, many telephone calls from one country to another are sent part of the way by radio. Some use communications satellites–small transmitter-receivers that orbit the Earth at such a speed that they match the Earth's rotation, so they always stay in the same relative place. Long-distance television signals travel by satellite.

On the other hand, many television and radio signals travel by wire from the studios where they originate to the transmitters.

There are many special forms of telephone service. Today most calls are made by dialling a number. The dial on your telephone automatically turns the numbers into electrical impulses, which activate devices at the telephone exchange to link your phone to that of the person you are calling. On a long-distance call this link may go through several telephone exchanges. If you are likely to be out a lot, you can instal a machine which records incoming calls so that you can replay them later.

Originally one pair of wires was needed to send each telegraph or telephone message. Today engineers have devised ways of sending messages at different frequencies (rates of vibration), so many calls can travel on the same pair of wires, and they have now invented a way of sending signals along fine glass fibres using lasers. The system may in time replace wires.

Spreading the news

What is news? Charles Anderson Dana, a great American journalist, once defined it this way: 'When a dog bites a man that is not news, but when a man bites a dog that is news'. In other words, news is the account of any unusual event, such as an earthquake; an action that will affect a lot of people, such as the passing of a new law; or some happening in the life of a well-known person, such as the marriage of a pop-star.

Newspapers are the oldest of these means of spreading news–the first true newspaper was founded in Germany in 1615. They are still the most important source of news because reports in a newspaper can be longer and give more details than those on radio or TV, and you can read them over again to study them more closely.

Producing a newspaper begins with the events that go into it–stories, journalists call them. Every newspaper employs a number of reporters whose job is to find out the facts of the stories and write them up. Newspapers also rely a good deal on local correspondents. These people are reporters who live in an area and report on events in that area. A correspondent is paid a small yearly fee, called a retainer, and then is paid for every story he sends in that a newspaper can use. In addition there are many news agencies which also employ reporters and correspondents. An agency supplies stories to a great many newspapers in return for a regular fee, and can thus cover events that would be too expensive for each newspaper to report on its own.

News reaches a newspaper in several ways. Many stories are telephoned in, and taken down on typewriters by skilled typists. News agencies send theirs by teleprinter. Others arrive by post or by hand, or are written in the office of the newspaper by its own reporters. All this mass of news has to be sorted out and graded for importance. Then it has to be edited for insertion in the paper. Some stories have to be shortened because they are too long; others must be rewritten from a number of different reports. As many facts as possible must be checked, and finally headlines are written. All this work is done by sub-editors or rewrite men. When the editing is finished the copy, as the manuscript of the stories is called, goes to the typesetters who set it into type. Some newspapers still use metal type, but others use a form of photographic typesetting. Once the type is set, other skilled men assemble it into pages, and from these pages printing plates are made. The plates are placed on the presses, and the actual printing begins. Newspaper presses are huge machines, and some are as big as a pair of two-storey houses.

Packers pack up the papers in bundles as they come off the presses and carry them to vans, which deliver them to newspaper sellers, or take them to trains and planes if they have to go considerable distances away. Some newspapers appear daily, others weekly. Some sell only a few thousand copies over a limited area, others may sell all over a country, and even in several countries.

In addition to news, many newspapers carry

Below: Taking a proof of the front page of a newspaper (the London 'Daily Telegraph'). This proof is checked before the paper is actually printed.

what are called features – articles on many subjects, book, theatre and cinema reviews, crossword puzzles, and strip cartoons. A separate group of editors deals with such matters. Both news and features are illustrated by photographs, most of which are taken specially for the paper. Producing a newspaper costs a lot of money. Part of this money comes from the sale of copies of the paper, and part from selling space to advertisers.

Radio and television news begins in the same way as for newspapers, but instead of being set in

A giant battery of presses prints copies of a 32-page (or bigger) newspaper, cuts them to size from a continuous roll of paper, and folds them. It also counts the copies, and turns one slightly to mark a quire (a newspaper quire is 27 copies). The papers are then bundled up for distribution.

type it is edited to be read by a newscaster. In addition, a broadcast news bulletin can include interviews with people in the news, or with eye-witnesses, and television can show pieces of film of the events it is reporting.

FINGERTIP FACTS ON TRANSPORT AND COMMUNICATIONS

THE WORLD'S MAIN RAIL NETWORKS

The United States has by far the greatest length of railway lines in the world – 600,000 kilometres (375,000 miles), more than four times as much as the Soviet Union, which has twice the area. The world's top ten rail networks are:

Country	Kilometres/miles
United States	600,000 (375,000)
Soviet Union	139,800 (87,375)
Canada	118,000 (73,750)
India	60,800 (37,500)
China	50,000 (31,250)
Australia	42,500 (26,562)
Argentina	39,800 (24,875)
Brazil	35,000 (21,875)
France	34,150 (21,343)
West Germany	32,500 (20,312)

Britain has about 18,000 kilometres (11,200 miles) of rail routes, and also some of the world's busiest lines, especially around London.

BUSY ROADS

In relation to the number of people living there, the United States has more vehicles than any other country –more than one for every two people. Leading countries in the busy roads stakes vary according to whether you count private cars or commercial vehicles (trucks, vans, and buses).

Motor-cars per 1,000 people	
United States	526
Canada	416
New Zealand	400
Luxembourg	400
Australia	384
Sweden	344
West Germany	333

Commercial vehicles per 1,000 people	
United States	146
Canada	116
Japan	110
Australia	94
France	46
United Kingdom	34

PIPELINES

Pipelines form an important means of transporting goods of various kinds. Their principal use is to carry water, natural gas and petroleum, but they can also carry finely broken coal, sewage and industrial waste.

The major pipeline networks are involved in moving oil and natural gas, and are in North America, western Europe, the Soviet Union, the Middle East, and North Africa. The North American network alone totals more than 1,600,000 kilometres (994,000 miles).

GIANTS OF THE SEA

The biggest ships afloat today are the giant oil tankers, and there are more than 50 in service each over 350 metres (1,150 feet) long. The largest is the Seawise Giant, launched in January 1981, owned by C. Y. Tung. She is 458.54 metres (1,504 feet) long, with a gross tonnage of more than 564,763.

THE MORSE CODE

The Morse Code is made up of a series of dots and dashes. These dots and dashes can be represented by sounds or by flashes of light, or by the movement of a single flag – known as 'wig-wag' signalling. The international code, still used to send messages by short-wave radio, is:

A •–	F ••–•	K –•–	P •––•	U ••–	Y –•––
B –•••	G ––•	L •–••	Q ––•–	V •••–	Z ––••
C –•–•	H ••••	M ––	R •–•	W •––	
D –••	I ••	N –•	S •••	X –••–	
E •	J •–––	O –––	T –		

1 •––––	6 –••••
2 ••–––	7 ––•••
3 •••––	8 –––••
4 ••••–	9 ––––•
5 •••••	0 –––––

OTHER SIGNS

Period •–•–•–	SOS •••–––•••
Comma ––••––	Start –•–
Interrogation ••––••	Wait •–•••
Colon –––•••	End of Message •–•–•
Semicolon –•–•–•	Understand •–•
Quotation Marks •–••–•	Error ••••••••

In wig-wag signalling you start by holding the single flag vertically. For a dot you swing the flag down to your right, for a dash you swing it down to your left. To mark the end of a word swing the flag down straight in front of you. Do this twice to mark the end of a sentence, and three times for the end of a message.

TWENTY FAMOUS SHIPS

Aaron Manby, British-built in 1821, was probably the first iron steamship.

Clermont, US-built in 1807, began the first steamboat passenger service on the Hudson River.

Cutty Sark, British-built in 1869, was one of the fastest sailing ships, and carried tea from China to England.

Golden Hind – originally named *Pelican* – was the ship in which Sir Francis Drake made his voyage round the world in 1577–80.

Great Britain, launched in England in 1843, was then the largest ship in the world at 98 metres (322 feet) long. She is preserved at Bristol, her home port.

Great Eastern, an even larger sister ship of the *Great Britain*, was launched in 1858. She laid four Atlantic cables.

Mauritania, British-built in 1906, held the Atlantic 'Blue Riband' (speed record) for 22 years.

Mayflower was the sailing ship in which the Pilgrim Fathers sailed from Plymouth to America to found a colony in 1620.

Normandie, French-built in 1932, was the first ship more than 300 metres (985 feet) long, and carried 2,170 passengers.

Queen Elizabeth was the largest passenger liner, and was British-built in 1934.

Queen Elizabeth 2 is the largest British passenger liner now in service, and was launched in 1969.

Queen Mary was a sister-ship of the *Queen Elizabeth*, and was also more than 300 metres (985 feet) long. She was launched in 1934 and 'retired' in 1968.

Santa Maria was the flagship of the little fleet in which Christopher Columbus made his epic voyage to the Americas in 1492.

Savannah was the first ship with steam-engines to cross the Atlantic. US-built, she made her voyage in

1819, using sail for most of the trip.

Savannah, US-built in 1962, was the first nuclear-powered merchant ship.

Sirius, British-built, made the first all-steam-powered voyage across the Atlantic in 1838.

Titanic, British-built in 1912 and reputed unsinkable, hit an iceberg on her maiden voyage and sank with the loss of more than 1,500 lives.

Turbinia, British-built in 1894, was the first ship to be driven by turbine engines.

Victoria was the first ship to sail round the world. She was the only survivor of five ships with which Ferdinand Magellan set out from Spain in 1519, and she returned under the command of Sebastian del Cano in 1522.

Vulcan, British-built in 1818, was the first all-iron sailing ship.

History of the world

History is the story of man from the time he became able to write. The period before he could write is called prehistory. We known about prehistoric man only indirectly, through traces he left behind. But in historic times men have written about their deeds and ways of life. During these times, from about 3000 BC, great civilizations and empires have risen and fallen. In the next 16 pages we describe some of the most important events and changes of the past 5,000 years.

Ancient civilizations

Civilization literally means 'life in cities'. The earliest civilizations developed in four so-called 'cradle lands'. These were the Fertile Crescent in Mesopotamia (modern Iraq), the Nile Valley in Egypt, the Indus Valley in Pakistan and the Yellow River Valley in China.

In Mesopotamia from about 2500 BC the Sumerians set up independent city-states, of which the greatest was Ur. They built fine temples and palaces. They also developed a form of writing called cuneiform which means wedge-shaped. Their religious beliefs greatly influenced later peoples in South-western Asia. In about 2360 BC a king called Sargon I imposed the rule of the city of Akkad throughout Mesopotamia, the Persian Gulf and Syria. In the 1800s BC the city of Babylon became the main power. Its greatest king, Hammurabi, created a mighty empire and introduced an important set of laws.

A people from Asia Minor (modern Turkey) called the Hittites overthrew Babylon and dominated the area for a while. The warlike Assyrians

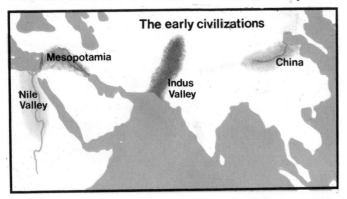

The early civilizations

Mesopotamia

China

Nile Valley

Indus Valley

A picture made of baked tiles on a wall at Persepolis in Persia. It shows King Darius's bodyguard.

conquered the Hittites. They were very like the Babylonians. Their main cities were Assur and Nineveh. Their empire reached its height under King Tiglath-Pileser I. By ruthless invasions he conquered Phoenicia (modern Lebanon).

The last great Assyrian ruler was Assurbanipal. We still have many books from his library. The books were 'written' by scratching letters on clay tablets. After Assurbanipal died in 627 BC Assyrian power collapsed.

Throughout its long history of more than 2,000 years ancient Egypt hardly changed its way of life or its religious practices. In this time 30 dynasties (families) of pharaohs (kings) rose and fell. Many of the colossal pyramids and temples that the Egyptians built still stand today. The Persians conquered Egypt in 525 BC. Five hundred years later Egypt became part of the Roman Empire.

The civilizations of the Indus Valley began about 2500 BC. The main cities were Harappa and Mohenjo Daro, and they were very luxurious. The houses were built of brick, the streets were well planned and the drainage system was efficient.

Invaders from north-western Asia overthrew this civilization in about 1500 BC. The invaders developed the Hindu religion and caste system that

1500 BC. Their people made fine bronze, jade and ivory objects and developed the first Chinese writing. During the rule of the succeeding Chou dynasty people followed the teaching of a wise man named Confucius (552–479 BC). For a few years China was ruled by a family named the Ch'in, and we still call the country 'China' after them. After the Ch'in came a family of emperors called the Han, and under their rule China had 400 years of peace.

have been so important in the history of India. In the 500s BC a holy man called Siddhartha Gautama, known as the Buddha, preached a new way of life. His ideas greatly influenced King Ashoka, who ruled most of India and Afghanistan in the 200s BC. The Buddha's teachings later spread throughout eastern Asia.

In China a family of emperors known as the Shang ruled on the banks of the Yellow River from about

This terracotta figure was found in the ruins of Mohenjo Daro, now in Pakistan. It shows the Mother Goddess, who was worshipped there 4,000 years ago.

The Sphinx, bearing the head of Pharaoh Khafre, has gazed over the Egyptian desert for 4,500 years. Khafre's pyramid is seen behind it.

The Classical Age

Early history is often mixed up with legend. This Greek vase, made in the 400s BC, shows the story of the Minotaur, a mythical creature half bull, half man, said to have been owned by King Minos. It was eventually killed by the hero Theseus from Athens, who found his way to its lair in the Labyrinth.

The ancient civilizations that most influenced the later history of Europe were those of Greece and Rome. Their time is often called the 'Classical Age'. The first Greek civilization was on the island of Crete, and it is called Minoan after a legendary king named Minos. Minoan civilization began about 3000 BC. The Minoans built splendid palaces with colourful wall paintings, and became wealthy traders. They developed a writing of their own.

The Aegean civilization, centred on the mainland Greek city of Mycenae, was also rich and powerful. The Greek poet Homer tells how its king, Agamemnon, led an army against the city of Troy. Invaders from the north overcame both the Minoan and Mycenean civilizations by 1100 BC.

In the Dark Ages that followed various invaders settled in Greece. The Ionians occupied the district of Attica, in which stands the city of Athens. The Dorians swept into the Peloponnesus, in south-western Greece. The cities the Dorians and Ionians founded were fiercely independent, though they did form alliances. Such an alliance defeated an invading army from Persia in 480 BC.

In time Athens became the most powerful city in Greece. During its Golden Age, from 461 to 431 BC, Athens was the head of a sea empire called the Delian League. Great Athenian writers, sculptors and architects created superb works of art. The Athenians' main rivals, the Spartans, were more warlike and less interested in the arts. The two cities fought the Peloponnesian War from 431 to 404 BC. Athens was forced to surrender and Sparta became the leader of Greece.

Later the power of the kingdom of Macedonia in the north of Greece grew quickly. In 338 BC its king, Philip II, won the whole of Greece by winning the Battle of Chaeronea. Philip's son, Alexander the Great, set out to conquer the world, but after capturing Egypt, Persia and part of India he died of malaria at the age of 32.

After Alexander's death his empire broke up, and Macedonia became part of the Roman Empire. Rome had developed into an important city by the 400s BC. It won three wars against its North African rival, Carthage (near modern Tunis). Rome also gained control of the whole of Italy. It extended its empire over the Mediterranean area and much of northern Europe, including Britain. At first Rome was ruled by elected officials, but from 27 BC emperors, beginning with Augustus, ruled the city.

In AD 30 Jesus Christ, whom many people believe to be the Son of God, was crucified at Jerusalem. Jerusalem was then part of the Roman Empire. For many years Jesus's followers, the Christians, were persecuted for their beliefs, but in AD 313 the Emperor Constantine made Christianity an official religion of the Roman Empire.

In the AD 300s, the Roman Empire was divided into two parts, the Eastern Empire and the Western Empire. In the 400s barbarian tribes from northern Europe burnt Rome, and the West Roman Empire came to an end.

The East Roman Empire, with its capital at Constantinople (now Istanbul), is better known as the Byzantine Empire, from an old name for Constantinople. Its greatest emperor was Justinian I, who enlarged it and encouraged Christianity. But in the 600s the Muslims began to overrun much of the empire. The Muslims were Arab followers of Muhammad, the founder of Islam, who was born at Mecca in western Arabia in 571.

In the 700s a group called the Franks, under Charlemagne, built a great empire in western Europe. Its capital, Aachen, became a centre for scholars. In 800 Pope Leo III crowned Charlemagne as 'Emperor of the West'.

In South America, the Maya Indians had developed a form of writing and a calendar system by the 700s, and also studied astronomy.

The T'ang dynasty controlled China from 608 to 906. Painters, sculptors and poets produced works of art that are much prized today.

Above: As Christianity spread it inspired pictures such as this one – the Last Supper. It was painted on the wall of a catacomb (underground cemetery) in Rome in the late AD 200s.

Left: The spread of Islam also inspired paintings. This one shows the prophet Muhammad visited by the Archangel Gabriel and some holy men. Muhammad is shown veiled because Muslims forbid pictures of his face, and also discourage any paintings showing both men and women.

The Middle Ages

The Middle Ages in Europe lasted from the fall of Rome in the 400s until the 1400s. They are called 'Middle Ages' because they come in the middle between classical and modern times. Most of the people lived within what is called a feudal system. This was supposed to protect the poor, but it enriched the powerful. The lord in his castle granted his vassal (tenant) protection, and also a plot of land. In return the vassal promised to work for the lord and to fight for him if necessary. But most country people were serfs, who were virtually slaves of the lord or his vassals. At the head of a feudal state was the king.

The Middle Ages were a period of strife and change. The Moors (Muslim Arabs) overran northern Africa, Spain and Portugal. They ruled their lands wisely. But when they occupied Palestine a number of Christian Europeans thought they must free this 'Holy Land' where Jesus had lived. They led a military expedition called a crusade, and captured Jerusalem. Later crusades were less successful, and in 1453 another group of Muslims, the Turks, captured the Christian city of Constantinople (now called Istanbul).

The Norsemen, or Vikings, from Scandinavia continually raided the coasts of northern Europe, Italy and Spain. King Canute of England was a Norseman. Another Viking, Leif Ericson, probably landed in North America.

William of Normandy in France led a Norman invasion of England in 1066. After a victory at the Battle of Hastings he soon subdued the whole country. He replaced the Anglo-Saxon way of life by the feudal system.

In 1337 the Hundred Years' War began between France and England. The English king at that time

Top Left: A scene from the Bayeux Tapestry, which describes William of Normandy's conquest of England.

Above: This stone carving, made in the 800s, shows a Viking ship. Such ships have been found sunk at sea.

Top Right: The pyramid of the Inscriptions, at the ruined city of Palenque in Mexico, conceals a tomb. It was built at the time of the Toltec Empire.

Right: An illustration from an early manuscript copy of 'The Travels of Marco Polo', the Venetian merchant who spent 17 years at the court of Kublai Khan in China. It shows the trial of a traitor.

ruled a large part of France. At first the French suffered defeats and also lost hundreds of thousands of its people in the Black Death, an outbreak of bubonic plague that swept through Europe in 1348. In the end the heroism of a French peasant girl, Joan of Arc, inspired the French, and they drove the English out of France. In England itself a series of civil wars, called the Wars of the Roses, greatly weakened the power of the nobles. The Wars ended in 1485 with victory by the first Tudor king, Henry VII. He made England rich and peaceful.

The great age of discovery began at the end of the 1400s, but a Venetian merchant, Marco Polo, made an amazing journey to the court of Kublai Khan at Peking in 1255. The Khan was the grandson of Genghis Khan, the ferocious leader of the Mongols of central Asia. Genghis founded a vast empire in the east which included China and southern Russia. Mongol rule in China was followed by the rule of two other dynasties, the Yüan and the Ming. In the late 1300s Tamerlane (Timur the Lame), a descendant of Genghis, again extended Mongol rule over much of Asia, but not over China.

In south-east Asia the Khmer Empire was at its height between 889 and 1434. At their capital, Angkor, the Khmers built great stone temples with rich carvings, which still stand deep in the forest.

In Africa the mysterious massive ruins of Zimbabwe in Rhodesia show that an advanced civilization existed there in the Middle Ages. More is known about the early civilizations of western Africa. The powerful Ghana Empire was followed by the Mali Empire. Mali's capital, Timbuktu, was famous as a centre of learning and trade. Modern Ghana and Mali are named after these ancient empires, but they are not in quite the same places.

In 1498 Portuguese ships captained by Vasco da Gama sailed round Africa and reached southern India. So European influence in Asia had its beginning. In the same year the great sailor Christopher Columbus, in the course of his third voyage to the west, set foot for the first time on the American mainland. At that time the Incas in South America ruled over an empire that stretched from northern Ecuador to Chile. In Mexico the Toltecs ruled a wide empire from their capital, Teotihuacán, later destroyed.

Renaissance and Reformation

From the 1300s to 1500s, people in Europe began to have new ideas in the arts, the sciences, and religion. This period, which came at the end of the Middle Ages, is known as the Renaissance. The word Renaissance means 'rebirth', and we call this period by that name because there was a rebirth of interest in learning at that time. You can read how artists worked at this time on pages 98–101.

The Renaissance began in Italy. Its ideas spread very quickly through Europe because a German goldsmith named Johannes Gutenberg invented printing from type in the 1400s. Before Gutenberg's invention people had to copy books slowly and laboriously by hand. As a result, books were very expensive and only a few people could afford to buy them. With printing, many copies of a book could be made quickly and cheaply.

The new ideas helped to bring about the Reformation. This was a movement begun by people who wanted to reform the Christian Church. At that time the Church in western Europe was ruled from Rome. The head of the Church was the Pope. Many people thought the Church was badly led. One of them was a monk in Germany named Martin Luther. He and his followers became known as Protestants, because they protested against the way in which the Church was run. Protestantism gradually spread through most of the countries of northern Europe. In southern Europe people stayed loyal to the Pope. They became known as Roman Catholics because they obeyed the teachings of the Pope in Rome.

During the Middle Ages princes and noblemen

Top: The cathedral at Florence, Italy, took more than 200 years to build. The dome, by the architect Filippo Brunelleschi, is a magnificent example of Renaissance work. Florence was a centre of the Renaissance.

Above: This old engraving shows how printing was carried on at the time of its invention and for hundreds of years afterwards. The man on the right is setting up the type ready for a book to be printed.

ruled most of Europe. Each one governed only a small area. In the 1500s, however, powerful kings began to rule over complete countries. They governed large areas. People in these countries began to think of themselves as nations. We call this period the rise of nationalism. But powerful countries became rivals, and went to war. At this time the kings of France and the emperors of the Holy Roman Empire (which covered modern Germany and Austria and part of Italy) began a conflict which lasted, with spells of peace, for hundreds of years.

There was also war between King Philip II of Spain, who was a Roman Catholic, and Queen Elizabeth I of England, who was a Protestant. Philip sent his soldiers to invade England. They sailed in a huge fleet called the Invincible Armada. English sailors, including the great explorer Sir Francis Drake, defeated the Armada in 1588 in a running battle up the English Channel.

Meanwhile the Ottoman Turks, who had a large empire in south-western Asia, began to invade southern Europe. Their sultan, Suleiman the Magnificent, captured Belgrade and nearly took Vienna. His forces also captured the Mediterranean island of Rhodes, and threatened to dominate the Mediterranean Sea. This threat was ended when a fleet from Spain, Venice and Genoa defeated a Turkish fleet at the Battle of Lepanto.

In 1526 a Mongol chief named Babar, a descendant of Genghis Khan, invaded India. He set up a Muslim state of northern India, known as the Mughal Empire. Under the rule of his grandson, Akbar, India became peaceful and prosperous.

Explorers went on looking for new lands. The Spaniards conquered Mexico, Central America and most of South America. They destroyed the empires of the Incas and the Aztecs, and looted their gold. The Portuguese began to conquer Brazil. In the north, the French explorer Jacques Cartier discovered the St. Lawrence River. And a Spanish expedition sailed right round the world, proving it was round (see pages 180–181).

This painting shows the Battle of Lepanto, fought in the Mediterranean Sea in 1571. It was the last big battle in which galleys (oared ships) were used.

The rise of empires

The 1600s in Europe were dominated by the Thirty Years' War, which began in 1618 as a religious struggle between Protestant and Roman Catholic states of the Holy Roman Empire (Germany). In the early part of the war a Roman Catholic army put down a Protestant uprising in Bohemia (now part of Czechoslovakia). Two Protestant kings, Christian IV of Denmark and Gustavus Adolphus of Sweden, intervened, but with little success. France, although a Roman Catholic country, now entered the war on the Protestant side, because Cardinal Richelieu, the clever adviser of the French king, feared the growing power of the Habsburg family which ruled the Holy Roman Empire.

By 1648 Germany was devastated, with millions of people dead and cities, farms and homes destroyed. The Peace of Westphalia, which ended the war, gave territory to France and Sweden and left the Habsburgs controlling only the area around the Danube, the Tyrol, Bohemia, and northern Italy.

England and the Netherlands were the strongest sea powers in the 1600s, and together they prevented France from becoming too powerful. The French king Louis XIV ruled as a dictator, but when England's king Charles I had tried to do likewise he was opposed by Parliament, and civil war broke out. Charles was defeated and executed for 'treason against the people'. After a few years of so-called republican government the people welcomed the monarchy back, and Charles's son Charles II became king. Under Charles and his brother, James II, England became friendly with France and waged war on its old ally, the Netherlands. However, in 1689 there was a bloodless revolution and James was driven from the throne. His sister Mary became queen, sharing the throne

A painting of New Amsterdam, capital of the Dutch North American colonies, about 1653. Soon after, the English captured it – it is now New York City.

with her husband, William, ruler of the Netherlands, and France became an enemy again.

During the 1600s Russia became an important world power. It had a strong government, and the rich nobles had enormous power over millions of poor serfs – people who were little better than slaves. In 1682 Peter the Great became tsar (emperor). He visited England and the Netherlands to study their industries and their governments. Then he went home and introduced the modern ideas he had learned into Russia. Peter defeated the Swedes and gained a port for Russian trade on the Baltic Sea. He called it St Petersburg (it is now Leningrad) and made it Russia's capital.

European countries began to gain overseas empires in this period. In 1607 English settlers set up a colony at Jamestown, in North America. The following year the French explorer Samuel de Champlain founded Quebec. In 1620 a group of religious refugees, the Pilgrim Fathers, founded a colony at Plymouth, Massachusetts. English settlers set up further colonies in North America, and in 1664 they captured the Dutch settlement of New Amsterdam and renamed it New York. Other English settlers took over much of the West Indies.

In south-eastern Asia the Dutch East India Company and the English East India Company were the main rivals for trade and land. The Dutch occupied Indonesia and controlled the rich trade in spices, while the English company set up trading centres at several places on the coast of India.

Many new ideas in science and philosophy

appeared during the 1600s. The Italian astronomer Galileo Galilei offended the Roman Catholic Church by declaring that the Earth moves round the Sun instead of the Sun around the Earth – which was how the Church thought it moved. René Descartes, a French thinker, showed how people should study nature, by careful reasoning. Two great English scientists made important discoveries: Isaac Newton developed the law of gravity and explained how light travelled, while the physician William Harvey discovered how blood circulates through the body.

Above: The Russian Tsar Peter the Great when he was working as a ship's carpenter in England in 1697.

Below: A contemporary 'map-picture' showing the Battle of Naseby in 1645. This was a key battle in the English Civil Wars, and the defeat of King Charles I there cost him his throne, and later his life.

Wars and revolutions

During the 1700s the great nations of Europe strove to be the most powerful not only in their own continent but also in the Americas and Asia. In a conflict called the War of the Spanish Succession (1701–14) Britain, the Netherlands and much of the Holy Roman Empire defeated France and its allies. At the Peace of Utrecht in 1714 Britain gained Gibraltar, Minorca, Newfoundland and Nova Scotia.

War soon broke out again. Prussia had become the strongest state in Germany. Its king, Frederick I, the Great, had a very efficient army. France joined Prussia in an attack on Silesia, part of the Austrian empire. British and Dutch aid helped to save Austria, but not Silesia.

In the Seven Years' War (1756–63) England supported Prussia against France, Austria and Russia. Prussia just managed to avoid complete disaster. Britain was most successful, mainly at the expense of the French. While France's armies were occupied in Europe British forces attacked its possessions in North America, in what is called the French and Indian War. In 1759 the British general James Wolfe captured Quebec after a long siege.

Under the Peace of Paris France lost all its mainland possessions in America. Britain received Canada and all French land east of the Mississippi River, while Spain took French possessions west of the Mississippi. Britain also had successes in India, where Robert Clive won a great victory at Plassey in 1757. By the terms of the peace Britain gained most of India, and France kept only a few trading posts there.

Two great revolutions occurred in the late 1700s. The first was the breakaway of 13 of the British colonies in North America. It began because the colonists would not pay the heavy taxes that Britain expected. In 1776 the Declaration of Independence was proclaimed. General George Washington led his people to victory and the United States of America was born, with Washington as its first president.

The other rebellion was the French Revolution. The people of France, like the Americans, were tired of heavy taxation. They were also sick of

The American War of Independence stirred cartoonists to action, just as events do today. This cartoon marked the Peace of Paris which formally ended the war in 1783. As you can see, the cartoonist thought England's sun was setting – but within a hundred years England, as part of Britain, was at the heart of a bigger empire than the one it had just lost.

THE BLESSINGS OF PEACE.

Above: The Industrial Revolution which began in the 1700s involved no bloodshed or battles, but it changed the world more than any other revolution. This picture shows women and children in a spinning mill. Children used to help their parents at home – so they joined them in the factories when they were built.

Left: Today's badges proclaiming support for a pop star or a political cause had their 18th century counterparts in buttons. The one shown here commemorated the Fall of the Bastille in Paris in 1789, which was the start of the French Revolution.

wars. Louis XV (1710–74) had spent money extravagantly and under Louis XVI and his wife Marie Antoinette things got worse. The people revolted, executed the royal family and set up an elected assembly. In the so-called Reign of Terror thousands of people, mainly nobles, were killed. At last the people grew tired of disorder and welcomed as dictator a successful young general named Napoleon Bonaparte–later Emperor Napoleon I.

Another, more peaceful, revolution began in the late 1700s with the development of machines and steam engines to drive them. Factories were built which produced thousands of objects instead of just a few. The Industrial Revolution, as it is called, started in Britain and quickly spread through Europe and North America. Its effect was felt first in the textile industry. With new inventions workers could spin thread and weave cloth much more quickly and efficiently. James Watt, a Scottish engineer, built a successful steam engine in 1769, making possible the first railway in 1825. New ways of making iron were also developed.

A British navigator, James Cook, made three voyages to the South Pacific in the late 1700s. He mapped the coast of New Zealand, landed at Botany Bay in Australia and discovered many new lands. Soon Britain began to send people convicted of crimes to Australia as a punishment. The first convict settlement was set up in 1788, and transportation, as the punishment was called, continued for more than 60 years. In that time over 150,000 convicts were sent to Australia.

Constitutions and colonies

The French ruler Napoleon Bonaparte dominated Europe during the early 1800s. He crowned himself emperor in 1804, and won victories at Austerlitz and Jena over the coalition, or alliance, formed against him. Then he made the fatal mistake of invading Russia in 1812. He reached Moscow but lost many men in the severe winter cold. In 1813 the allied armies of Britain, Prussia, Austria and Russia defeated Napoleon at Leipzig, and the following year he abdicated and retired to the Mediterranean island of Elba. In 1815 he returned in triumph to rule France for a further hundred days until the British under the Duke of Wellington and the Prussians under Prince Gebhard von Blücher completely defeated him at Waterloo. He was imprisoned on the lonely island of St Helena, where he died six years later.

Between 1815 and the beginning of World War I in 1914 there were few serious conflicts between countries, but there were many revolutions. The poor industrial and agricultural workers wanted to improve their condition and gain some political power. Several revolutions took place in the same year, 1848. In Italy the Roman Republic was set up, but it did not last long and it was not until 1861 that the various states of Italy became a united country. Other revolutions took place in Austria, France and Germany but they had little lasting effect, except that France temporarily became a republic again.

The states of Germany came together as one country in 1871 under the leadership of Prussia and its prime minister, Otto von Bismarck. Prussia had just defeated France, and the other German states were eager to join this powerful country. Bismarck proved himself the cleverest statesman in Europe until he resigned in 1890. He formed several alliances, and hoped to keep Europe peaceful while Germany grew in power.

Most European countries during the 1800s introduced written constitutions – basic systems of laws which gave the people protection against injustice, and in many cases granted the right to vote. Even Russia, which was backward in many ways, received a constitution after a revolution in 1905. Even so, many people from all over Europe sailed to the United States to find a freer life.

By 1914 there were only three independent countries in Africa – Liberia, South Africa and Ethiopia. Britain, France, Italy, Germany, Spain, Portugal and Belgium had all set up colonies there. They grew rich on the trade the colonies brought, but did not give much to the people who lived in them. Some colonies were founded following the discoveries of great British explorers such as John Speke and David Livingstone. As a result of the Boer War (1899–1902) Britain took over the states in southern Africa that had been founded by Dutch settlers, who were known as Boers.

In the United States a bitter struggle broke out

between the industrial North and the rural South over the question of slavery. Many Southern states left the Union when Abraham Lincoln, who opposed slavery, became president. The North won the resulting civil war (1861–65) and slavery ended. Over the rest of the century the United States became more and more prosperous.

Spain and Portugal lost their vast American empires in the 1800s. Mexico gained its independence from Spain in 1821, while in South America the freedom fighter Simón Bolívar helped Bolivia, Colombia, Peru and Venezuela to gain their freedom from Spanish rule also.

In Asia China was compelled to open five ports to British traders. Japan, too, opened its ports to foreign trade, became powerful and fought successful wars against China and Russia. The French took over Indo-China in south-eastern Asia, and Spain gave the Philippine Islands to the United States. Australia's population increased rapidly. The states remained colonies of Britain until 1901 when they united to form the Commonwealth of Australia.

Left: The Emperor Napoleon I reviewing his troops. With soldiers like these he made France and himself masters of most of Europe – but only for a while.

Below: The Battle of Fredericksburg in 1862 was one of many fierce encounters in the American Civil War. The South won it, but only to lose the war eventually.

Some of the soldiers who conquered an empire for the French in Algeria and other parts of Africa. The senior officers were French, all others Muslims.

World wars and after

'Over the Top', a dramatic painting of World War I, shows something of the suffering endured by the troops in that grim conflict. This attack from the trenches was made in the snow, but others were carried out in rain in a sea of shell-torn mud.

During the early 1900s quarrels between the great powers of Europe grew more bitter. Britain and France formed various alliances to protect themselves from the growing military strength of Germany. Only a spark was needed to start war. It came when the heir to the Austrian throne was shot by a student from Serbia (now part of Yugoslavia). Austria attacked Serbia; Russia, Serbia's ally, attacked Austria; and Germany, Austria's ally, attacked Russia and its ally, France, drawing Britain in as well. Bulgaria and Turkey backed Germany and Austria.

Most of the fighting took place on the Western Front in France and Belgium. Armies found it easier to defend than attack, and as a result there were fierce battles just to gain a few kilometres of muddy ground. The war was finally won in 1918 after the United States joined Britain and France. The Russians fought on the Eastern Front until a revolution overthrew the government of the tsar in 1917. About 15,000,000 people were killed in the war, soldiers and civilians.

The Russian Revolution brought the Bolsheviks to power, first under Vladimir Lenin and then under Joseph Stalin, under whose rule life remained harsh for many people.

Germany was heavily punished for the war,

losing all its colonies and some of its own land. The Germans became angry and bitter. Many were out of work, and the mark, the German currency, became so worthless that people had to take their week's wages home in wheelbarrows. As a result, Germans welcomed Adolf Hitler, leader of the Nazi Party, when he promised to restore their pride and power. Hitler became dictator in 1934. His great ally was Benito Mussolini, who had become dictator of Italy in 1922. The League of Nations (ancestor of the United Nations) was weak and did nothing to stop Hitler when he seized Austria and Czechoslovakia, but when he attacked Poland in 1939 Britain and France decided he must be stopped.

World War II was even more violent than World War I. Hitler's armies occupied most of Europe, including France. In 1941, unable to invade Britain, he attacked Russia, which proved to be as big a mistake as Napoleon's invasion back in 1812. The same year Japan began an all-out attempt to conquer an empire in eastern Asia, which brought the United States into the war. The run of German and Japanese successes came to an end in 1942. In 1943 the Russians began driving the Germans back, and in 1944 the British and Americans invaded France. In May 1945 Germany, crushed and with many of its cities in ruins, surrendered.

Japanese forces were also being driven back, but that part of the war was brought to an abrupt end when the Americans dropped two atomic bombs.

After World War II the Americans and Russians, who had been allies, grew to distrust each other, and a so-called 'Cold War' dragged on for many years. Most eastern European countries came under Communist rule and were allies of Russia. Even when the Cold War ended, scientific rivalry between Russia and the United States continued.

Colonial rule came to an end almost everywhere in the years after World War II. All African colonies became independent between 1951 and 1977. In 1947 the British left India, which split up (it is now India, Pakistan and Bangladesh). The Dutch East Indies became Indonesia, and French Indo-China split into the independent countries of Laos, Cambodia (Kampuchea), North Vietnam and South Vietnam. China, under the leadership of Mao Tse-tung, became Communist and grew into a world power.

The United Nations, to which nearly all countries belong has helped to keep the peace. Its peace-keeping forces have seen duty in Korea, Vietnam, the Middle East and in other parts of the world where local military conflicts have threatened to escalate into major wars.

This painting by Charles Cundall shows one of the most dramatic moments of World War II – the evacuation of British forces from the beaches at Dunkirk, under fire from German guns and planes. A fleet of little ships ferried the soldiers home to England.

One of the many Communist leaders who came to power after World War II is Kim Il-Sung of North Korea. As in China, posters like this are issued to honour the chairman and demonstrate unity.

177

Exploration
by land

The young Venetian merchant Marco Polo spent years exploring eastern Asia in the Middle Ages. When he returned to Italy people just did not believe all he told them. This illustration from a manuscript copy of his book exaggerates his stories more than he did.

Exploration has been a very important part of the world's history. It has led to the discovery of new lands, and the opening up of others. The great countries of Australia, New Zealand and the Americas all sprang from the work of explorers, and though those lands were discovered by sea, their secrets were found out by men trudging over-land through unknown and often dangerous country. Because there are few tracks in such terrain most exploration—until comparatively recent times—has been carried out on foot. In rare cases explorers have been able to use horses, camels or river boats to help them.

For thousands of years, when the Earth's population was small, men were exploring all the time. Exploration in the modern sense began in Asia, with the expedition of the Greek warrior-king Alexander the Great. He crossed Iran and Afghanistan to what is now Pakistan. Another important

explorer of Asia was a Buddhist monk from China, Hsüan-tsang. He crossed the great Gobi Desert of central Asia in the AD 600s, and came down through Afghanistan and over the mountains to India. Two European monks also explored Asia in the 1200s, John of Pian del Carpine and William of Rubruquis. The greatest explorer of the 1200s was Marco Polo, a young Venetian merchant, who went to the court of Kublai Khan at Peking with his father and uncle. A few years later Asia was further explored by a Muslim from Tangier, Ibn Battuta.

The exploration of North and South America began in the 1500s. At first it was carried out by Spanish *conquistadores*, bloodthirsty adventurers in search of gold and loot. They included Hernán Cortés, who conquered Mexico; Francisco Pizarro, who conquered Peru; and Vasco de Balboa, who was the first European to fight his way across the Isthmus of Panama and see the mighty Pacific

The Victoria Falls, called 'The Smoke that Thunders' by people living near it, was discovered by the Scottish missionary David Livingstone in 1855.

Ocean. Once colonisation began every settler was an explorer, moving always westwards into unknown territory. Among the greatest pioneers were René Cavalier, Sieur de la Salle, who explored the Mississippi River, and Alexander Mackenzie, who explored a large part of Canada. In 1804–1805 two American soldiers, Meriwether Lewis and William Clark, explored the north-western part of what is now the United States.

The early colonies of Australia lay along the south-east coast, and the way inland was barred by steep mountains. A farmer, Gregory Blaxland, found a way over the mountains to the fertile Bathurst Plains in 1813. An army officer and a surveyor, Charles Sturt and John Stuart, penetrated deep into the interior in the 1840s. The most daring expedition was that of Robert O'Hara Burke and William John Wills in 1860. They crossed Australia from south to north, but only one man of their party survived.

The exploration of Africa came fairly late. It was called the 'Dark Continent' because so little was known about it. The greatest of Africa's explorers was a Scottish missionary, David Livingstone. He crossed the Kalahari Desert, in southern Africa, and then set out to explore the Zambesi River, on which he discovered the Victoria Falls—known to the Africans living near it as Mosi-oa-Tunya, the Smoke that Thunders. In the 1860s Livingstone set out to find the sources of the Nile and Congo (Zaïre) rivers. He found Lake Tanganyika, but died soon after. Henry Morton Stanley, a journalist who was sent to look for Livingstone, later travelled all the way down the Congo. A British soldier, John Hanning Speke, discovered the source of the Nile–Lake Victoria–in 1862.

Exploration of the polar regions came in the 1900s. Robert Peary, an American naval officer, sledged across the ice to reach the North Pole in 1909. Two years later the South Pole was conquered by the Norwegian traveller Roald Amundsen–a few weeks ahead of a British party led by Robert Falcon Scott. Amundsen returned to base just before bad weather set in. Scott and his party were caught in a blizzard, and died less than 18 km. (11 mi.) from safety.

Below left: Three explorers meet at the South Pole in 1958: Rear Admiral George Dufek of the United States, Sir Edmund Hillary of New Zealand, and Dr. (now Sir) Vivian Fuchs of Britain.

Below: A 'Snocat' vehicle, on the same expedition, which nearly vanished into a deep crack in the ice.

Exploration by sea

The first sea explorers about whom we know much were the Phoenicians, who lived along the coast at the eastern end of the Mediterranean Sea. They were great traders, and their ships plied everywhere in the Mediterranean. There is a tradition that about 600 BC a Phoenician fleet set sail from the Mediterranean coast of Egypt and travelled right round Africa, returning to Egypt up the Red Sea. The voyage took them three years. Three hundred years later a Greek, Pytheas of Massilia (Marseille), sailed northwards out of the Mediterranean, up the English Channel to Britain, and further north into a region of fog and cold to an island he called Thule – probably Iceland or perhaps a Norwegian island. Next in the story of sea exploration came the Vikings, a fierce, bold race of warriors and pirates, who sailed from their Scandinavian homeland to raid the coasts of Europe, and colonised Iceland and Greenland. About the year 1000 one Viking, Biarni Heriulfsson, was driven west of Greenland by a storm and sighted land. Two years later an expedition led by Leif Ericsson sailed to look for this land, and reached North America.

Trade caused the next great exploration. People in Europe imported spices from the islands of south-east Asia, which were carried overland at great expense. The Portuguese set out to find a sea route to the Indies around Africa. Their ventures required great courage because many people

An early primitive painting showing Christopher Columbus arriving in the Bahamas.

This contemporary painting by John Cleveley shows
the death of the British explorer Captain James Cook.
He was killed in Hawaii in a scuffle with some of the
local people, who had been accused of pilfering.

thought the Earth was flat, and sailors feared they
would fall off the edge or be roasted alive by the
heat of the Sun. While Portuguese sailors were
gradually creeping further and further south and
east along the coast of Africa, an Italian from
Genoa, Christopher Columbus, who did realise
that the Earth was round, thought of trying to
reach the Indies the other way by sailing westward.
Financed by the king and queen of Spain, he set
sail in August 1492 with three little ships—the
biggest 35·5 metres (116 feet) long. After three weeks
he reached land, and thought he had found Japan.
In fact he had rediscovered America, Leif Ericsson's epic voyage having been forgotten long before.
Columbus actually reached the West Indies, but

soon other explorers found the great continent
beyond, which was named America after one of
them, Amerigo Vespucci.

However, America barred the westward route to
the Indies, and sailors spent a long time trying to
find a way round. The first person to do so was
Ferdinand Magellan, a Portuguese navigator. He
discovered the Magellan Strait to the south of
America, and sailed for the first time into the
Pacific Ocean. Magellan and many of his men died
on the voyage, but one ship with 18 survivors
aboard sailed right across the Pacific and back to
Europe by way of Africa—the first men to circum-
navigate the globe. Attempts to find a northern
route, the North-West Passage, ended in disaster,
until the Norwegian, Roald Amundsen—who later
conquered the South Pole—battled his way through
the ice in 1903–1906.

Later explorers spent much time looking for a
great southern continent, which they thought
must exist. The Dutch navigator Willem Jansz
sighted Australia in 1606, while another Dutchman,
Abel Janszoon Tasman, discovered Tasmania, New
Zealand, Tonga and Fiji in 1642–1643. The final,
thorough exploration of the southern Pacific was
carried out in the 1770s by an English navigator,
James Cook. He mapped the coasts of New Zealand
and eastern Australia, and proved finally that the
great southern continent did not exist.

Modern sea exploration is mostly under water.
Among present-day explorers is the Swiss scientist
Jacques Piccard, who descended 10,900 metres
(35,800 ft.) into the Mariana Trench, the deepest
part of the Pacific Ocean, in 1960. He used a kind of
submarine called a bathyscaphe. The French diver
Jacques-Yves Cousteau has spent a lot of time
exploring shallower parts of the sea bed.

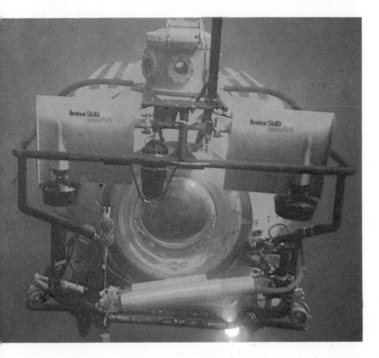

Modern underwater exploration is carried out by divers
in fairly shallow water but in deeper water miniature
submarines like this one are used. They carry two or three
men with supplies for a week.

Exploration in space

Man's exploration of space began thousands of years ago, when people used to gaze up at the heavens and wonder what the stars were, and if they were more than just lights in a great black dome overhead. With nothing except their own eyes to help them, astronomers discovered the existence of the planets, which moved, and the so-called 'fixed' stars, which moved so slowly they seemed to be standing still. The first telescopes were invented in the early 1600s, and with their aid the great Italian Galileo Galilei discovered the mountains on the Moon, the satellites of the planet Jupiter and Saturn's rings.

Gradually astronomers found out more and more about the rest of the universe. Aviators in balloons and aeroplanes soared great distances above the Earth's surface. Yet man's venture into space outside the Earth's atmosphere began as recently as 1957. On October 4 that year Russian scientists sent the first artificial satellite, *Sputnik 1*, into orbit, a small sphere weighing only 84 kilogrammes. The second satellite, *Sputnik 2*, launched four weeks later, carried a dog named Laika–the first living thing to go into space.

During the next three years Russian and American teams sent many more satellites into orbit around the Earth, hurling them clear of the Earth's gravity with the aid of powerful rockets. These rockets were originally developed as weapons carrying high explosives during World War II. The first man into space was a Russian cosmonaut, Yuri Gagarin. He made one complete orbit of the Earth on 12 April, 1961.

Soon afterwards the American President John F. Kennedy announced that the Americans would put a man on the Moon by 1970. In a series of daring space flights American astronauts made flight after flight around the Earth, spending longer and longer in space and learning all the time how to fly their strange new craft. Meanwhile the Russians sent an unmanned spacecraft all the way to the Moon in 1966. It landed safely and sent back television pictures of the Moon's surface.

In order to land on the Moon and take off again the Americans built the Lunar Module. This small spacecraft could be carried close to the Moon on a larger spacecraft, detach, and fly down to the Moon and back to its mother-craft. Then came the

This drawing of the late 1800s shows the Italian astronomer Galileo demonstrating his telescope to the rulers of Venice. Galileo's views on astronomy got him into trouble with the Church: the Pope and his cardinals thought they contradicted the Bible.

first real venture: in December 1968 three men aboard spacecraft Apollo 8 flew in a great loop around the Moon and back to Earth. They were the first men to see the back of the Moon.

Two more trial missions followed: Apollo 9 tested the flying of the Lunar Module in orbit around the Earth, while Apollo 10 tried out a module in a flight going very close to the Moon's surface. Then came the first Moon flight, Apollo 11. On 20 July 1969 a lunar module, code named Eagle, landed on the Moon, and astronaut Neil A. Armstrong became the first man to set foot on its dry, dusty surface. He was accompanied by Edwin E. Aldrin.

Five more Moon landings were made, the last in December 1972. On the last three trips astronauts drove electric buggies over the Moon's surface.

Since the ending of the Apollo Moon missions Russian and American space programmes have concentrated on setting up orbiting space laboratories, from which astronauts can be ferried back to Earth by 'space shuttle' craft. On 11th January 1978 the Russians became the first to link two spacecraft with an orbiting laboratory, while the Americans were the first, in 1981, to make more than one flight in a re-usable space shuttle. They have also sent unmanned spacecraft to fly close to Mars and Jupiter, and to land on Mars and Venus. These spacecraft have sent TV pictures back to Earth.

Above: The Russians issued this stamp in 1957 to commemorate the launching of Sputnik 1, the first spacecraft. It shows the craft orbiting the Earth.

Below: The American lunar module 'Eagle' made the first manned landing on the Moon in 1969 – only 12 years after the launching of the first spacecraft.

FINGERTIP FACTS IN HISTORY

BRITISH KINGS AND QUEENS

Saxon and Danish rulers

Egbert	802–839
Ethelwulf	839–858
Ethelbald	858–860
Ethelbert	860–865
Ethelred I	865–871
Alfred the Great	871–899
Edward the Elder	899–924
Athelstan	924–939
Edmund	939–946
Edred	946–955
Edwig	955–959
Edgar the Peaceful	959–975
Edward the Martyr	975–978
Ethelred II, the Redeless	978–1016
Edmund Ironside	1016
Canute	1016–1035
Harold I, Harefoot	1035–1040
Hardicanute	1040–1042
Edward the Confessor	1042–1066
Harold II	1066

The Normans and their successors

William I, the Conqueror	1066–1087
William II, Rufus	1087–1100
Henry I, Beauclerc	1100–1135
Stephen	1135–1154
Henry II	1154–1189
Richard I, Coeur-de-Lion	1189–1199
John, Lackland	1199–1216
Henry III	1216–1272
Edward I	1272–1307
Edward II	1307–1327
Edward III	1327–1377
Richard II	1377–1399
Henry IV	1399–1413
Henry V	1413–1422
Henry VI	1422–1461
Edward IV	1461–1483
Edward V	1483
Richard III, Crookback	1483–1485
Henry VII	1485–1509
Henry VIII	1509–1547
Edward VI	1547–1553
Mary I	1553–1558
Elizabeth I	1558–1603
James I (VI of Scotland)	1603–1625
Charles I	1625–1649
The Commonwealth	1649–1660
Charles II	1660–1685
James II	1685–1688
William III and Mary II (Mary died 1694)	1689–1702
Anne	1702–1714
George I	1714–1727
George II	1727–1760
George III	1760–1820
George IV	1820–1830
William IV	1830–1837
Victoria	1837–1901
Edward VII	1901–1910
George V	1910–1936
Edward VIII	1936
George VI	1936–1952
Elizabeth II	1952–

Scottish rulers

Malcolm II	1005–1034
Duncan I	1034–1040
Macbeth	1040–1057
Lulach	1057
Malcolm III, Canmore	1058–1093
Donald Bane	1093–1094
Duncan II	1094
Donald Bane	1094–1097
Edgar	1097–1107
Alexander I	1107–1124
David I	1124–1153
Malcolm IV, the Maiden	1153–1165
William I, the Lion	1165–1214
Alexander II	1214–1249
Alexander III	1249–1286
Margaret, the Maid of Norway	1286–1290
John Balliol	1292–1296
Robert I, the Bruce	1306–1329
David II	1329–1371
Robert II	1371–1390
Robert III	1390–1406
James I	1406–1437
James II	1437–1460
James III	1460–1488
James IV	1488–1513
James V	1513–1542
Mary, Queen of Scots	1542–1567
James VI	1567–1625

TWENTY MEN WHO CHANGED THE COURSE OF HISTORY

Alexander the Great (356–323 BC), King of Macedonia, set out to conquer the world. He subdued Greece, Palestine, Egypt and Persia and invaded India, but died of fever at the age of 32.

Augustus (63 BC–AD 14) became Rome's first emperor in 27 BC. His real name was Octavius, and 'Augustus' was a title meaning 'exalted'. He made the Roman Empire strong and brought it peace.

Simón Bolívar (1783–1830) was a soldier and statesman who led wars of independence in South America against the rule of Spain. He became known as *El Libertador* – 'the liberator'.

The **Buddha** (c. 563–c. 483 BC) was an Indian philosopher. Originally a prince named Siddhartha, he became a great preacher and teacher, and was given the name of the Buddha, the 'enlightened one'. His teachings form the basis of Buddhism.

Christopher Columbus (1451–1506) was an Italian seaman whose real name was Cristoforo Colombo. While he was in the service of the King of Spain he set out to find a sea route to India by sailing west, and so discovered America.

Confucius (c. 551–479 BC) was a Chinese philosopher, real name K'ung Fu-tzu. He taught people how to live a good life. His teachings form the basis of the Chinese religion Confucianism.

Albert Einstein (1879–1955) was one of the greatest scientists. He evolved the Theory of Relativity, and also established the relation between mass and energy which helped to make atomic power possible.

Mohandas Gandhi (1869–1948) was an Indian nationalist who devoted his life to winning independence for India from British rule. His religious views earned him the title 'Mahatma' – 'great soul'.

Genghis Khan (1162–1227), a Mongol chief, united all the Mongols under his rule and conquered China, Korea, and other parts of Asia.

Adolf Hitler (1889–1945) became dictator of Germany in 1933. His ambition and his hatred for Jews led him to try to conquer Europe. This brought on World War II. Millions of Jews were killed under his orders.

PRESIDENTS OF THE UNITED STATES

Name	Political Party	Years in Office	Name	Political Party	Years in Office
George Washington	Federalist	1789–1797	Rutherford B. Hayes	Republican	1877–1881
John Adams	Federalist	1797–1801	James A. Garfield	Republican	1881
Thomas Jefferson	Democratic-Republican	1801–1809	Chester A. Arthur	Republican	1881–1885
James Madison	Democratic-Republican	1809–1817	Grover Cleveland	Democrat	1885–1889
James Monroe	Democratic-Republican	1817–1825	Benjamin Harrison	Republican	1889–1893
John Quincy Adams	Democratic-Republican	1825–1829	Grover Cleveland	Democrat	1893–1897
Andrew Jackson	Democrat	1829–1837	William McKinley	Republican	1897–1901
Martin Van Buren	Democrat	1837–1841	Theodore Roosevelt	Republican	1901–1909
William H. Harrison	Whig	1841	William H. Taft	Republican	1909–1913
John Tyler	Whig	1841–1845	Woodrow Wilson	Democrat	1913–1921
James K. Polk	Democrat	1845–1849	Warren G. Hardin	Republican	1921–1923
Zachary Taylor	Whig	1849–1850	Calvin Coolidge	Republican	1923–1929
Millard Fillmore	Whig	1850–1853	Herbert C. Hoover	Republican	1929–1933
Franklin Pierce	Democrat	1853–1857	Franklin D. Roosevelt	Democrat	1933–1945
James Buchanan	Democrat	1857–1861	Harry S. Truman	Democrat	1945–1953
Abraham Lincoln	Republican	1861–1865	Dwight D. Eisenhower	Republican	1953–1961
Andrew Johnson	Democrat	1865–1869	John F. Kennedy	Democrat	1961–1963
Ulysses S. Grant	Republican	1869–1877	Lyndon B. Johnson	Democrat	1963–1969
			Richard M. Nixon	Republican	1969–1974
			Gerald R. Ford	Republican	1974–1977
			James E. Carter	Democrat	1977–1980
			Ronald Regan	Republican	1980–

BRITISH PRIME MINISTERS OF THE TWENTIETH CENTURY

Name	Political Party	Years in Office	Name	Political Party	Years in Office
Arthur J. Balfour	Conservative	1902–1905	Winston S. Churchill	Coalition	1940–1945
Sir H. C-Bannerman	Liberal	1905–1908	Winston S. Churchill	Conservetive	1945
Herbert Henry Asquith	Liberal	1908–1915	Clement R. Attlee	Labour	1945–1951
Herbert Henry Asquith	Coalition	1915–1916	Winston S. Churchill	Conservative	1951–1955
David Lloyd George	Coalition	1916–1922	Sir Anthony Eden	Conservative	1955–1957
Andrew Bonar Law	Conservative	1922–1923	Harold Macmillan	Conservative	1957–1963
Stanley Baldwin	Conservative	1923–1924	Sir Alec Douglas-Home	Conservative	1963–1964
J. Ramsay MacDonald	Labour	1924	Harold Wilson	Labour	1964–1970
Stanley Baldwin	Conservative	1924–1929	Edward Heath	Conservative	1970–1974
J. Ramsay MacDonald	Labour	1929–1931	Harold Wilson	Labour	1974–1976
J. Ramsay MacDonald	Coalition	1931–1935	James Callaghan	Labour	1976–1979
Stanley Baldwin	Coalition	1935–1937	Margaret Thatcher	Conservative	1979–
Neville Chamberlain	Coalition	1937–1940			

Jesus of Nazareth (c. 6BC–c. AD 30) is regarded by Christians as the Son of God and the Saviour of mankind. He was a great healer, and his teachings emphasized the love of God. A Jew, his name in Hebrew was Joshua; Jesus is the Greek form. He was accused of blasphemy and crucified.

Vladimir Lenin (1870–1924) was a Russian statesman who led the communist revolution in Russia in 1917. He founded the modern Soviet Union. His name was originally Vladimir Ulyanov.

Abraham Lincoln (1809–1865) was the 16th president of the United States. He led his country during the civil war of 1861–1865, and helped to end slavery in the United States.

Mao Tse-tung (1893–1976), Chinese Communist leader, made his country a Communist state in 1949, and worked to modernize and reform it.

Karl Marx (1818–1883) was a German politician and thinker who was the main founder of modern Communism.

Muhammad (570–632) was an Arab merchant who felt he must do something to help his people. He became a prophet and teacher, and founded the religion of Islam. His teachings are recorded in the *Koran*, the holy book of Islam.

Napoleon I (1769–1821) was a Corsican soldier (original name Napoleon Bonaparte) who became Emperor of France and set out to conquer Europe. He was overthrown in 1815 and spent the rest of his life in exile.

Franklin Delano Roosevelt (1882–1945) was the 32nd president of the United States. He served for 12 years during which he led his country out of a great financial depression and almost to victory in World War II. He was crippled by polio.

George Washington (1732–1799) commanded the United States army in the American War of Independence, and became his country's first president in 1789.

William I the Conqueror (1027–1087), Duke of Normandy in France, invaded and conquered England in 1066, making England a powerful country.

Sports and games

Sports and games are physical activities which people indulge in because they enjoy them. Some sports, such as football or cricket, are professional–people get paid for playing, at top levels at least. Others, such as athletics and swimming, are amateur–people take part without payment. Paid or unpaid, team or individual, all sports have one thing in common: people striving to do better, better than they have done themselves, better than other people can do.

Athletics

Athletics–track and field to Americans–is a mixture of different activities which can be organised on or around a running track. The sport includes running, walking, jumping, throwing, and all-round contests for both men and women.

The sprints–the 100, 200, and 400 metres events–are races for the fastest runners. A good start is vital, so the runners press their feet against starting blocks. The 100 metres race is run along a straight course. The 200 and 400 metres races include the curves of the track. A standard athletics track is 400 metres round.

Middle-distance running is the basis of the sport. The standard Olympic Games events–the 800, 1,500, 5,000 and 10,000 metres races for men and 800, 1,500, and 3,000 metres races for women–give both runners and spectators a chance to get involved in tactical and personal battles. Because of this, many of the athletes specializing in these events have become the best known.

Long-distance races normally take place on

Above left: Throwing the hammer. The competitor whirls around inside a marked circle.

Above: The high jump. Many different methods are used to clear the bar. Here the competitor successfully uses the flop technique.

Left: Mary Peters of Northern Ireland winning a 100-metres hurdles event in 1973.

roads, rather than on athletics tracks. As a rule only men take part in them. The length of these races extends from a few kilometres through the marathon (the Olympic event of 42·195 kilometres) to ultra-long races of over 80 kilometres. Cross-country running, with distances of up to 16 kilometres, is popular during winter months. It has some link with another sport, orienteering, which is basically cross-country running following a map over unknown ground.

Hurdles events are in two forms. The sprints – 110 and 400 metres for men, 100 and 400 metres for women – are run over collapsible barriers. The 3,000 metres steeplechase has more solid obstacles. It is a race for very strong male runners only.

Of the jumping events, the high jump and long jump are for both men and women. The pole vault is for men only. So is the triple jump, which is also known as the hop, step and jump.

In the throwing events competitors have to see how far they can throw an object. The javelin is a kind of spear, while the shot is a solid metal ball, something like the shot which used to be fired from cannon years ago. The discus is a smooth, round wood-and-metal disc. Both men and women can throw the javelin, shot, and discus, but women use lighter ones than men. The other object used in throwing events is the hammer. Originally a sledgehammer was thrown, but today a heavy metal ball on the end of a long steel wire is used. Only men compete in the hammer-throwing events.

There are two all-round competitions, in which the athletes have to complete several different events. The men's all-round competition consists of 10 events – four races, three jumps, and throwing the discus, shot and javelin. It is called the decathlon, from two Greek words meaning 'ten contests'. The women's competition has five events, and is called a pentathlon. The events are two races, two jumps, and putting (throwing) the shot. In the all-round competitions competitors are awarded points for each event. The athlete with the most points at the end of all the events wins.

Bat and ball games

Many games are played in which a ball is hit by a bat or a stick. They include cricket and the related games of baseball, softball and rounders; hockey and similar games such as hurling and shinty; and lacrosse, in which the ball is caught and thrown by a stick with a net on the end of it. Of all these games the two of greatest international importance are cricket and baseball.

Cricket is the traditional English summer sport, and it is played widely in most parts of the Commonwealth. The main cricketing countries are England, Australia, New Zealand, India, Pakistan, the West Indies as a group, and South Africa. The game is generally played by men, but there are a few women's teams.

Two teams play against one another, one batting while the other fields. The batsmen have to score runs–counted by running between the wickets– and do this by striking the ball away from the fielders, while the fielding side must either catch the ball or hit a wicket to get the batsmen out. A catch has to be taken after the batsman hits the ball and before the ball bounces.

The pitch measures 22 yards (20 metres) from one wicket to the other. A wicket is three stumps with crosspieces (the bails) balanced on them. Several of the fielding team act as bowlers; they bowl the

ball by swinging the arm over, but must not throw the ball with the elbow bent. Some bowlers make the ball move fast, others spin it so that it bounces awkwardly. Much of the skill is in trying to make the batsman hit the ball towards the places where fieldsmen have been stationed. One fieldsman stands behind the wicket and is called the wicket-keeper. He and the batsmen wear protective clothing of leg pads and gloves. Play is from alternate ends: each bowler bowls six balls, and then play changes ends and another bowler bowls.

A batsman can also be out if he blocks the ball with his pads, or steps outside his defensive position, when a fieldsman may hit the stumps with the ball and stump him. The batsmen do not need to run if the ball crosses the boundary of the field, scoring four runs if the ball runs along the ground, or six if it sails through the air.

A match is divided into innings (turns to play). The most important matches are Test Matches between countries, and the next most important are county or state matches inside a country.

Baseball developed from cricket and from the children's game rounders. It was first played in its present form about 1846 – cricket is about 500 years older. It is popular in Australia, Japan and Central America, but it is the United States game, with its World Series, that is the most important.

Baseball is played between two teams of nine men on a 90-foot (27-metre) infield called the diamond, with a large outfield. There is a base at each corner of the diamond, and the batter stands at one of these bases, called the home plate. The pitcher throws the ball from a mound in the middle of the diamond. To score a run the batter must hit the ball through the infield and run all round the bases, one or more at a time. A home run is scored when the hitter gets round all four bases in one hit. Otherwise he has to wait at one of the bases until the next batter scores a hit, when he can run on.

Each game is made up of nine innings. There is no wicket, but a pitcher must throw the ball over the home plate. The batter is out if the ball is caught, or if he is run out, or tagged by a fielder with a ball. An innings is closed when three batters are out. Protective clothing is worn by the catcher, who stands behind the batter, and each fielder may wear one glove for catching.

The World Series is a championship play-off between the winners of the two great U.S. leagues – the National League and the American League – who play a best-of-seven series. 'Little leagues' cater for players aged eight and upwards.

A contrast in styles between the world's two greatest bat and ball games. On the left, cricketer Tony Greig, in the Sussex team, plays down and forward to a slow ball. The wicket keeper stands just behind the stumps, ready to make a catch. On the right, baseball striker Bobby Valentine, playing for the Californian team San Diego Padres, swings high and back ready to meet a fierce pitch. Generally speaking, baseball is a much faster game than cricket.

Football

Football in its various forms is the most popular sporting pastime in the world, and is played in almost every country. Rugby, Gaelic, Australian rules, American and Canadian football have areas of local interest, but association football is the only kind that is played world wide. It is rapidly gaining popularity in the United States.

Association football, usually called soccer or just 'football', has its roots deep in history. The Chinese, Japanese, Greeks and Romans played games with footballs, and in 1314 the English king Edward II declared the game illegal in cities. The first rules were drawn up in 1846, but local variations remained until the English Football Association (FA) was formed in 1863. Football was then an amateur game centred on big private schools and the universities of Oxford and Cambridge. In 1885 the FA first allowed professionals to play. The game quickly spread to other countries, and in 1904 an international organisation was formed–the Fédération Internationale de Football Association (FIFA). It still controls the game.

Football is a team game, each team being made up of 11 men with one or sometimes two substitutes allowed. The game is controlled by a referee and two linesmen. Each team is made up of a goalkeeper, defensive players (backs), midfield players and

Top: Rugby football is a fast, tough game. This is an international match between Wales and Japan.

Above: A scene during a World Cup match between Scotland and Zaïre. By contrast to rugby, the players in soccer games must not handle the ball.

forwards. Soccer is played on a pitch about 100 by 70 metres (110 by 75 yards). The goals measure 7·3 metres wide by 2·4 metres high (24 ft. by 8 ft.). The game lasts 90 minutes, divided into two halves of 45 minutes, with additional time for injuries and other stoppages. The game starts with a toss-up, the winner having the choice of ends and the loser kicking off. A kick-off also restarts the second half and is taken after each goal. Teams change ends at half time, so that neither has an advantage.

The rules are simple, but sometimes difficult for referees and players to follow. The most important rule is that the ball may be played with any part of the body except the hands and arms. The goalkeeper is the only player allowed to handle the ball.

When the ball goes out of play behind the goal line a goal kick is taken if the attacking side last touched the ball: if the defending side put the ball behind, then a corner kick is taken. If the ball goes out at the side of the field a throw-in is taken. Fouls on the field are punished with a free kick. If a foul occurs within the penalty area—a region near each goal—a direct free kick or penalty may be given. Repeated foul play or a major foul make a player liable to be sent off the field.

Football's major international competition is the World Cup, held every four years since 1930 except 1942 and 1946, during World War II. This competition and the European Championship are competitions for national teams. The major annual European club competitions are the European Cup (for national league winners), the European Cup Winners Cup (for winners of national knock-out competitions such as the FA Cup), and the UEFA (Union of European Football Associations) Cup. Most national football is organised along the British pattern, with league and cup competitions.

Association football is unique in the football world because the use of the hands is banned. In other games the ball is oval (except for Gaelic) and handling is allowed. The most important handling game, rugby union, is an amateur 15-a-side game played in every continent, though principally in Europe, South Africa and Australasia. Rugby league is its professional counterpart, with 13-man teams. The rules are slightly different.

American football, played between two heavily padded 11-a-side teams, is related to rugby, as is the 12-a-side Canadian football.

Australian rules football, played almost exclusively in Australia on an oval field up to 183 metres long between teams of 18 men, is a fast and furious game. It incorporates some elements of Gaelic football, in which fisting and kicking the ball are allowed, but throwing is not.

In American football the players wear heavy protective clothing – a helmet and face mask, padding on the shoulders, body and legs, and shin guards. A full team can consist of as many as 40 members, but not more than 11 can be on the field of play. Teams change players according to whether they are attacking or defending, or for injury.

Court games

Games played on courts divide into two types: those played over a net, such as tennis, and those played against a wall, such as squash. The basic idea common to all these games is to hit a ball (or a shuttle) with a racket or the hand so that one's opponent cannot return the ball or is forced into making an error.

Lawn tennis is the most popular court game with a net. It is increasingly played on surfaces other than a grass lawn, such as wood, tarmac, shale and all-weather courts. The game evolved from 'royal' or 'long' tennis, popular with the nobility hundreds of years ago (England's King Henry VIII was a keen player). Lawn tennis, originally called sphairistiké, was first played in 1872. It proved popular, and in 1877 the first championships were played at Wimbledon on the lawns of the All England Croquet Club. A number of different rules were combined, and today's vary only a little from those in use then. In particular, the size of the court (26 by 9 yards; 23 by 8 metres), the scoring system derived from royal tennis (the points of love, 15, 30, 40 and advantage), the division of the match into sets and games and the allowing of one service fault without penalty, were fixed in 1877 and remain in force today.

Tennis was originally an amateur game. Though this is still largely true, tennis has become so commercial that few amateurs remain at the top level. Prize money is plentiful and sponsors generous. Top players travel the world.

The rules of tennis are complex. The basic idea is that each player serves alternate games. A game is won by the first player to reach four points and be two points clear. The first point is 15, the second 30, the third 40, and the fourth either 'game' or advantage. If each player has one point the score is 15-all, then 30-all, but 40-all is 'deuce', from the French *quarante à deux*. Thereafter, the score is in games: the first player to win at least six games and be two games clear wins a set. Usually the best of three sets decides the match, but some men's matches are the best of five sets.

Tennis is played in three forms: in men's and women's singles; men's and women's doubles; and mixed doubles.

Games having a strong affinity with tennis include table tennis, badminton (very similar to tennis but played with a higher net and a shuttle instead of a ball), and the team game volleyball.

Squash rackets is the king of a whole family of

Left: Players such as America's Jimmy Connors, one of the stars of tennis in the 1970s, make big money from their game, but they have to travel to all the big tournaments of the world to stay at the top.

Right: A thrilling moment in the final of the women's volleyball event at the 1972 Olympic Games in Munich, West Germany. A Russian team beat a Japanese team.

games played with a ball against a wall. In essence the game resembles tennis, but instead of a net there is a wall with a tin 'telltale' along the bottom. The ball is out of play if it hits the telltale, which makes a loud clang when struck.

Squash matches are normally decided on the best of five games. A game is won by the first player to score nine points. The server keeps the serve as long as he wins points. The receiver cannot score a point, but must first win the service point from the server before he begins scoring.

In the Spanish-speaking world pelota games are popular. In jai alai, or pelota vasca, each player has a wicker basket on his hand instead of holding a racket. With this he can propel the ball at speeds up to 240 kph (150 mph). The courts have three walls and a clear screen through which spectators can watch. Another game of the squash family is court handball, in which the players strike the ball with a gloved hand. There may be one, two, three or four walls in a handball court. Some forms of handball are known as fives, and are named after three well-known English boys' schools where they were first played – Eton, Rugby and Winchester. Paddleball is a similar game, but the players use paddles, bats like large table-tennis bats.

Below: Squash rackets, played on an enclosed court, is a fast and furious game. The game is played in more than 30 countries and is particularly popular in Britain – where it originated – Australia, Canada and the United States.

Road and track sports

Motor-cycling is a very personal sport – the rider feels at one with his machine, just as a jockey does with his horse. In this picture Britain's Barry Sheene comes into a corner at speed. Japanese machines dominate the sport today.

Since bicycles and cars were invented their owners have felt obliged to race against each other. At first the public roads were the scene of such contests. Later circuits were built especially for this purpose. Although motor racing circuits resemble roads, they have special safety features included. Cycling, being slower, can happily adapt itself to public roads, but also takes place on small oval tracks.

The first race between motor-cars took place in 1895, only a few years after the first machines were built. It soon became too dangerous to race on roads not especially prepared for racing, and the rules of motor sports are continually being changed to protect the lives of drivers and spectators.

Today motor racing is almost universal and is big business in Europe and the Americas. The rules of the sport divide races among various groups of cars, ranging from ordinary production vehicles to the refined Formula One or grand prix car, which can cost hundreds of thousands of pounds to design and construct.

A series of grand prix races is held all through the year in different countries. This series constitutes the World Drivers' Championship. The series was started in 1950, and was at first dominated by the great Argentine driver Juan Fangio, who won in 1951 and 1954–57, though Commonwealth drivers were more successful in the 1960s and 1970s.

Sports car racing is the next most important branch of motor racing, and it has a world championship run on similar lines to the grand prix circuit. Two of motor sport's most important events are for sports cars: the Le Mans 24 hours race in France, and the tough 792-kilometre (492-mile) Targa Florio race in Sicily.

Another famous motoring event is the Monte Carlo rally, the classic event of this branch of the sport. In rallying the idea is to cover a certain distance partly over public roads, in a particular time. Some rallies, like the East African Safari and the London-Sydney run, are brutally tough, even though technique and the ability to finish are more important than sheer speed.

Motor-cycles raced against the early motor-cars until this mixture became too perilous. Since 1903 motor cycling has been a separate sport. Its format roughly follows that of motor racing, and its world championship, fought out on similar lines, has been contested since 1949. The world championship, with five classes dependent on engine capacity, is the pinnacle of the sport, but moto cross (scrambling), grass track racing, trials riding and motor-cycle speedway each has its supporters.

Cycling has as many variations as the motorized road sports, but in addition has a specialized track

section. Cycle races range from the three-week long Tour de France, a multi-stage road race, to the last explosive 200-metre section of the tactical 1,000-metre sprint on the track. Continental Europe is where the sport is taken most seriously, as the successes of French, Italian, Belgian and Spanish riders show.

Track racing itself takes many forms. The sprint races are perhaps the most fascinating, though the kilometre time trial and pursuit events (individual and team) are equally enthralling. These are Olympic and world championship events. Six-day racing is immensely popular, and track meets feature many other variations.

Road racing takes two forms. In time trials cyclists ride solo against the clock over various distances. Hill climb trials too are popular. Road racing takes place on traffic-free roads and develops into long solo chases culminating in massed sprints at the finishing tape.

Left: Niki Lauda, one of the world's ace drivers, in car No. 11, takes the lead in the Swedish Grand Prix. Skill and courage are necessary in the sport.

Below: In track racing, cyclists ride stripped-down machines without mudguards or brakes, but with fixed-wheel gearing. For road events they ride on specially-built machines of more orthodox design.

Water sports

Sports in and on water are popular wherever there is sufficient water to allow them. Swimming—for pleasure or competition—is universal, and where there are boats, there too will be sport—sailing, rowing, canoeing and water-skiing.

Competitive swimming is a modern sport, but in Japan it is said to have been practised in 36 BC. Today, a swimming 'meet' at any level is made up of five basic disciplines. In freestyle swimming the swimmer can use any stroke to make progress, but the front crawl stroke is the most popular. Back-stroke is merely swimming on the back, but here again the back crawl stroke is most effective. Then there are two strokes in which the arms and legs move simultaneously and symmetrically: breast-stroke, in which the arms move under water; and butterfly, in which part of the arm movement is made above the water. The fifth discipline is the medley, races made up of an equal distance swimming with each stroke in turn.

The standard programme of events for world championships and other major meets is: freestyle: 100, 200, 400, 800 (women), and 1,500 metres (men), and 4 × 100 (women); and 4 × 200 metres (men) relays; breast-stroke, butterfly and backstroke: 100 and 200 metres; individual medley: 200 and 400 metres, and 4 × 100 metres medley relay. Competitions right down to schools level follow roughly this format, with reduced distances.

The International Swimming Federation governs world amateur swimming. As well as competitive

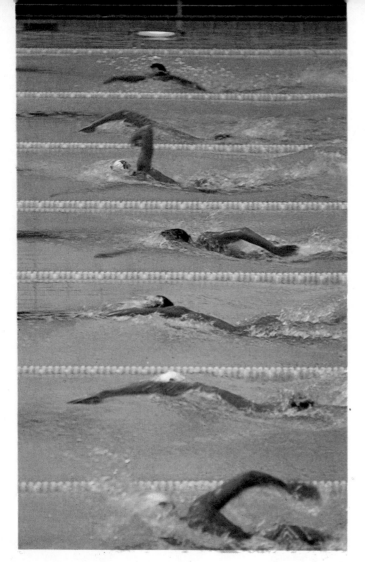

Above: Competitors using a variety of strokes in a freestyle race. Lanes in the swimming bath are marked out with cords to keep the swimmers on track.

swimming, the federation also governs synchronized swimming (a form of water ballet), water polo and diving. Of these the most significant is diving. There are two forms of diving, for both men and women—highboard (10 metres) and springboard (3 metres), though lower boards are also used.

Outside the federation's rules is long-distance swimming, a semi-professional world sport. There are many long-distance swims, though the best-known is probably the English Channel crossing, first made by Captain Matthew Webb in 1875.

Small-boat racing, with open boats up to about 6 metres (20 feet) long, takes place on lakes and in sheltered parts of the sea near coasts. Races are over triangular courses designed to test the design of the boat and the ability of its sailor. Larger boats compete in ocean races. The most famous race is for the *America's Cup,* first won by the schooner *America* in 1851. Since then boats from many countries have tried to take the cup from the United States, without success. From time to time major races are held across the Atlantic and Pacific oceans, sometimes with one-man crews, and there have been round-the-world events also.

The first sailing races were held in England in the

Small yachts designed for offshore racing in a mixed fleet. Craft of this kind do not compete in ocean races, but take part in sea races close to the coast. They have their own racing clubs, dedicated to improving the standard of small-boat sailing.

Towed behind a fast-moving power-boat, a water-skier leaves a fan of spray behind him. Water-skiers cut elaborate tracks through the water, and even leap with the aid of specially-built ramps.

1600s during the reign of Charles II. Rowing also began as a sport in England, and the oldest recorded race, the Doggett's Coat and Badge, has been rowed ever since 1715, over a course on the River Thames. Competition rowing is done in specially designed boats, called pairs, fours or eights according to the number of oarsmen. A single oarsman uses a pair of oars, called sculls. The most important rowing events are regattas, and among the most famous are the Henley Royal Regatta on the Thames, the Australian Henley Regatta on the Yarra River at Melbourne, and the European, American and world championships.

Canoeing is a complete sport in its own right. There are two kinds of canoes: Canadian in which the canoeists use a single-bladed paddle, and the kayak, in which a double-ended paddle is used.

Surfing is especially popular in Australia, Hawaii, South Africa and the mainland United States. Here there are stretches of beach where suitable waves roll in and the water is not too cold. A surfer rides his surfboard on the back of a wave in much the same way as a skateboarder controls his board. A water-skier achieves a similar effect by being towed through the water behind a powerboat.

Winter sports

The term winter sports includes all those sporting and leisure activities which take place on snow and ice – skating, skiing, and sledging. They are popular in all snowy lands, especially Switzerland and other parts of the Alps, Scandinavia, the Soviet Union, the United States and Canada, and Japan.

Skating on ice is said to have originated in Scandinavia, where the first skates were made of bone. The metal skate was invented in 1850, and the first artificially frozen rink was opened in 1876 in London. The pastime of skating soon developed into a sport, and world championships for men were first held in 1896.

There are three events in competitive figure skating: solo men and women, and pairs. In the solo events skaters have to perform six compulsory figures, which they follow with a programme of freestyle skating to a musical accompaniment.

Downhill skiing is one of the most exciting sports. Ski tows pull the skiers back up the mountain.

Sometimes a shorter programme containing certain specified movements is also skated. In pairs skating only the two freestyle sections are performed. In ice dancing there are no acrobatics as there are in figure skating. Competitors dance three compulsory dances out of nine, plus a freestyle programme.

Speed skating is another branch of the sport, and it takes place on outdoor 400-metre tracks. The Olympic programme is, for men: 500, 1,500, 5,000 and 10,000 metres; for women: 500, 1,000, 1,500 and 3,000 metres. It is a sport in which competitors often excel at all distances, the world championships including an all-round championship as well.

Ice hockey is a tremendously fast and sometimes rough team game played on ice rinks. Instead of a

set in the snow so as to test the skier's technique to the maximum. The giant slalom combines the essential elements of both slalom and downhill, the gates being set some distance apart. In both slalom events skiers have two runs over different but similar courses. In many championships a combined title is also awarded to the best all-round performer.

A different type of skiing developed in Scandinavia, known as Nordic skiing. The principal events in this are cross-country skiing, biathlon and ski-jumping. Cross-country skiing, or langlauf, is a long-distance sport, the championship events being for men: 15, 30 and 50 kilometres, and 4 × 10 kilometres relay; for women 5 and 10 kilometres, and 3 × 5 kilometres relay. The biathlon is a combination of cross-country skiing and shooting, and the best people in this sport tend to be soldiers from the Scandinavian countries. Only men compete in ski-jumping, a spectacular sport in which the skiers hiss down long ramps and may soar through the air for distances as great as 160 metres (525 feet). Marks are awarded for distance and style, though there is a less well-known sport of ski-flying where the emphasis is on distance.

Sledging is popular wherever there are snow-covered hills. It, too, has been made into a highly exacting sport. The simplest event is tobogganing, in which the sledger lies face down, guiding the sledge with his feet and body weight. In luge tobogganing, which is for one and two-person sledges, the sledgers lie almost on their backs, going feet first down the icy runs. Bob sledding is a more complicated event with bigger and stream-lined sleds which may reach 145 kph (90 mph).

A bob sled hurtles down a specially-built track. On corners the sleds ride up the outer wall of the run until they are almost hanging vertically.

ball a rubber puck–a small thick disc–is used. The heavily-padded teams normally consist of from 11 to 18 players, six of whom may play at any one time. The game is divided into three periods of 20 minutes each actual play. Substitutes are allowed at any time during play.

Alpine ski racing was pioneered by British skiers, notably Sir Alfred Lunn who organized the first downhill race at Montana, Switzerland, in 1911. The sport consists of three events for both men and women: downhill, slalom and giant slalom, the object in each case being to ski down a set course as fast as possible. The downhill consists of a single run of from 2.4 to 4.8 kilometres with a 760–915-metre descent. There are no artificial obstacles. In the slalom the skier covers a shorter distance, the drop being between 200 and 300 metres, but has to ski through as many as 75 'gates', pairs of poles

FINGERTIP FACTS ON SPORT

THE OLYMPIC GAMES

The ancient Greeks held a series of Olympic Games at Olympia in Greece from 776 BC until the abolition of the Games in AD 393. The idea of reviving the Games was that of a French sportsman, Baron Pierre de Coubertin. The Olympic Games were not held in 1916, 1940, or 1944 because of the two world wars.

An Olympiad is a period of four years beginning with a year divisible by four: thus 1896 was the first year of the first Olympiad of the modern era of the Games.

Year	Place held	Number of competitors
1896	Athens, Greece	285
1900	Paris, France	1066
1904	St Louis, USA	496
1908	London, Great Britain	2059
1912	Stockholm, Sweden	2541
1920	Antwerp, Belgium	2606
1924	Paris, France	3092
1928	Amsterdam, Netherlands	3015
1932	Los Angeles, USA	1408
1936	Berlin, Germany	4069
1948	London, Great Britain	4689
1952	Helsinki, Finland	4925
1956	Melbourne, Australia	3343
	(The equestrian events were held in Stockholm, Sweden)	
1960	Rome, Italy	5337
1964	Tokyo, Japan	5558
1968	Mexico City, Mexico	6059
1972	Munich, West Germany	7147
1976	Montreal, Canada	6815
1980	Moscow, USSR	5784
1984	Los Angeles, USA	

Above: A Greek bronze of Zeus, illustrating the Greek ideal of an athlete.

WINTER OLYMPIC GAMES

Year	Place held	Number of competitors
1924	Chamonix, France	293
1928	St Moritz, Switzerland	491
1932	Lake Placid, USA	307
1936	Garmisch, Germany	756
1948	St Moritz, Switzerland	713
1952	Oslo, Norway	732
1956	Cortina, Italy	924
1960	Squaw Valley, USA	665
1964	Innsbruck, Austria	1111
1968	Grenoble, France	1293
1972	Sapporo, Japan	1128
1976	Innsbruck, Austria	1368
1980	Lake Placid, USA	1283
1984	Sarajevo, Yugoslavia	

THE ENGLISH CHANNEL SWIM

Most crossings
Michael Read (Great Britain)   *22*

Fastest crossing
Penny Dean (USA)   *7 hrs 40 min*
(England to France, July 29, 1978)

Youngest swimmer
Marcus Hooper (Great Britain), aged 12 years 53 days, swam from England to France in *14 hours 37 minutes* on August 6, 1979

First swimmer
Matthew Webb (Great Britain) swam from England to France in *21 hours 45 minutes* on August 24, 1875

BRITISH COMMONWEALTH GAMES

The Commonwealth Games were first held in 1930 and have been held every four years since, except for 1942 and 1946. They include nine sports: athletics, swimming, and seven others from a list of 11. Perhaps the best known incidents in this series of meetings occurred in 1954 in Vancouver, when Roger Bannister won the mile from John Landy, both men beating four minutes, and Jim Peters suffered a dramatic collapse in the marathon within sight of the finishing tape.

Year	Place held
1930	Hamilton, Canada
1934	London, England
1938	Sydney, Australia
1950	Auckland, New Zealand
1954	Vancouver, Canada
1958	Cardiff, Wales
1962	Perth, Australia
1966	Kingston, Jamaica
1970	Edinburgh, Scotland
1974	Christchurch, New Zealand
1978	Edmonton, Canada
1982	Brisbane, Australia

THE MAGIC SEVEN

Some people think seven is a magic number—and it certainly seemed to give good luck to the American swimmer Mark Spitz at the Munich Olympic Games in 1972. He was entered in seven events, four individual and three teams, and he won them all, and all in world record times. He added his seven Munich golds to his medals from the previous Games in Mexico City—two golds, a silver, and a bronze—to make him the most successful swimmer in history. For the record, his Munich wins and times were:

100 metres freestyle	51.22 sec
200 metres freestyle	1 min 52.78 sec
100 metres butterfly	54.27 sec
200 metres butterfly	2 min 00.70 sec
4 × 100 metres freestyle (USA team)	3 min 26.42 sec
4 × 200 metres freestyle (USA team)	7 min 35.78 sec
4 × 100 metres medley relay (USA team)	3 min 48.16 sec

HISTORY OF SPORT

Some prominent dates in sporting history

1715	Rowing–Doggett's Coat and Badge sculling race first held on Thames
1780	Racing–The Derby first run
1787	Cricket–formation of MCC
1829	Rowing–first Oxford v Cambridge boat race
1846	Football–standard soccer rules drawn up at Cambridge
1860	Golf–first Open Championship played
1867	Boxing–Queensberry Rules drawn up
1872	Football–first international played: England v Scotland
1877	Cricket–first Test match: Australia v England
1894	Motor racing–first race: Paris to Rouen
1896	Olympic Games revived in Athens
1911	Festival of Empire Sport held in London
1924	First Winter Olympic Games
1926	Swimming–European championships established
1930	British Empire Games first held
1930	Football–Uruguay win first World Cup
1939	Television–first televised boxing match
1954	Athletics–Roger Bannister runs first sub-4-minute mile
1955	Football–European Champions Clubs Cup first played
1966	Television–an estimated 500 million people see England win World Cup
1970	Football–Brazil win World Cup for third time
1970	Politics–MCC cancels South African tour of England
1972	Politics–terrorists kill 11 Israeli participants in Olympic Games Swimming–Mark Spitz wins 7 Olympic gold medals
1976	Politics–30 countries withdraw from Olympic Games
1977	Cricket–Kerry Packer sets up commercialized cricket in Australia
1981	Athletics–Sebastian Coe beats 3 world records

A GREAT AFTERNOON

Jesse Owens was suffering from a sore back on May 25, 1935, but it did not show in his performances that afternoon in the annual 'Big Ten' inter-university athletics meeting at Ann Arbor, Michigan. He competed in four events, with the following staggering results:

100 yards 9.4 sec
equalled world record

Long jump 26 ft 8¼ in
world record (unbeaten for 25 years)

220 yards low hurdles (straight) 22.6 sec world record
(also a record for 200 metres)

220 yards (straight) 20.3 sec
world record (also a record for 200 metres)

So in the space of less than an hour Owens had set five world records and equalled another!

THE WORLD CUP

The world association football championship is held every four years. For many years the winning team held the golden Jules Rimet trophy, but in 1970 Brazil won the cup permanently and presented the football world with a second trophy called simply the World Cup.

Year	Place	Final score
1930	Montevideo	Uruguay 4 Argentina 2
1934	Rome	Italy 2 Czechoslovakia 1
1938	Paris	Italy 4 Hungary 2
1950	Rio de Janeiro	Uruguay 2 Brazil 1
1954	Berne	West Germany 3 Hungary 2
1958	Stockholm	Brazil 5 Sweden 2
1962	Santiago	Brazil 3 Czechoslovakia 1
1966	London	England 4 West Germany 2
1970	Mexico City	Brazil 4 Italy 1
1974	Munich	West Germany 2 Netherlands 1
1978	Buenos Aires	Argentina 3 Netherlands 1
1982	Spain	

FINGERTIP FACTS ON SPORT

ASSOCIATION FOOTBALL RECORDS

THE WORLD CUP	Most wins	3	Brazil 1958–62–70
	Appearances	5	Antonio Carbajal (Mexico) 1950–54–58–62–66
	Goals	14	Gerd Muller (West Germany) 1970–74
		13	Just Fontaine (France) 1958
	Highest score	9	Hungary(v South Korea, 1954)
		9	Yugoslavia(v Zaïre, 1974)
	in final	5	Brazil (v Sweden, 1968)

INTERNATIONAL MATCHES	Most 'caps'	150	Hector Chumpitaz (Peru)
		120	Rivelino (Brazil)
		115	Bjorn Nordqvist (Sweden)
	Most goals	90	Pele (Brazil)
		83	Ferenc Puskas (Hungary, Spain)
		75	Sandor Koscis (Hungary)

INTERNATIONAL CLUB COMPETITIONS	THE EUROPEAN CUP		
	Most wins	6	Real Madrid (Spain) 1956–57–58–59 60–66
	Individual goals	7	Ferenc Puskas (Real Madrid)
		6	Alfredo di Stefano (Real Madrid)
	SOUTH AMERICAN CUP		
	Most wins	6	Independiente (Argentina) 1964–65–72–73–74–75

BRITISH CLUB RECORDS	Highest score	Arbroath 36 Bon Accord 0 (Scottish Cup, 1st round, 1885)
	International	England 13 Ireland 0 (1882)
	FA Cup	Preston 26 Hyde 0 (1st round, 1887)
	League Div 1	West Bromwich Albion 12 Darwen 0 (1892) Nottingham Forest 12 Leicester Fosse 0 (1909)
	Scottish Div 1	Celtic 11 Dundee 0 (1895)
	Goals in a season	
	League Div 1	128 Aston Villa (42 games 1930–31)
	Scottish Div 1	132 Hearts (34 games 1957–58)

BRITISH INDIVIDUAL RECORDS	International 'caps'	England	108 Bobby Moore
		N. Ireland	87 Patrick Jennings
		Scotland	78 Kenny Dalglish
		Wales	68 Ivor Allchurch
	Football League matches		824 Terence Paine (Southampton)
	Scottish League matches		626 Bob Ferrier (Motherwell)

TEST MATCHES

Most runs in a career 8,028 by Geoff Boycott (England)

Highest score in a Test match 365 not out by Garfield Sobers (West Indies v Pakistan at Kingston, 1957–58)

Best career average 99.94 by Donald Bradman (Australia)

Highest team score 903–7 declared by England v Australia at the Oval in 1938

Lowest team score 26 by New Zealand v England at Auckland in 1954–55

Most wickets in a career 309 by Lance Gibbs (West Indies)

Best bowling in a match 19–90 by Jim Laker (England v Australia at Manchester in 1956)

Best bowling in an innings 10–53 by Jim Laker (as above)

Best career average 10.75 (112 wickets for 1,205 runs) by G. A. Lohmann (England) in 18 Tests.

ALL FIRST-CLASS MATCHES

Most runs in a career 61,237 by Jack Hobbs (England)

Highest score 499 by Hanif Mohammad (Pakistan) for Karachi v Bahalwapur at Karachi in 1958–59

Best career average 95.14 by Donald Bradman (Australia)

Highest team score 1,107 by Victoria v New South Wales at Melbourne in 1926–27

Lowest team score 12 by Oxford University v MCC and Ground at Oxford in 1897

12 by Northamptonshire v Gloucestershire at Gloucester in 1907

Most wickets in a career 4,187 by Wilfred Rhodes (England)

Best bowling in a match – see Tests

Best bowling in an innings 10–10 by Hedley Verity for Yorkshire v Nottinghamshire at Leeds in 1932

WICKET-KEEPING
(all matches)

Most dismissals in a match 12 by E. Pooley for Surrey v Sussex at The Oval, 1868; Don Tallon for Queensland v NSW at Sydney, 1938–39; Brian Taber for NSW v South Australia at Adelaide in 1968–69

Most dismissals in an innings 8 by Wally Grout for Queensland v Western Australia at Brisbane in 1959–60

Most dismissals in a career 1,526 by John Murray (England)

Most catches in a career 1,273 by Bob Taylor (England)

Most stumpings in a career 415 by Leslie Ames (England)

ALL-ROUND RECORDS

Best all-round career Test performance 8,032 runs and 235 wickets by Garfield Sobers (West Indies)

Best all-round career performances 58,969 runs and 2,068 wickets by Frank Woolley (England)

54,904 runs and 2,876 wickets by W. G. Grace (England)

Emblems

Emblems are pictures, or mixtures of colours and shapes, which stand for something else. For example, a country's flag makes you think of that country when you see it. Our alphabet began as a series of pictures representing sounds, and changed over many years into the simple shapes we know today.

Emblems still play a very big part in our everyday lives. The controls on a motor-car dashboard are often labelled in this way, so that they can be understood by a driver no matter what language he speaks. If you are driving in Europe you will find that many road signs are pictorial–and the pictures are the same in each country you pass through.

In these pages we see some of the most colourful emblems–badges, medals, flags, and coats of arms (heraldry).

Badges and medals

People often wear emblems to show who they are or what group they belong to. For example, a soldier wears a badge on his cap or on his tunic to show what regiment or corps he belongs to. Scouts and guides wear badges to show which troop they are in, and a great many children have badges which indicate which school they attend. Other badges indicate membership of a club or a sporting team.

Some badges are personal ones and indicate the wearer's status or family. Such badges are closely allied with coats-of-arms, which are described on pages 206–207. Famous examples of family badges are the Red Rose of Lancaster and the White Rose of York, worn by rival branches of the English royal family during the Wars of the Roses in the 1400s. A member of a Scottish clan may wear a badge consisting of the clan chief's crest surrounded by a strap and buckle.

Many badges indicate that the wearer has achieved something, or has a particular ability. Scout and guide badges are of this kind, and they indicate that the wearer has passed proficiency tests in such activities as signalling, sewing or cooking. Members of the armed services of many countries receive badges for good conduct.

Decorations take the theme of achievement still further. A decoration is generally a metal medal (a coin-shaped emblem) or a cross on a coloured

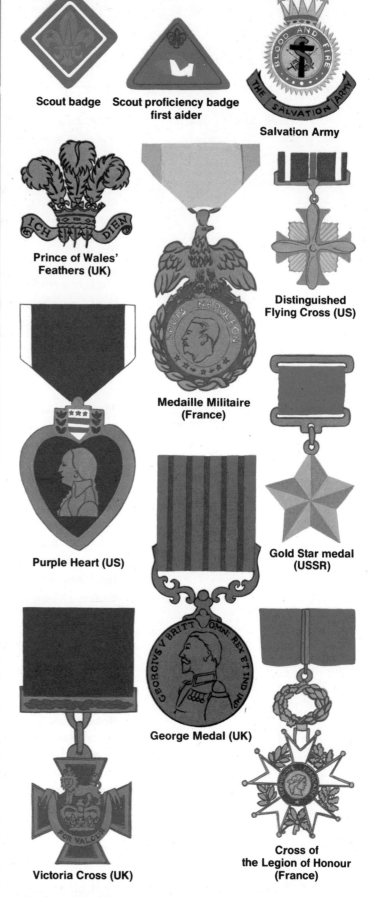

Scout badge   Scout proficiency badge first aider

Salvation Army

Prince of Wales' Feathers (UK)

Distinguished Flying Cross (US)

Medaille Militaire (France)

Purple Heart (US)

Gold Star medal (USSR)

George Medal (UK)

Victoria Cross (UK)

Cross of the Legion of Honour (France)

A selection of badges and medals of various kinds. The first identifies the wearer as a scout, the second denotes achievement. The third shows membership of the Salvation Army. The Prince of Wales' feathers are the personal badge of the heir to the British throne. The remaining medals and crosses are awards for bravery in different countries, or – in the case of the Cross of the Legion of Honour – for service. The Purple Heart is given to wounded.

ribbon. Decorations are awarded for great courage, and examples of such awards include Britain's Victoria Cross, the United States' Congressional Medal of Honor, and France's Croix de Guerre. Medals for courage are generally awarded by a government on behalf of a whole country, but societies and institutions also give medals for achievement. For example, many explorers have been given the gold medal of Britain's Royal Geographical Society.

Medals may be awarded for service rather than for any one deed or achievement. People who fight in wars generally receive medals to show that they took part. Sometimes a medal is issued for a particular campaign in a war.

Another group of emblems shows membership of an order. An order is a society based on the orders or bands of knights in the Middle Ages, and in Britain and some other countries of the Common-

Proud emblems of their countries, a group of flags – one for each nation taking part – flying at the 1972 Olympic Games in West Germany. Flags play an important part in identifying countries and their peoples, not only at events like this but also in trade and travel. Ships and aircraft display their flags, and so do embassies in foreign countries.

wealth members of many orders still receive the title of knight. The most famous order of knighthood is the Order of the Garter, founded by Edward III in 1349. Many countries, including Britain, have Orders of Merit, which do not confer the title of knight. The United States is one of the few major countries which has no orders.

As a rule, people wear decorations and the emblems of orders only on formal occasions, but most soldiers, sailors and airmen wear little strips of ribbon on their uniforms at all times to show that they have won these awards.

chief embattled

barry wavy

bordure

Left: Medieval knights wore heraldic devices on their shields and surcoats for identification.

Heraldry

In the days when knights wore complete suits of armour in battle, it was very difficult to tell who was friend and who was foe. So the custom grew up of each knight having his own badge or device painted on his shield. He also had it embroidered on his surcoat, a kind of loose linen tunic worn over the armour to keep it clean. In time, such devices became known as coats of arms. Each family had its own coat of arms. To make sure they were all different, the designs were controlled by royal officials called heralds, and the study of these designs is called heraldry for this reason.

Heraldry has its own language, called blazonry, based on old French. The colours used are called tinctures. Two are metals: *or* (gold) and *argent* (silver); five are called colours: *azure* (blue), *gules* (red), *vert* (green), *sable* (black) and *purpure* (purple). There are also some patterned tinctures called furs, including *ermine*, *pean* and *vair*.

The pattern on a shield is its charge. The most popular charges are basic shapes such as crosses, bars, and bends (diagonal bars), animals, particularly lions, and flowers such as roses and lilies. The lily has its French name, *fleur de lys*.

A shield can be divided in various ways, some of which are shown on these pages. For example, a bend is a broad diagonal stripe. If you divide the shield in two diagonally, this is called per bend, while two diagonal stripes are known as bendlets. If the shield is alternate stripes of colours, heralds describe it as bendy. Most of the shield divisions are made with straight lines, but the lines may be of different shapes, such as wavy, indented, or dovetailed.

A basic rule of heraldry is that you should never put one metal on another, or one 'colour' on another. So you would not put *argent* on *or*, nor *gules* on *sable*; but you could put *argent* on *sable*, for example.

When describing a shield, heralds use the term dexter (right) to describe the right-hand part of the shield as seen from behind – what would be left as you look at it. Sinister is the term for left (right as you look at it). They begin by naming the tincture

Royal Coat-of-Arms

A full coat of arms, called an 'achievement' – in this case that of the British sovereign. It shows the shield, surrounded by the sash and motto of the Order of the Garter. On either side are the supporters – a lion and a unicorn – and above the shield is a helmet, surmounted by the crest. The motto is underneath.

Shield of Merano, Italy

Shield of Poland

Arms of Jamaica

The arms of a city – Merano in Italy – and a country – Poland, together with an achievement of arms for a country, Jamaica. Like the British royal coat of arms, this one shows shield, supporters, helmet, crest and motto.

chief · fesse · pale · bend · chevron · saltire

cross · per fesse · per pale · per bend · per chevron · per saltire

quarterly · cross patée · crosslet · bendy · checky · gyronny

Maltese cross · Calvary cross · bowen knot · vair · ermine · fleurs de lys

hawk's bells · weavers' shuttles · tower · beehive · cock · bear

of the background, followed then by the charge and its colour. For example, the arms of St Peter shown here would be described as '*Gules, two crossed keys or*'.

When families intermarried they often combined their coats of arms. A favourite way of doing this is called quartering–dividing the shield into four sections. The British royal arms are quartered, with the arms of England (twice), Scotland and Ireland.

Above you see some examples of basic shield divisions, such as chief, fesse, pale and bend, followed by further divisions based on them, such as per bend and bendy. Then come some examples of charges, such as crosses and animals. Vair and ermine are furs. Top left on the opposite page are an example of a fancy line dividing a shield, while 'barry wavy' means wave-shaped bars. A bordure is a border round a shield. Below are three examples of the different poses adopted by heraldic lions, and examples of actual arms–those of St Peter, the City of London, and Washington, DC–the same as the Washington family.

lion sejant

lion passant

lion statant

St Peter

City of London

Washington DC

People at work

All living things, not only humans, have to 'work' to stay alive. A green plant 'works' by using the energy of sunlight to make its food from chemicals in the soil and water. Animals also 'work' to get their food.

Early Stone Age people lived by hunting wild animals and gathering wild plants. Except for the very young and the very old, everybody had to join in the hard work of getting food–or starve. When farming was developed, about 10,000 years ago, it was possible to produce a surplus of food–more than was immediately needed for everyone to eat. This meant that many people became free to do other kinds of work and to

develop new skills, such as pottery, weaving, basket-making and metalwork. These craftsmen could exchange the products of their work for food. It became possible for many people to build and live in cities, where still more skills such as writing and different kinds of jobs could develop. This was the beginning of civilization (which just means 'living in cities').

So we can see that civilization depends on what is called the division of labour. This means people doing specialized work, instead of many tasks just in order to survive. In this chapter we shall look at some of the many different jobs which exist in the modern world.

Working on the land

To work we must eat, so everything depends on farming. The simplest kind of farming is called subsistence farming. In this kind of agriculture the farmer (then usually called a peasant) and his family raise just enough crops and animals for their own needs, and maybe a bit extra to sell in order to buy tools and things they cannot make for themselves. In poorer parts of the world, such as India and the countries of Africa and Latin America, most of the people are subsistence farmers.

Producing crops and animals for sale, rather than to eat yourself, is called cash farming. This is the usual kind of farming in the richer, more developed parts of the world, such as the United States and Europe. Cash farming is very important because it provides food for people who live and work in cities and cannot grow their own.

To produce large crops cash farming needs plenty of modern equipment, such as tractors and combine harvesters, and also chemical fertilizers to enrich the soil. It is just these things which peasant farmers in poor countries cannot afford–which is why they stay poor.

There are many specialized kinds of farming, which concentrate on raising one particular kind of crop or animal. Many New Zealand farmers, for instance, concentrate on dairy farming–raising cattle for their milk products (butter and cheese). In Ghana, West Africa, many farmers live by

These women are picking tea on an estate in Kerala, in south-western India. After picking, the tea is dried, heated to make it keep, and then graded and packed. India is one of the largest tea producers.

Top: Modern farming – harvesting quickly by machine.

Above: Traditional farming – ploughing the slow way with a camel. Horses and oxen also work with ploughs.

growing cocoa beans. Pig farming for bacon and pork is important in Denmark. Huge cereal crops are grown on the prairies of the United States and Canada and on the fertile steppelands of the Soviet Union. Sheep farming for wool is important in Australia and New Zealand.

In another type of farming, called plantation agriculture, growers also concentrate on a single crop, such as coffee in Brazil, sugar cane in the West Indies and rubber in Malaysia.

Tree-farming, or forestry, is important in many countries. Tropical countries produce many valuable hardwoods, such as mahogany and teak. In cold places, such as Canada and Norway, foresters grow pine trees, which are the raw material for paper-making.

Working in industry

Very few of the things that we take for granted as part of modern life could exist without industry. Telephones, radio, television, cars, railways and aeroplanes are just a few examples. So are the clothes we wear and the books we read.

Most people think of industry as making goods in factories, using powered machines. This kind of factory industry started about 200 years ago with the Industrial Revolution, when the use of steam-driven factory machinery speeded up the production of goods hundreds of times. Today factory machines are powered by electricity rather than steam, though steam may be used to generate power.

Factory industry is the main way of producing wealth in the world's developed countries, such as the United States, Japan, the Soviet Union and the countries of Europe. In these countries from about one-third to half the people work in factories.

There are two basic kinds of industry: consumer industry and heavy industry. Consumer industry is making the necessaries and luxuries that people 'consume'—that is, buy and use—in their day-to-day lives, such as refrigerators, clothes and make-up. Heavy industry makes things such as steel, locomotives, ships and the machines used to make consumer goods.

The many different jobs in industry are often classed according to the kind and amount of skill they need. Many factory jobs are unskilled or semi-skilled. Assembly-line work is an example, in which a complicated job, such as putting cars together, is broken down into many simple repeated tasks, each of which is done by a particular worker or group of workers. This kind of work is often terribly boring. Unfortunately it is also the only

nature. Many of them are minerals from the Earth's crust, which have to be extracted by mining, quarrying or drilling. These processes are called extractive industries.

Mining and quarrying are used for solid minerals such as metal ores, stone and coal. If the minerals are near the surface, the soil is stripped away and mechanical diggers scoop up the mineral. This is called strip-mining. Quarrying is removing minerals such as limestone or marble from the sides of hills and mountains, either by cutting them away or by blasting them free with explosives. If the minerals are far from the surface, underground mining is necessary. This has always been one of the most dangerous and unpleasant of jobs, even though much of the work can be done by machinery.

Drilling is used to extract oil and natural gas. A borehole is drilled down to the deposit and the oil or gas comes up under its own pressure. In recent years much oil has been found under sea beds, particularly in the North Sea. To extract this oil huge drilling rigs are towed out to sea and positioned over the oil fields. The oil is taken back to the land by tanker or pipeline. Working on these oil rigs, in all kinds of weather, is a very tough job indeed, and is highly paid.

Above: Building motor-cars on an assembly line in an Argentine factory. In this process each group of workers does one particular job, over and over again.

Left: Cutting coal by machine in a British mine. This work, carried out far underground, is highly skilled.

way to make many kinds of goods quickly enough to earn a profit. Industry also needs highly-skilled workers such as scientists and designers to invent and develop new products. Other jobs in industry include managers and administrators, who organize the work of other people.

The opposite of factory industry is known as 'cottage industry'. In this, skilled craftsmen work by themselves or in small groups to produce mainly hand-made goods. This is much more satisfying work than factory assembly-line work, because each person or group makes a complete product, rather than just a bit of one. Before the Industrial Revolution most industry was organized in this way. Today, however, cottage industry is only practical for goods in which handcraft quality is important, for instance pottery or jewellery.

To make goods, industry needs raw materials to work with and energy to do the work. These basic necessities are 'natural resources' provided by

A traditional form of industry – making baskets in the Andes. Basketry is one of the few crafts that has proved almost impossible to mechanize.

Working in transport

Efficient ways of moving people and goods about are just as important in the modern world as factories and other kinds of industry. Transport is a vital industry in itself, and includes many different kinds of jobs.

Many people drive their own cars to work, but if everyone did this the roads would become hopelessly jammed in rush-hours. So in any big city public transport is necessary. This usually consists of bus fleets and overground railways. Most capital cities, such as Paris, New York and London, have underground railways as well. Drivers, conductors, guards, ticket-office staff and porters are just some of the jobs in public transport. Mechanics are also needed to maintain buses and trains, and many office staff are involved in planning timetables and other administrative work.

Long-distance transport is carried on by road, rail, sea and air. Road freight is mostly carried by big trucks, sometimes called 'juggernauts'. Long-distance truck-driving is an exhausting job, and most countries have laws to prevent drivers from doing more than a certain number of hours at a stretch. This helps safety on the roads.

The captain of a ship is responsible for the safety of the crew, passengers and cargo, and, of course, the ship itself. He has to have had years of experience to qualify for his master's ticket (Captain's Certificate). Other important crew members include the first lieutenant, first mate, the engineer (who looks after the ship's engines) and the radio and radar operators (who handle communications).

An airline pilot's job is, if anything, even more demanding than a ship's captain's, though he is in charge of a smaller crew. The control panel in the cockpit of a modern jet airliner presents a bewildering array of dials, knobs and switches. The pilot must be able to read all the information about the aircraft's performance and to react instantly if there is any danger.

Equally important is the job of the air-traffic control staff in the control tower of the airport, who supervise the take-off and landing of aircraft.

Air traffic controllers in the control tower of a busy airport have a very responsible job. They must tell all aircraft when they can land and take off and what paths they must follow close to the airport. The airspace around them is like a busy main highway.

Working on construction

The construction industry includes as many different kinds of job as any other branch of industry. First the architect must draw up the plans for the building, and the surveyor must carefully measure the site. The amounts of materials needed must be worked out and costed by an estimator.

When all this has been done the construction workers move on to the site. The first stages of work are clearing and excavating the site. Bulldozers clear rubble, uproot trees and level the ground. Excavators then dig into the ground so that the foundations can be laid.

The frame of an office block or skyscraper is usually made of steel girders, which are swung into place by cranes and joined by riveting, bolting or welding. This job is known as steel-fixing or

In the United States trucking, as it is known there, is a major industry. Some of the journeys are very long – a two-man team with a load of fresh fruit from California would take 3½ days to reach New York City, the other side of the country. While one man drives, the other can sleep in a bunk behind the cab.

steel-erecting. As the frame of the building rises, other workers place reinforced concrete walls and floors in position. They are followed by plumbers, electricians, carpenters, heating engineers, glaziers (who put the glass in the windows) and painters.

One of the most important jobs in traditional housebuilding is bricklaying. A skilled bricklayer lays his bricks and cements them in place at great speed, keeping them straight by means of a stretched line. Plastering is another skilled building job. It

Building bridges is an important part of the construction industry, as more and more roads are needed to carry the ever-increasing volume of traffic.

is usually done by a two-man team. The hod-carrier brings the freshly-mixed plaster in a wooden holder (the hod) and the plasterer spreads exactly the right amount on to the wall with his trowel. He has to work fast because plaster dries out quickly and then cannot be worked smooth.

Providing services

Many kinds of job do not produce raw materials or make goods, but provide services to other people. This non-productive work includes commercial services, such as selling in shops, and office work, banking and insurance. It also includes the various jobs involved in working for the country and the government, such as the civil service, the police and the armed services (army, navy and air force).

Once goods have been made, they must be distributed to the people who want to buy them. As we have seen, transport is a vital part of distribution. The other part involves the actual selling. This breaks down into two main parts, wholesaling and retailing. Wholesalers buy goods in very large amounts from factories and store them in warehouses. Usually wholesalers do not sell directly to the public. Instead they sell goods to retailers—that is, shops—in much smaller quantities.

Retail work is very important, because to sell goods successfully they must be attractively displayed and conveniently arranged so that people who come into a shop can easily find what they need. A good shop assistant knows about the range of wares that he or she is selling, and can give customers helpful advice and information about what they are buying.

Almost all services involve a good deal of office work. This can range from making up people's wage packets to the sorting and filing of bills and other documents, and writing letters.

Banking and insurance provide financial services to industries, businesses and the ordinary public. Banks not only look after people's money, but make loans to industry and business. Insurance embraces a wide range of needs, from covering ships and aircraft to people's houses and possessions. An insurer charges his customers a small yearly sum, called a premium, to cover his goods or his buildings. If the customer suffers a loss, for example by fire or theft, the insurer pays him a sum in compensation. Insurance works because although a large number of people insure, only a few actually suffer a loss and claim compensation. In this way a small payment guarantees a large payout in case of need.

In most countries today many thousands of people are public employees, who work for the state in a wide variety of jobs, including many services. The social services are an example. They are designed to help people who are in need, such as the unemployed, the sick and the homeless.

The police, with responsibility for keeping law and order, are an important group of public servants. Their work is hard and often dangerous. As well as

Shops and stores provide an essential service to the community. This butcher's shop is in the covered market in the university city of Oxford. Straw hats are traditional wear for butchers in England.

Sailors line up on an American aircraft carrier. The armed forces provide a very special service to a country in defending it and helping to preserve peace.

Traffic wardens, like this one in London, help to keep busy city streets clear. Their work is all part of the maintenance of order and law in our society.

preventing and detecting crime, the police are responsible for controlling traffic and keeping public order, for instance at political demonstrations. Firemen are another group of public servants with a difficult and dangerous job.

Defending a country in wartime is the job of its armed services. In peacetime some countries rely on a full-time professional or volunteer army, with soldiers who work for wages, as in any other job. In other countries most young men have to serve in the army for a certain amount of time as conscripts. In return they get their keep and pocket money. As well as defending against enemy attacks, a country's armed forces are often called on to help with emergencies such as floods, earthquakes and other disasters.

People who work in government offices, such as the various ministries, are called civil servants. It is the job of civil servants to advise the government and to carry out its policies, for instance in health, education and housing.

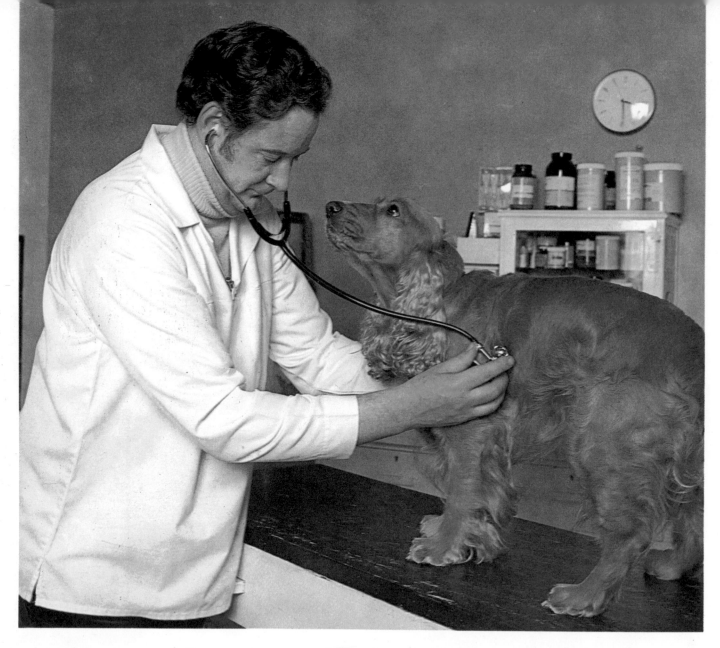

The professions

What is the difference between a job and a profession? In a general way someone's profession is whatever he or she does for a living. So we can say that a housewife and mother, who looks after a family and home, is just as much a professional person as a judge or a doctor.

In a more exact way the word professional is often used to mean the opposite to an amateur. Amateurs are people who take up a subject, such as painting, writing or music, as a spare-time hobby. As it is not their job it does not matter how well or badly they do it, so long as they enjoy themselves. But anyone who becomes good enough at doing something to make money at it is a professional.

Usually a profession means the sort of job for which a high standard of education and training are needed. Most professional people are graduates –that is, after leaving school they have spent several years studying for a degree at a university or college. Many of them also have to take examinations which are set by associations or other bodies controlling their particular professions.

The traditional professions include medicine,

law, the Church, teaching and engineering. Each of these includes several different kinds of jobs.

For instance, the medical profession includes psychiatrists and surgeons as well as hospital doctors and general practitioners–the doctors whose surgeries you visit to get a prescription. If you want to be a surgeon you first take a degree in medicine and then take further examinations in surgery while working at a hospital.

Animal medicine, or veterinary surgery, has its own special importance. Many people who live in cities think of 'vets' as people who treat sick pets, but in the countryside vets spend most of their time looking after farm animals. This is vital work because most farm animals are prone to diseases which can wipe out entire herds. Just like doctors, vets can expect to be called out at any time of day or night, and often they have to work in the open in all kinds of weather.

The legal profession, like medicine, is divided into several different 'compartments'. In most countries law is such a complicated business that lawyers specialize in different parts of it, just as doctors specialize in different kinds of medicine. The two main kinds of law are civil law, which deals with disputes–for instance over contracts–

and criminal law, which deals with crimes such as robbery and violence. There is also international law, which deals with disputes between countries.

In the early Middle Ages in Europe all professional people came from the Church because the clergy were almost the only people who knew how to read and write. In modern times, however, a clergyman's job is often limited to conducting church services and doing social work in the community. To qualify for his job a clergyman spends some years studying theology (religious knowledge) and the doctrines of his church.

Teachers include school teachers and lecturers in colleges and universities. The top jobs in universities are held by professors, who are the leading experts in their subjects. They usually spend less time teaching than lecturers because they are busy with their own research. In other words, a professor's main job is to add to the fund of already existing knowledge.

In many ways teaching is the most important of all professions. This is because it is one of the main ways in which the skills and knowledge of society are passed on from one generation to the next. However, public respect for teachers is not the same in every country. In Britain, for instance,

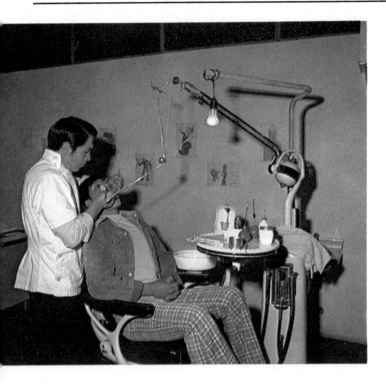

Above: Care of the teeth is an essential part of health, and the profession of dentistry is one that requires great skill and long training.

Left: Animal medicine, also called veterinary surgery, is a vital service—not only for pets, like this dog, but also to prevent and cure disease in farm animals.

Below: A barrister, wearing wig and gown, walks through Lincoln's Inn, London base for many lawyers. A barrister is a lawyer who is qualified to appear before a judge in English courts.

teachers are not very highly regarded. In Germany, on the other hand, they are among the most respected people in the community, as they are in most poorer countries, where there is a shortage of schools and teachers.

'Scientist' is a general term for anybody whose job is to make new discoveries in the sciences, such as physics, chemistry and biology. Scientists work for many different kinds of organizations, including universities, industries and governments. Often, of course, scientists may be professors.

Nowadays accountancy has become an important profession. An accountant's job is to keep account of all the money that is spent and received by any organization or business, and to advise his employers on the best way to arrange the company's finances. Each year every company must by law publish a statement of its profits and losses, and this must be audited (checked) by an independent accountant.

The profession of journalism includes reporters and other people who write for newspapers, journals and magazines. A journalist writing for a national or local newspaper is expected to keep up high standards of accuracy and truthfulness, and to avoid bias. At the same time, a reporter needs a keen sense of what is news, and persistence and resourcefulness to 'get a story'. He (or she) must also know how to get on with people, and so be able to ask questions and obtain the information required. Not all journalists are reporters: to prepare

Teaching is one of the most important of the professions, because a good education is essential for all young people. This teacher is taking a class in Penang, a state in Malaysia.

The artist Pietro Annigoni is seen here at work on a mural illustrating 'The Last Supper'. Although the profession of artist is not essential for day-to-day living, it is of enormous value in helping to make people's lives worthwhile.

a newspaper for press there are also many editors and sub-editors who check each story for accuracy, and make sure it is written with good grammar and to the right length.

People whose profession is writing books are known as authors. The author's profession is one of the hardest, because if his books do not sell, he does not get paid. However, writing is also one of the most respected of professions.

Literature and the other arts, such as music, acting and painting, are usually regarded as professions. Artists are in a different position from that of other professional people such as doctors or lawyers. For one thing, artists often work as

freelances—that is, they do not have regular jobs and salaries. Their pay depends on people being interested in their work. Then again, art is not so obviously 'useful' as the services of a doctor or lawyer. All the same, the artistic professions are very important because they are the main way in which a society expresses its culture and ideas.

Professional people such as accountants, doctors and lawyers are paid more than people in most other kinds of jobs, such as factory workers. One reason is that it takes more time and money to train for a profession than it does to work in a factory. However, many people in factory managerial and administrative jobs, who help to arrange other people's work, also rank as professional. You can study management techniques and take examinations in them.

Like artists, actors do not contribute directly to the wealth of a country, but their work provides pleasure for thousands. These performers are appearing in William Congreve's play 'The Way of the World' at a London theatre.

Index

222

The publishers would like to thank the following individuals and organizations for their kind permission to reproduce the photographs
in this book.

A-Z Botanical Collection 22 below right, 25 below right; A.F.A. 39
above; Heather Angel 27 centre, 53; Ardea (P. Germain) 38 above,
(E. Mickleburgh) 39 centre, (P. Morris) 35 below, (R. & V. Taylor)
43–44 below, (W. Weisser) 40 below; BBC 6–7, 111 above left, 116; Beken
of Cowes 161, 196 below; Bodleian Library 167 below, 178; Paul Brierley
122–123, 124, 125 right, 126, 127, 129 right, 139 above and below; British
Airports 212 right; British Antarctic Survey 179 below left and right;
Trustees of the British Museum 103 below left, 172, (J. R. Freeman)
171 below; Camera Press Ltd. (R. Crane) 219 left, (L. Dean) endpapers,
83 above, (R. Halin) 74; Bruce Coleman Ltd. 142, (S. C. Bisserot) 51
above right, (J. Burton) 1, 33 above, 47 below, 48 below, 51 below, (L. R.
Dawson) 40 above, (Jeff Foott) 46, (C Hughes) 36 above, (D Hughes) 90,
(G. Pizzey) 32 below, (G. D. Plage) 34 above, (F. Prenzel) 2–3, (M.
Quarishy) 36 below, (H. Reinhard) 34 below, (S. Trevor) 37 above;
Colorsport 113, 188, 190 above and below, 191, 193 below, 194, 195 below,
196 above, 197, 198–199, 199 below; Cooper-Bridgeman Library 173
below; Courtauld Institute 100 above; Gerry Cranham 193 above;
Anthony Crickmay 112 below right; Ben Cropp 51 above left; Daily
Telegraph Colour Library 181 below, (T. Marshall) 158, (P. Morris) 89,
(L. L. T. Rhodes) 189; P. M. David 47 above, 49 below; Douglas Dickens
13, 16 above, 17 below, 56 below, 57 below, 69, 71, 72–73, 79, 80 above
left, 81, 82, 83 below, 87 above and below, 88 above, 91 above and below,
94 left, 95, 105 above, 107, 150 above, 179 above, 208, 209 below, 218;
Walt Disney Productions 118 right; C. M. Dixon 200; Eastman Kodak
Co. 114 above and below right, 115 above, centre, below left and right;
Electricité de France 143; England Scene 68, 123 right, 213, 214, 215
below, 216, 217 below; Mary Evans Picture Library (F. Bernard) 106
above; Explorer (J. Dupont) 19 above left; Francoise Foliot 162–163;
J. R. Freeman and Co. 168 below; GPO 154 above, 155 above and below
left, 156, 157 above and below; Giraudon (M. Picardie) 110; R. & S.
Greenhill 78; Sonia Halliday 102 above, 108; Keith Hammond 4–5;
Victor Hand 148–149 below, 149 above; Carol Hay 152; Andre Held
165 above; Historical Society of Pennsylvania 175; Michael Holford
86, 103 above, 163 below, 165 below, 166 above and below, 171 above
right, (The Bobrinsky Collection) 98 below, (J. Chapman) 167 above,

(G. Clyde) 80 above right, (Musée Guimet) 163 above right, (The
Rienits Collection) 181 above, (Ianthe Ruthven) 58; The Huntingdon
Library, San Marino, California 106 below; Alan Hutchinson 15 below;
Imperial War Museum 176, 177 above; Jacana Agence de Presse (P.
Dupont 33 below); Keystone Press Agency 159; Jean Kingsnorth 103
below right; R. Klinger Ltd. 128 above; Frank Lane 43 above, (C. P.
Rose) 38 below; Musée Louvre (Giraudon) 164, (M. Holford) 99 below;
Patricia Mandell 175 above, 177 below; Mansell Collection 173 above;
Wendy Martensson 134; John Massey-Stewart 75 above, 141 right; P.
Morris 50; NASA 11 above, 136 below; National Coal Board 210;
National Gallery 100 below, (M. Holford) 99 above left; National
Maritime Museum (M. Holford) 169; NHPA 41, (A. Bannister) 22–23
above, (J. Blossom) 43 below, (S. Dalton) 43 above, (E. Degginger) 27
left, (A. Huxley) 24, (G. E. Hyde) 29, (G. Pizzey) 39 below, 42 below, (I.
Polunin) 25 above right, (J. Talton) 26; Natural Science Photos (J. N.
Wood) 42 above; Morris Newcombe 109 above, (Old Vic Theatre) 219
right; New York City Museum (J. Clarence Davies Collection) 170–171
above; New York State Historical Association 180; Novosti Press
Agency 75 below, 183 above; Oxford Scientific Films 16 below, 23 below,
28, 32 above, 48 above, 59 below, 62–63, 130, (J. K. Burras) 27 above;
Photo Feuillée 104 below; Picturepoint 30, 112 above left, 140–141
below, 150 below, 168 above, 205; Pinewood Studios 119; Dick Polak
117; Quantas 153 above; Radio Times Hulton Picture Library 148
above; Rocket Records 111 right; Ann Ronan Picture Library 182;
Royal Astronomical Society © California Institute of Technology and
Carnegie Institute of Washington 8–9; Science Museum, London 114
above left; Kenneth Scowen 105 below; Sheffield City Art Gallery 99
above right; Shell International Petroleum Ltd. (Photographic Library)
151; Ronald Sheridan 102 below; Spectrum Colour Library 104 above,
134 below; Syndication International 62, 186 above and below, 187,
192, 195 above; The Tate Gallery 101 above left and right, 101 below;
John W. R. Taylor 153 below; John Topham Picture Agency 74 (G.
Villiers) 140 above; Trans-Antarctic Expedition 94 right; United
Artists 119; Mireille Vautier 56–57 above, 59 above, 60 below, 64, 65, 70,
109 above, 146, (Decool) 211 above, (De Nanxe) 211 below, 212 left, 215
above, 217 above; Warner Bros. 118 left; Worldwide Butterflies Ltd.
(R. Goodden) 49 above; D. & J. Wright 88 below, 147; ZEFA (R. Everts)
17 above right, (Janoud) 128–129, (H. Helbing) 209 above.